ETHIOPIA

A Post-Cold War African State

THEODORE M. VESTAL

Westport, Connecticut
London

Library of Congress Cataloging-in-Publication Data

Vestal, Theodore M.
  Ethiopia : a post–Cold War African state / Theodore M. Vestal.
    p. cm.
  Includes bibliographical references and index.
  ISBN 0–275–96610–0 (alk. paper)
  1. Ethiopia—Politics and government—1991– 2. Ya 'Ityopyā hozboč
'abeyotāwi démokrāsiyāwi genbār. 3. Democracy—Ethiopia—
History—20th century. 4. Ethiopia—Foreign relations—United
States. 5. United States—Foreign relations—Ethiopia. I. Title.
DT388.V47 1999
320.963'09'049—dc21   99–21190

British Library Cataloguing in Publication Data is available.

Library of Congress Catalog Card Number: 99–21190
ISBN: 0–275–96610–0

First published in 1999

Praeger Publishers, 88 Post Road West, Westport, CT 06881
An imprint of Greenwood Publishing Group, Inc.
www.praeger.com

Printed in the United States of America

∞™

The paper used in this book complies with the
Permanent Paper Standard issued by the National
Information Standards Organization (Z39.48–1984).

10 9 8 7 6 5 4 3 2 1

Copyright Acknowledgments

For freedom-loving Ethiopians everywhere.

Contents

Contents

Unnumbered photo section follows p. 116.

Preface

In the mid-1960s, it was my good karma to work with Kennedy's Children on the roof of Africa. As a Peace Corps executive, I traveled throughout Ethiopia, a heaven-blessed land of natural beauty and potential abundance, meeting Ethiopians from all walks of life. I encountered a fascinating culture and a handsome people whose intelligence and courteous ways were beguiling. The Peace Corps' aspirations were high as was the altitude in the highlands where we worked. The country was at peace, and the Peace Corps was appreciated for what it was accomplishing. At that time, historian Arnold Toynbee said that in the Peace Corps, the world was seeing the Western tradition at its best. This frequently was the case with the volunteers in Ethiopia, especially in those happily naive days before the Vietnam war and Watergate scandals.

Most of the Peace Corps Volunteers were teachers who helped expand Ethiopia's system of education and made a qualitative improvement in the English language competence of an entire generation of Ethiopians. In the process, they forged bonds of amity and goodwill with their hosts, and the ramifications of those ties are still being played out in the histories of the two nations. The Peace Corps workers were part of a succession of thousands of Americans who, beginning in World War II, pioneered ideas of bilateral aid in Ethiopia and developed a special relationship, some would say the most extraordinary relationship, between the United States and an African nation.

For almost all of the Americans, service in Ethiopia was a first time in Africa experience. The nation was known to us principally because of the Emperor Haile Selassie's moving address to the League of Nations in 1936 asking that organization to choose between support for collective security or international lawlessness. Some knew of the Italian fascists' use of poison gas and air raids against the poorly equipped Ethiopians. Few realized that the liberation of Ethiopia was the first victory of the Allies in World War II. Because we knew so little about the history and culture of Ethiopia, the Americans presented a *tabula rasa* primed to be filled. With the help of Ethiopian co-workers and friends, we learned a good deal about the fascinating country that was only starting the process of modernization.

My work took me to all of the country's provinces where the wonders I observed remain strongly etched in memory: the rainbow-wreathed mist of the mighty Blue Nile Falls during the rainy season; the castles of Gonder, emblematic of a feudal system that was still extant; the angel heads on the ceiling of the church of Debra Berhan Selassie, their eyes ever watchful for the faithful; a Grand Canyon in the Semien larger than the Arizona model; the mysterious stele, standing and fallen, at Aksum, not far from "Sheba's bath"; the pastel buildings and Mediterranean ambiance of Asmara; the rock-hewn churches of Lalibela, so submerged that it's difficult to see they dwarf the temples of India's Mahabalapuram and Ellora; the walled city of Harar, where Harari women, dressed in colorful garb reminiscent of the Middle East, weave and sell renowned basketry, and the hyena man calls and feeds his bone crunching denizens of the night; the haunting, three-part harmony of the Lalibelas, mendicants, greeting the dawn at verdant Yirga Alem; on the Jimma road, the rain forest shrouded in fog with a colony of colobus monkeys providing black and white accents to the treetops; the German poet's *Blaue Nebelland* on the blue mountained horizon of Bonga; the damp, freezing cold on the heights of Debre Berhan, and the dry heat of lowland Gambella; the thud of the crocodile banging into the side of the dugout canoe in the middle of the Baro; the open air market at Bati where stately Afar nomads from the Denakil desert ascend the escarpment to hawk their camel loads of goods to the highlanders; the pink island of flamingos standing in the shallows of Lake Abaya; the Big Rains, the rival of India's monsoon, followed by the blooming of the "New Flower"; Addis Ababa, when yellow daisy-like Masqal flowers pervade the hills. In the mornings, in our Addis Ababa home, we opened the shutters to look out over the trees and valley to the mountains. There usually was a haze that softened the colors and contours, and as an artist described it, "the sunlight was brilliant, yet cool and soft."

Other Americans in their *sui generis* experiences shared in similar feasts of learning about another people and culture. They saw things and visited places all but unknown to Westerners even today. And the learning was two way: Ethiopians, in small towns as well as in cities, got to know Peace Corps Volunteers and thirsted for more knowledge of the broader world. Together, in the land where coffee originated, we drank freshly roasted brews, and we ate the firey injera and wat long before it became popular abroad. We tasted the bag of the bee, both strong and sweet, on the edge of the abyss into which the Empire was about to descend. Perhaps naively, we thought we knew about the Great Rift until the monarchy was replaced with government by committee, and the real meaning of the term was revealed.

After the revolution of 1974 overthrew Emperor Haile Selassie and brought the repressive Derg (Amharic for "committee") regime to power, official relations between the United States and Ethiopia chilled, but amiable links between the people continued. Ethiopians fleeing the horror of the Derg and a bitter civil war set out in a great diaspora with large numbers coming to the United States. When the oppressive rule of the Marxist-Leninist dictator Mengistu Haile Mariam finally came to an end in 1991, there was hope that a new era might begin for a democratic Ethiopia.

Instead, with the backing of the United States another Marxist- Leninist group, the Ethiopian People's Revolutionary Democratic Front (EPRDF or "the Front"), came to power. The EPRDF has been accused of creating a repressive regime that thwarts democratic processes, abuses human rights, and purposefully intensifies ethnic distrust among the people. According to critics, the repressions of the EPRDF are on a scale the equivalent to those of the world's worst dictatorships. But events in Ethiopia are little reported in American media, and few are cognizant of the record of the post-Derg government or of the condonation of its purported oppressive acts by the United States and other donor nations. More widely publicized are official United States concerns about deficits of democracy for numerous nations with which Americans historically have not had strong ties. In Ethiopia, the African nation with which Americans have worked closely and invested in human resources for over fifty years, the United States government has been strangely quiet about alleged shortcomings in the process of democratization.

This book attempts to bring some balance to description and analysis of events in Ethiopia since the EPRDF came to power. Its aim is threefold: 1) to describe the plight of the Ethiopian people under the EPRDF regime and the role of the U.S. in enthroning and sustaining the Front; 2) to counter questionable pronouncements of the Ethiopian government and the United States Department of State about conditions in the Federal Democratic Re-

public of Ethiopia (FDRE);[1] and 3) to suggest alternate strategies for bringing about democratization in Ethiopia for the benefit of *all* Ethiopians.
Specific analysis focuses on how the EPRDF's power was established, exercised, and maintained in the existing political order. Comparisons are
made between what the EPRDF/FDRE said they were going to do with
what they actually did. Definitions of significant terms and their nuances
are given to provide normative standards (what ought to be) by which to
judge the EPRDF's "democracy," "democratization," and "ideology" and
its commitment to "constitutionalism."

Part I of the book provides a critique of the Transition Period from
1991–1995 when the Transitional Government of Ethiopia was used by the
EPRDF to consolidate its power and to ensure the hegemony of a political
minority over the majority of the people. Part II addresses the record of the
FDRE and the EPRDF's continuing struggle to attain the goals of its ideological creed, "revolutionary democracy." Two secret documents that lay
out the EPRDF's organizational structure and long-term goals and strategies for attaining them are examined to help in an attempt to formulate a political theory for the Front. The book concludes with suggestions for
revision in U.S. policy toward Ethiopia and for peaceful negotiations between a united Ethiopian political opposition and the EPRDF to develop a
liberal democracy for their troubled nation.

The ruling parties of Ethiopia and Eritrea developed from insurgent
groups during the civil war. In the 1980s the Eritrean People's Liberation
Front (EPLF) had emerged as the dominant liberation front among various
anti-Derg factions in Eritrea, the northernmost province of the nation. The
EPLF had a strong political organization and highly disciplined military
units and enjoyed broad-based popular support among Eritreans in its demands for an independent state. During the civil war, the EPLF provided
military training and equipment to Tigray People's Liberation Front
(TPLF) cadre from neighboring Tigray province and helped mold them into
an efficient fighting force.

The TPLF had started as a "national liberation front" with the political
objective of establishing an independent "Democratic Republic of Tigray."
In a February 1976 manifesto, the TPLF defined a Tigrayan as anyone who
spoke Tigriña and described the geographic boundaries of Tigray as extending to the borders of the Sudan and including land previously in Begemdir
and Wollo provinces and "Afar lands including Assab."[2] When the Derg's
army collapsed, the TPLF expanded its goals and proceeded to militarily
occupy the rest of Ethiopia. Leaders of the TPLF had used an armed conflict
in 1943 as a foundational myth to mobilize Tigrayans. The conflict called

"the Woyane" or "revolution" was a popular uprising of Tigrayans against
the Emperor Haile Selassie and what they perceived as "Amhara domination." The TPLF uses the term "the Woyane" as the title of its struggle, and
the term is used synonymously for the TPLF. In 1989 the TPLF joined or
created other ethnic insurgent movements to form a united front, the
EPRDF. Although separate organizational structures were set up for the
EPRDF and its component groups, the TPLF has dominated the leadership
of the united front. Hence, in the chapters that follow, the EPRDF occasion-
ally is referred to as "the Woyane" as well as "the Front," but in the background, remains the directing hand of the TPLF. The proliferation of
acronyms, most of which have no easy synonyms or simple explanatory
names, for Ethiopian political organizations challenge one trying to fathom
the country's political system.

Fortunate indeed is the author who has enjoyed so much support and help
from friends of the enterprise as I have had in writing this book. To thank all
of them in print would be a daunting task, but I symbolically tip my hat to
the probity of a few of the judicious friends with whom I consulted and conferred and who provided mega-aid: my colleague, Conrad Evans, the splen-
did veteran of twelve years residence and work in Oklahoma State
University's programs in Ethiopia who started a chain of serendipitous
events that led to my return to Ethiopia in 1992 to serve as a consultant to the
new government; the late Deborah Hauger who facilitated my testifying before the House Committee on Foreign Affairs, Subcommittee on Africa; the
faculty of Addis Ababa University (AAU) and the alumni of Alemaya University of Agriculture (AUA); in Washington, DC, Chris and Gene Rosen-
feld, LaVerle Berry and the Friends of Ethiopia, and Dr. Aklilu Habte and
the Alliance for Democracy and National Unity of Ethiopia (ADNUE); the
Japanese Ethiopianists of the Japan Association for Nilo-Ethiopian Studies
(JANES); Donald N. Levine of the University of Chicago, the dean of
Ethiopianists; Dr. James McCann and the faculty and staff of Boston University's African Studies Center who provided a congenial setting for a sab-
batical leave; the hospitable Ethiopian community of Boston, and
especially Bisrat Jemaneh, Girma Asfaw, and Dr. Tsehai Berhane-Selassie;
former Peace Corps Volunteers who served in Ethiopia; Dr. Selameab
Wolde Tsadik who supplied helpful information about the AAPO; Dr. Shumet Sishagne who carefully critiqued my manuscript; Elias Kifle who gen-
erously provided photographs; Dr. Getatchew Haile, an intrepid watcher
and an unsurpassed commentator on the Ethiopian scene; and the editors
and publishers of the *Ethiopian Register* and the *Ethiopian Review* who
keep the world informed about what really is happening in Ethiopia. And fi-

nally, special thanks to my wife Pat whose support makes possible all my adventures.

NOTES

1. See the caption of Robert Mankoff's cartoon: "Has there ever been a country that had the word 'Democratic' in its name that was?" *New Yorker*, 2 June 1997, 72.

2. TPLF, *Manifesto*, February 1976.

Acronyms

AAI	African American Institute
AAPO	All Amhara People's Organization
AAU	Addis Ababa University
ADNUE	Alliance for Democracy and National Unity of Ethiopia
ALF	Afar Liberation Front
ANDM	Amhara National Democratic Movement
APDM	Agew People's Democratic Movement
ARDUF	Afar Revolutionary Democratic Unity Front
AUA	Alemaya University of Agriculture
BPRDM	Bench People's Revolutionary Democratic Movement
CA	Constituent Assembly
CAFPDE	Council of Alternative Forces for Peace and Democracy in Ethiopia
CDC	Constitution Drafting Commission
CEOPO	Coalition of Ethiopian Opposition Political Organizations
CETU	Confederation of Ethiopian Trade Unions
COEDF	Coalition of Ethiopian Democratic Forces
COR	Council of Representatives
CPJ	Committee to Protect Journalists

CPR	Council of Peoples' Representatives
EAL	Ethiopian Airlines
EDU	Ethiopian Democratic Union
EFFORT	Endowment Fund for the Rehabilitation of Tigray
ENC	Ethiopian National Congress
EOC	Ethiopian Orthodox Church
EPDM	Ethiopian People's Democratic Movement
EPLF	Eritrean People's Liberation Front
EPRDF	Ethiopian People's Revolutionary Democratic Front
EPRP	Ethiopian People's Revolutionary Party
ESDL	Ethiopian Somali Democratic League
ETA	Ethiopian Teachers Association
EU	European Union
EUCC	Ethiopian Unity Coordinating Committee
FC	Federal Council
FDRE	Federal Democratic Republic of Ethiopia
FJAC	Federal Judicial Administrative Council
GNDA	Gambella National Democratic Alliance
GO	Government Organization
GPRDF	Gedio People's Revolutionary Democratic Front
IEAC	International Ethiopian Action Committee for Unity and Democracy
IFBIN	Industrial Federation of Banking and Insurance Trade Unions
IFLO	Islamic Front for the Liberation of Oromia
IMF	International Monetary Fund
ISCEPC	International Solidarity Committee for Ethiopian Prisoners of Conscience
JAC	Judical Administration Commission
JANES	Japan Association for Nilo-Ethiopian Studies
JIOG	Joint International Observer Group
KPRDO	Keffa People's Revolutionary Democratic Organization
MEDHIN	Ethiopian Medhin Democratic Party
MEISON	All-Ethiopian Socialist Movement
NDI	National Democratic Institute
NEB	National Election Board

NEC	National Election Commission
NGO	Non Government Organization
OAU	Organization of African Unity
OC	Organizational Center
OFL	Oromo Liberation Front
ONC	Oromo National Congress
OPDO	Oromo People's Democratic Organization
PC	Propaganda Center
PDRE	Peoples' Democratic Republic of Ethiopia
PGE	Provisional Government of Eritrea
PM	Prime Minister
POC	Propaganda and Organizational Committee
REST	Relief Society of Tigray
SEPDC	South Ethiopia Peoples' Democratic Coalition
SEPDF	Southern Ethiopian Peoples' Democratic Front
SPDO	Sidamo Peoples' Democratic Organization
SPO	Special Prosecutor's Office
TAND	Tigray Alliance for National Democracy
TDA	Tigray Development Agency
TGE	Transitional Government of Ethiopia
TPLF	Tigray People's Liberation Front
TTESD	Tigray-Tigrea Ethiopians for Social Democracy
UDN	United Democratic Nationals
USAID	United States Agency for International Development
WPE	Workers' Party of Ethiopia

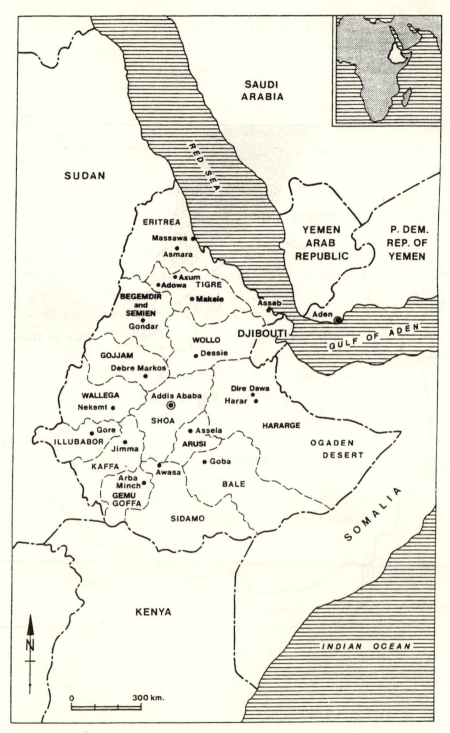

Map 1. Administrative Divisions of Ethiopia, 1974.

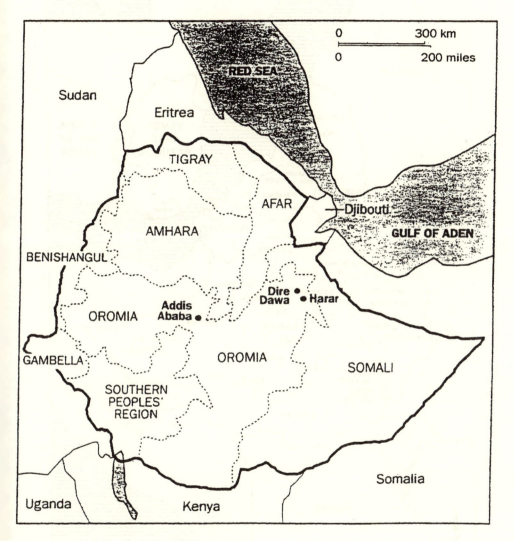

Map 2. Administrative Division of the FDRE.

Part I

THE TRANSITION PERIOD, 1991-1995

CHAPTER 1

The EPRDF Comes to Power

One of the last detritus of the melt down of the Cold War in the early 1990s was the Marxist-Leninist dictatorship of Ethiopia headed by Mengistu Haile Mariam. As Ethiopia's patron states, the USSR and Eastern bloc nations, made tectonic shifts toward democracy and abandoned their support of the African comrades-come-lately-to-communism, the People's Democratic Republic of Ethiopia (PDRE) was cursed with plagues that would daunt a Pharaoh, much less a Derg. Africa's longest running civil war had laid waste large areas of the nation. Devastating famine left hundreds of thousands dead and suffering and engendered a massive relief dependency upon the generosity of the world's benevolent donors—a galling experience for a proud people. Inexpedient domestic policies decimated the economy, snuffed out human rights, and alienated the masses. The ravages of these plagues drove multitudes to flee their homes to fight the evil system or to seek refuge elsewhere.

Mengistu Haile Mariam, the "Red Pharaoh" of the Blue Nile, presided over this carnage. His massive military was losing the civil war to insurgent forces, the strongest of which were two originally Marxist organizations from the north, the Eritrean People's Liberation Front (EPLF) and the Tigray People's Liberation Front (TPLF). In 1989 the TPLF joined or created other ethnic insurgent movements and led a united front known as the Ethiopian People's Revolutionary Democratic Front (EPRDF) that battled Derg forces outside of Eritrea.[1] Another ethnic movement, the Oromo Liberation Front (OLF), also fought against the government in a more limited way but was not closely allied with the EPRDF.

For almost two decades the Derg and its foes had decimated each others ground forces. There was no victory, only defeat. There was massive death but it led to nothing except the gradual attrition of both sides without advantage to either. Then in 1990 the EPLF and EPRDF became kings of their respective hills at the same time the Derg's once powerful army, demoralized and lacking popular support and leadership, lost any heart for battle and collapsed. Had the demise of the Derg occurred sooner or later, other rebel groups might well have been more important players in the peace agreement that followed, and Ethiopian history would have been different.

In retrospect, it is obvious that the EPLF and EPRDF, Tigriña-speaking allies in the north of the country where the civil war mainly was fought, shared mutually supportive post–civil war objectives. The EPRDF would champion the EPLF's goal of independence for Eritrea and in return the EPLF would provide military backup to keep the EPRDF in power in Ethiopia.

The coordinated strategy of these fronts produced military victories that impelled Mengistu, *de mal en pis*, to an abrupt and belated volte-face to liberalize the nation's economy and political structure.[2] As the Derg came under intense pressure from EPRDF forces, the Red Pharaoh also let the children of Israel, Ethiopia's Falashas, cross the Red Sea to their promised land—at a price.[3] Unbeknownst to observers of the Horn at that time, the departure of Beta Israel by air was a precursor to other Ethiopians' severing ties with their homeland on the ground.

In May 1991 the U.S. government responded to a call from Mengistu's regime and the insurgent groups to hold a peace conference in London for all parties in the Ethiopian civil war.[4] While the U.S. Assistant Secretary of State for African Affairs Herman Cohen attempted to broker peace, the EPLF and EPRDF broke the back of the remnant Derg military. The EPLF occupied all of Eritrea while the EPRDF breached the defenses of Addis Ababa. At that point, the U.S. government arranged for the departure of Mengistu to exile in Zimbabwe.[5]

To give the Devil his due, it was fortunate that Mengistu chose not to fight to a Tewodros-like death and lead his demoralized forces to the grim slaughter comparable to those precipitated by other failed tyrants in Somalia and Liberia. Instead Mengistu took the money and ran, and unlike the Greek archer Philoctetes, who also had shot himself in the foot, he did not wait to be cast out by his companions because of his permanently open, stinking, suppurating, unhealed wound. Indeed, upon the dictator's departure, a new breeze of hope blew, if only for a brief while, in refreshing fragrance upon the highlands of Ethiopia.

THE LONDON PEACE CONFERENCE

In London, the Marxist-Leninist skeletons in the closets of the EPLF and EPRDF were kept firmly under lock, while their leaders, Issayas Afeworki and Meles Zenawi respectively, took on the rhetorical mantles of democrats to win support of Western powers.

Issayas and Meles played Cohen like a well tuned *masinko*, the Ethiopian one-stringed "violin." In effect, the United States anointed the EPLF with *de facto* sovereignty over Eritrea, and the EPRDF was given a green light to enter Addis Ababa to "restore public order and prevent further bloodshed."[6] Cohen maintains that he had no choice in the matter because the EPLF and EPRDF had won the war.[7] The EPRDF was the dominant military force outside of Eritrea, and according to Cohen, no other group was better equipped and positioned to bring stability to Ethiopia in the frantic time following the fall of the Derg. From the State Department's point of view, "the United States sanctified, legitimated, and thereby made cleaner and less violent an ending that it did not cause andcould not change."[8]

Some Ethiopians in Addis Ababa at that time dispute this gospel according to Cohen and believe that the United States had options other than handing over Ethiopia on a silver platter to Meles. Cohen's sanctioning of the EPRDF's action while admonishing Meles to implement democratic reforms in return for continuing U.S. support appears to critics to be too simple a solution for the problems of 1991. They contend that what concerned the United States then (and now) was containment of the spread of Islamic fundamentalism and sustaining of regional equilibrium by the nations with large Christian populations that are dominated by the EPRDF and EPLF. Other issues and other actors were given secondary importance.[9]

The Ethiopia subjected to the power play of the EPRDF and EPLF in May 1991 was a shattered remnant of the land of promise that Western donor nations had analyzed and subsidized before the revolution. The nation's psyche was badly damaged from almost two decades of the hell of the Derg in which virtually all aspects of Ethiopian life fell under the shadow of the ruling party. As the hopes of the early revolutionary reformers dimmed in light of Mengistu's heavy handed reign, the population was polarized into the oppressors and the numerically larger oppressed. Survival became the cardinal principle for the great majority who lived and worked in the tension-filled milieu created by the unpredictable dictatorship. Others refused to endure the decimation of their homeland and in three large streams left their homes to contest or to avoid the ravages of the Derg.

Some went to the battlefields. Since the time of the Emperor's reign, rebels in Eritrea had waged civil war seeking independence from Ethiopia. They were joined by other insurgent groups, armed and aided by foreign nations, to battle the massive military of the Derg—and frequently each other. From this internecine warfare were developed the major "liberation fronts" that were to play dominant roles in post-Mengistu politics. Lost to the nation in this carnage was a sizable number of a generation of young men and women just reaping the benefits of an expanded national system of education. Others, who survived, had dropped out of college or high school, blocked from returning to normal, formal education, getting instead instruction on the battlefield. These veterans of combat claimed the right to rule because they had remained in the country and slain the "evil enemy" of the people while others had fled or eschewed the fight.[10]

A second stream of Ethiopians fleeing the ravages of Mengistu became refugees in neighboring countries, including the Sudan, Somalia, Kenya, and Djibouti. Many were poor and trekked out of the country through Tartarean passageways carrying their meager possessions with them. While a substantial number eventually returned to their native land, others have remained outside of Ethiopia until the present: refugees of extraordinary permanence in a war-inspired melange of suffering émigré peoples in the Horn of Africa. These men and women without a country prefer to stay where they are until they are sure that the rule of law is firmly entrenched in Ethiopia enabling them to return to a welcoming homeland to pursue a way of life they were compelled to abandon.

The third stream escaped the Derg in a diaspora to North America and Europe. This group included many of Ethiopia's "brightest and best" who entered professions, started businesses, and pursued higher education in their new surroundings. Some excelled in their chosen work and lived well.[11] All experienced first hand the virtues and problems of democratic governance and free market capitalism. They comprised what had never existed before—a critical mass of Ethiopians who understood such concepts as democracy, constitutionalism, and human rights by having partaken of them and who earnestly wanted something similar for their fatherland once the demons of the Derg were expelled. These educated cosmopolitan democrats held starkly different views of the theory of governance from that of the authoritarian liberation front leaders for whom war and mass death were the only route to personal power and survival. Between the two groups existed a strong sense of cognitive dissonance, the condition of minds stocked with starkly incompatibilities and desires.

It was from the ranks of expatriate Ethiopians who could speak their minds without fear of retaliation by Ethiopian government officials that the most meaningful political opposition to the EPRDF was to exist.

SETTING UP THE TRANSITION PERIOD

In July 1991 the EPRDF, with the diplomatic backing of the United States, held its Founders Party and organized a national conference in Addis Ababa with over twenty other groups, mostly ethnic liberation fronts, some of which were created by the EPRDF for the occasion.[12] Meles Zenawi, leader of the EPRDF and head of the Marxist-Leninist League of Tigray, presided at the meetings. The EPLF sent observers, as did the United States, the USSR, the United Nations, and other representatives of the international community.[13] Although the absence of discord at the Conference raised hopes for Ethiopia's future, critics charged that the meeting had been carefully stage-managed by the EPRDF. Several important groups long opposed to the Derg but politically at odds with EPRDF were excluded or chose not to participate, creating what critics of "The Conference of Nationalities" termed a problem of inclusion and lack of a national consensus from the start of the transition. Among organizations left out were the American- and European-based Ethiopian People's Revolutionary Party (EPRP), whose army had fought the TPLF in bitter military struggles in Tigre during the civil war; the All-Ethiopian Socialist Movement (MEISON); and the Coalition of Ethiopian Democratic Forces (COEDF). Precluded from the process, these groups went their separate ways principally to opposition exile bases abroad.[14]

On 22 July 1991 the national conference adopted the Transition Period Charter designated the supreme law of the land during what was supposed to be a two-and-a-half-year transition period. The Charter set up institutions and processes to begin restructuring political, economic, and social life in the war-torn nation. Under the Charter, the Transitional Government of Ethiopia (TGE) was established to supervise a transition process culminating in the drafting of a democratic constitution to be ratified by a newly elected National Assembly. This Charter of anomalies expressed democratic sentiments, which most of the world wanted to hear, interlaced with caveats to keep power in the hands of the EPRDF.

The TGE was comprised of the offices of the President (Meles was elected to that post by the national conference) and Prime Minister (a position appointed by the President); a seventeen-member multiethnic Council of Ministers; and the Council of Representatives (COR), originally an eighty-seven- member legislature composed of "national liberation movements, other political organizations and prominent individuals." Members of the COR were not elected by the people but were appointed by the organizations they represented. Although the EPRDF had only thirty-two seats in the COR, critics charge that the seat allocation was manipulated to give the EPRDF and its allies a built-in majority.[15] The Charter did not establish the judiciary as part of the TGE, but proclamations subsequently passed by the COR authorized a system of central and regional courts.[16] Separation of powers was not a concern of the COR in setting up the judiciary, and the courts were far from independent from the executive and legislative branches.

Under the Charter, the TGE was committed to abide by the United Nations' Universal Declaration of Human Rights guaranteeing that "individual human rights shall be respected fully, and without any limitation whatsoever"; to seek an end to armed conflict, including Ethiopian-supported insurgencies in neighboring countries; and to establish elected local and regional councils.

The most controversial provision of the Charter affirmed "the right of nations, nationalities and peoples to self-determination" including a guarantee of the right of such ethnic groups to secede. When first announced, this blue print, with its emphasis on ethnic self-determination and autonomy for the nation's eighty ethnic groups, was considered visionary. Each major ethnic group would get autonomy within its own region, called a *killil*, including powers of police, economic policy and the right to use local languages. Instead of trying to subsume ethnic identities, Ethiopia would embrace them. Some thought Ethiopia would serve as a model—not just for Africa but for other fragile nation-states beset by ethnic strife.[17] Subsequent events in Rwanda, Zaire, and the former Yugoslavia demonstrated the fragility of the overly optimistic Ethiopian approach to encouraging ethnic differences. The secessionist mantra of the EPRDF also was viewed by skeptics as the hidden agenda of the TPLF and its Tigrayan leadership: should their continued dominance of Ethiopia fail, they could abandon the greater Ethiopian ship of state, exercise their right of secession, and possibly join into a new boreal federation with Eritrea.[18]

The National Conference committed the TGE to honor the outcome of an internationally-monitored referendum on Eritrean independence, a covenant previously agreed to by the EPLF and the EPRDF during the civil war. This decision, cited as "courageous" by some outside observers,[19] put an end to a conflict that started in the 1960s and escalated after 1974, sapping the Ethiopian economy, devastating Eritrea, and dashing hopes for development in both areas. This settlement was not popular to a majority of Ethiopians, many of whom condemned the United States for having "given away"

Eritrea. The boundaries of Eritrea included Ethiopia's only ports. It was said that Meles had given up Ethiopia's access to the sea to pay a debt of gratitude to the EPLF which had provided every bit of the TPLF's equipment and military know-how.[20]

The TGE and its counterpart in the north, the Provisional Government of Eritrea (PGE), were committed to the free market and privatization of much of the economy. The two governments developed close working relationships in both the economic and political spheres. With official blessing of the TGE, Eritrea held its referendum and became independent on 24 May 1993. Issayas Afeworki, a leader of the EPLF, was the new nation's first president.

In late 1991 the transitional "parliament," directed the reorganization of Ethiopia into new administrative divisions composed of twelve regions based on nationality or ethnicity and two cities (Addis Ababa and Harar) with regional status (See Map 1 and Map 2).[21] These divisions were given broad powers over security, budget, language, and cultural affairs. Regions were further divided into districts (*weredas*) and neighborhoods (*kebeles*). Critics contended that ethnicity could be a viable organizing principle for an insurgent group but not for a political party which aspires to govern.[22]

There was no unified national military force, and political organizations, most of which were "liberation fronts," were required to register their armed forces and confine them to camps prior to elections with certain exceptions for the EPRDF functioning as the State Defense Army. Encampment agreements were negotiated between the EPRDF and OLF. The agreements set up tripartite (EPRDF-OLF-EPLF) commissions to resolve disputes over encampment and ensure free political competition.

As they began governing under the Charter, Ethiopia's new leaders generated high expectations by committing themselves to such democratic ideas as multiparty elections, a pluralist society with a free press, respect for human rights, and the rule of law with equal status for all peoples of the country.[23] Such commitments were necessary, for the U.S. State Department made it clear that the EPRDF would have to implement democratic reforms if it wanted to continue receiving American support.[24]

In contrast to the nadir achieved by the Derg in political, economic, and human rights spheres, the record of the TGE looked good during its first few months of rule. The human rights and democratic promises made by the leaders of the TGE soon were put to the test, however.

NOTES

1. In the mid-1980s the TPLF orchestrated the establishment of allied ethnic organizations, such as the Ethiopian People's Democratic Movement (EPDM)

and Oromo People's Democratic Organization (OPDO), to broaden its national appeal beyond Tigray. Makau Wa Mutua, "Ethiopia," *Africa Report* (November-December 1993): 51; for analysis of the success of the EPLF and TPLF during the civil war, see Harold Marcus and Kevin Brown, "Ethiopia and Eritrea, Nationalism Undermines Mass and Technology," in *Ethiopia in Broader Perspective*, eds. Katsuyoshi Fukui, Eisei Kurimoto, and Masayoshi Shigeta, (Kyoto: Shokado, 1997), II: 139–157.

2. United States response to Mengistu's belated reforms and "charm offensive" to improve relations with the West was "guardedly positive." Terrence Lyons, "The Transition in Ethiopia," *CSIS Africa Notes* (27 August 1991): 3.

3. Mengistu reportedly received US $35 million from Israel in exchange for letting some 15,000 Beta Israel emigrate from Ethiopia to Israel in May 1991. The money was deposited in a bank in the United States, but it was never collected by the dictator or his cronies. See, Thomas P. Ofcansky, "National Security," in *Ethiopia: A Country Study* eds. Thomas P. Ofcansky and LaVerle Berry, (Washington, DC: Library of Congress, 1993), 300–301.

4. The London peace conference was part of a lengthy process started by the U.S. Department of State which earlier had established contacts with guerrilla groups including the TPLF and the EPLF. For background on the London conference and its precursors, see Lyons, 3. See generally, John W. Harbeson, "Post-Cold War Politics in the Horn of Africa: The Quest for Political Identity Intensified," in *Africa in World Politics: Post Cold-War Challenges* eds. John W. Harbeson and Donald Rothschild, (Boulder: Westview Press, 1995), 127–146.

5. For Mengistu's version of his removal from power, see Mengistu Haile-Mariam, "I Had to Break Silence . . ." *Ethiopian Review* 4 (March 1994): 38–41; contra, Paulos Milkias, "Mengistu Haile Mariam, Profile of a Dictator," Part VI, *Ethiopian Review* 4 (February 1994): 56. Robert Frasure, a National Security Council Africa specialist, Robert Houdek, charge d'affaires in the U.S. Embassy in Addis Ababa, and Cohen persuaded and pressured Mengistu to step down as early as January 1991. Paul B. Henze, "Off the Sidelines and Discreetly into the Fray," *Los Angeles Times*, 29 May 1991. According to the *New York Times*, Frasure asked Mengistu a blunt question: What would it take for him to leave? "The Ethiopian President looked startled at the suggestion but did not seem to rule it out completely." Jane Perlez, "New View of Ethiopia," *New York Times*, 31 May 1998, A10. The answer to Frasure's question has not been made public.

6. On May 26 acting Derg president, General Tesfaye Gebre Kidan, telephoned Houdek to report that he could no longer control his troops. In response, Cohen concurred in Meles' proposal to bring EPRDF forces into Addis Ababa to prevent anarchy and destruction. Paul B. Henze, *Ethiopia in 1991—Peace Through Struggle*, RAND, p-7743, 1991, 11; Edmond J. Keller, "Government and Politics," in *Ethiopia: A Country Study,* eds. Thomas P. Ofcansky and LaVerle Berry, (Washington, DC: Library of Congress, 1993), 262–65.

7. Lyons, 3–6.

8. Terrence Lyons, "The International Context of International War: Ethiopia/Eritrea," in *Africa in the New International Order: Rethinking State Sovereignty and Regional Security* eds. Edmund J. Keller and Donald Rothchild, (Boulder: L. Rienner, 1996), 91–92.

9. Editorial, "Ethiopia's Bigger Picture—the Horn, the Middle East, and the West," *Ethiopian Tribune*, 1 February 1995, 2.

10. Christopher Clapham, *Africa and the International System: The Politics of State Survival* (Cambridge: Cambridge University Press, 1996), 242.

11. Admasu Shunkuri, "Ethiopians in the U.S.," *Ethiopian Review* 5 (March 1995): 22, 24, 26–27. For Prime Minister Meles' thoughts on the "best and brightest," see letter, Meles to Vestal, 30 November 1995, published as "Focus," *Ethiopian Register* 3 (August 1996): 26–27.

12. According to Cohen, after the EPRDF occupied Addis Ababa, the United States was no longer mediating but was serving in a "de facto advisory role for the three opposition groups." Lyons, "The Transition in Ethiopia," 5.

13. The future president of Eritrea, Issayas Afeworki, was an EPLF observer.

14. The EPRP and MEISON were excluded from the conference on the grounds that they had "declared war on the new regime." Political groups identified with the Derg, such as the Workers' Party of Ethiopia (WPE), were not invited to participate. Lyons, "The Transition in Ethiopia," 6.

15. The OLF was allowed twelve seats; the Afar Liberation Front (ALF), the Islamic Front for the Liberation of Oromia (IFLO), and the Workers' Representatives received three seats apiece. The remaining thirty-five seats went to individuals or organizations beholden to the EPRDF. Makau Wa Mutua, "Ethiopia," *Africa Report* (November-December 1993): 51.

16. International Human Rights Law Groups, *Ethiopia in Transition, A Report on the Judiciary and the Legal Profession*, Washington, DC (January 1994): vi.

17. "Ethiopia's Endangered Dream," *Newsweek*, International edition, (6 July 1992): 19; Donald Crummey, "Ethnic Democracy? The Ethiopian Case," in *Proceedings of the 37th Annual Meeting of the African Studies Association*, Toronto, Ontario, 3–6 November 1994.

18. Theodore M. Vestal, "Deficits of Democracy in the Transitional Government of Ethiopia Since 1991," in *New Trends in Ethiopian Studies,* ed. Harold G. Marcus, Vol. 2 (Lawrenceville, NJ: Red Sea Press, 1994), 188–204.

19. Marina Ottaway, "An Update on the Democratization Process," *Ethiopian Review* 3 (August 1993): 32; cf., Patrick Gilkes, "The Eritrean Referendum," *Ethiopian Review* 3 (April 1993): 59–61; Alemayehu Gebre Mariam, "The Tangled Web of Nationality and Citizenship in Ethiopia," *Ethiopian Review* 3 (April 1993): 75; Minasse Haile, "Legality of Secessions: The Case of Eritrea," *Emory International Law Review* 8 (Fall 1994): 480–537; Edmund J. Keller, "The United States, Ethiopia and Eritrean Independence," in *Eritrea and Ethiopia: From Conflict to Cooperation* ed. Amare Tekle, (Lawrenceville, NJ: Red Sea Press, 1994). For an optimistic evaluation of Eritrean nationhood, see Ruth Iyob,

"The Eritrean Experiment: A Cautious Pragmatism?" *Journal of Modern African Studies* 35 (1997): 647–673.

20. Lara Santoro, "At the Root of an Odd African War: Money," *Christian Science Monitor*, 22 June 1998; see also John Young, "The Tigray and Eritrean Peoples Liberation Fronts: A History of Tensions and Pragmatism," *Journal of Modern African Studies* 34 (March 1996): 105–20.

21. Proclamation 7/92; see Walle Engedayehu, "Ethiopia: Democracy and the Politics of Ethnicity," *Africa Today* 40 (Spring 1993): 29–53.

22. Sandra Fullerton Joireman, "Opposition Politics and Ethnicity in Ethiopia: We Will All Go Down Together," *Journal of Modern African Studies* 35 (1997): 387–407; cf., Kidane Mengisteab, "New Approaches to State Building in Africa: The Case of Ethiopia's Ethnic-Based Federalism," *African Studies Review* 40 (December 1997): 111–32.

23. Henze, *Ethiopia in 1991*, 3.

24. Lyons, "The Transition in Ethiopia," 5. The EPRDF showed its heavy-handed response to critics by suppressing demonstrations against the Front during its first few days of occupation of Addis Ababa. When thousands took part in demonstrations protesting against the United States role in bringing the EPRDF to power, Woyane forces opened fire on demonstrators in front of the American Embassy and in other locales reportedly killing ten or more people. Clifford Krauss, "Several Rioters are Killed as Ethiopians Vent Anti-American Anger," *New York Times*, 30 May 1991, A10; "2 Ethiopian Rioters are Killed as Rebels Fire on Anti-U.S. Rally," 31 May 1991, A10.

CHAPTER 2

The Importance of Political Definitions

Before reviewing and analyzing the record of the TGE, it is important to establish some semantic guidelines—to give definitions to significant words and phrases used in the Ethiopian political lexicon. Throughout the transition period, such terms as "democracy," "democratization," "authoritarianism," and "ideology" were bandied about without giving them meaningful explanations. Frequently, terminological distortions were deliberately fostered by government officials with a view to deceiving their audience.[1] Indeed, the current political rhetoric used in justifying or criticizing events in Ethiopia often amounts to what Giovanni Sartori calls "confused democracy" in which almost anything—rules, laws, policies, and decisions—can be defined as, or justified in the name of, democracy,[2] or in the case of the EPRDF, "revolutionary democracy." Major actors in the politics of Ethiopia could be accused of exploiting and manipulating language for their own selfish ends—of "calling in ambiguity of language to promote confusion of thought."[3]

The four sections that follow will use the terminology of contemporary political science to bring a sharper, if not incisive, definition to key terms and phrases needed to understand the TGE's professed efforts at democratization. Political science is the study of power relationships, and this critique will focus on questions of how power was established, exercised, maintained, and transferred in the political order of the transition. Political science methodology also will be employed to compare empirically-grounded knowledge (what is) with normative theories (what ought to be) to evaluate the TGE and its legacy.

While fully aware that definitions of "democracy" and other important concepts are complex and contested, an attempt at making more clear the meaning of the language used, at least in the English discourse or translations, by TGE apologists and critics alike will facilitate more astute analysis. After defining basic theories of democracy and authoritarianism and postulating on the elusive concepts of "democratization" and "ideologies" and investigating what the TGE did, this section of the book will conclude with a comparison of the acts of Meles and his followers with those normative standards to identify which, if any, were missteps on the path of democratic transition.

WHAT IS DEMOCRACY?

Democracy is a relative term, best illustrated by American humorist James Thurber's answer to the question, "How's your wife?" Replied Thurber, "Compared to what?" At best, a government can be said to be relatively democratic when compared to other regimes.[4]

Conceding the relativity of democracy, what are the parameters of the concept? Some definitions have stood the test of time. Schumpeter, writing in the early post–World War II era, defined democracy as an "institutional arrangement for arriving at political decisions in which individuals acquire the power to decide by means of a competitive struggle for people's votes."[5]

In power terms, democracy is a political system in which political power is widely shared in the sense that citizens have ready access to positions of decision making. Such access has two meanings: the citizen's ability to contact decision makers to attempt to influence their decisions and the citizen's capability to stand for (compete for in an election) decision-making positions.

Decision making in a traditional democratic system would be based on such principles as: 1) the sovereignty of the people;[6] 2) equality in voting (the votes of all adults are given equal weight);[7] 3) effective participation (which needs not be universal but should be representative);[8] 4) inclusion of all those subject to the laws of the state;[9] 5) majority rule restricted and limited by rights of minorities;[10] and 6) the free flow of information to enlighten understanding (each citizen should be given the opportunity for arriving at a considered judgment as to the most desirable outcome of political decisions).[11]

A democracy, by necessity, has a free market place of ideas. Freedom of speech and press are essential to civic understanding, for when rulers monopolize or distort information, citizens cannot develop enlightened understanding. Nor can they effectively criticize those who rule. The significance of the "Madisonian principle" in the U.S. experience is instructive. The Madison principle holds that citizens have an absolute right to criticize, without fear, government officials whom they have designated to temporarily rule in their behalf.[12] Related to this is citizen access to government media resources, access to technologies to create the press, and the right to demand information from government.

Post–Cold War political theorists have added nuances to traditional democratic theory to define requirements for a "liberal democracy." Valerie Bunce identifies five such requirements: 1) dominance of rule of law (with an independent judiciary to interpret the laws); 2) extensive civil liberties guaranteed by law (including freedom of expression, freedom of the press, freedom to form and join organizations—sufficient to ensure the integrity of political competition and participation); 3) representative government (simultaneously representative, accountable, and powerful); 4) a Weberian bureaucracy that is rule-bound, merit-based, and responsible to elected public officials; and 5) a system of some dispersion of economic resources (by disseminating economic resources, there is less chance that political rights will be a prerogative of wealth, especially where it is concentrated in the hands of the government).[13]

Liberal democracy features *certain* political procedures, but *uncertain* political results. Authoritarian regimes, on the other hand, feature *uncertain* political procedures, but *certain* political results. In a liberal democracy, procedures for handling political conflict are regularized. There is consensus on rules of the game, and these rules are codified into law. Democratic politics are thus regularized but risky—what could be called "continuing experiments."[14]

A liberal democracy "is characterized not simply by a pluralism of comprehensive religious, philosophical, and moral doctrines but by a pluralism of incompatible yet reasonable comprehensive doctrines." In such a system, "a plurality of reasonable yet incompatible comprehensive doctrines is the normal result of the exercise of human reason within the framework of the free institutions of a constitutional democratic regime."[15]

Fair and free multiparty competitive elections are key indicators of democracy in a pluralistic society. In such a setting, it is inevitable that any majority will have to be made up of a number of minorities. The parties will have to produce platforms which "accord due weight to minority opinion and coordinate compromises and trade-offs on the voters' behalf."[16] Democratic electoral processes permit opposing forces to depose and replace current officeholders, in contrast to authoritarian electoral systems which do not permit the electoral defeat of those in power and serve as an instrument of mass mobilization and legitimation for the regime.[17] Those elected serve in representative institutions that have considerable policy-making powers and feature public deliberations, including public votes.

Democratic electoral systems are most likely to evolve in societies where politically relevant resources exist outside the control of the central government. Politically relevant resources include wealth, communications, education, and organization, as well as the capacity to employ armed forces.[18]

History has discredited so-called one-party democracy as practiced in some African nations and in Marxist-Leninist regimes. The principle underlying one-party democracy is that a single party can be a legitimate expression of the overall will of the community. This institutional arrangement theoretically allowing for mediation, negotiation, and compromise among struggling factions, groups, or movements did not work well in reality. When given a choice, many of those ruled by one-party governance opted for a system of institutions to promote discussion, debate, and competition among divergent views. The people chose a pluralistic system encompassing the formation of relatively autonomous organizations, movements, pressure groups, and political parties with leaderships to help press their cases.[19] This suggests that another facet of liberal democracy is the separation of state from civil society.[20]

WHAT IS AUTHORITARIANISM?

In contrast to a democracy where political power is widely shared, an authoritarian system has a highly concentrated and centralized power structure. Indeed, the two governing systems are mirrored opposites of each other. In an authoritarian system, power is generated through control of a repressive system that excludes potential challengers and through political parties and mass organizations that mobilize people around the goals of the government.[21]

Principles of authoritarianism might include: 1) rule of men, not rule of law; 2) rigged elections; 3) all important political decisions made by unelected officials behind closed doors; 4) a bureaucracy operated quite independently of rules, the supervision of elected officials, or concerns of constituencies they purportedly serve; 5) the informal and unregulated exercise of political power.[22]

Authoritarian leadership is self-appointed and even if elected cannot be displaced by citizens' free choice among competitors. The authoritarian regime does not guarantee civil liberties nor does it tolerate meaningful opposition.[23] Control of mass media makes it impossible for the people to learn of political alternatives. There is no freedom to create a broad range of groups, organizations, and political parties to compete for power or question the decisions of the rulers. Instead there is an attempt to impose controls on virtually all elements of society.[24]

Authoritarian political systems are characterized by several features that contribute to their stability: 1) control over and support of the military to provide security to the system and control of society; 2) a pervasive bureaucracy staffed by the regime; 3) control of internal opposition and dissent; 4) creation of allegiance through various means of socialization.[25]

Inadequate performance in response to demands of the people is likely to lead to the downfall of an authoritarian political system. The answer to challenges to the system tends to be tighter control, not adaptation. Authoritarian political systems tend to be too rigid to adapt to changes or to accommodate growing demands on the part of the populace or even groups within the system. This inability to adapt is a crucial factor contributing to the erosion of authoritarian control, for its legitimacy to govern relies heavily on its performance.[26] Such was the case in the USSR and Eastern Europe where "actually existing socialism" failed.[27] Popular pressure can induce a reluctant authoritarian regime to democratize—as seen in the dying gasp of Mengistu's regime. But the building of pressure takes time.

Authoritarian regimes, such as Marxist-Leninist single-party systems, enjoy a political and economic monopoly through one-party rule and through their capacity to both own and plan the economy. Because they are able to expand their powers by placing everyone within the system in a position of uncertainty, the party enjoys indefinite political tenure. Thus, a transition from authoritarianism to democracy requires a virtual inversion of the political system.[28] It requires rulers to make a clean break with their authoritarian past—a course of action that few autocrats are willing to follow.[29]

WHAT IS DEMOCRATIZATION?

"Democratization" is a transition from an authoritarian system to a form of government that ensures civil liberties and provides its citizens with means to influence or attempt to influence policy outcomes. If successful, this dynamic process produces an open contest for public office without a preordained winner. If the voters, rather than the transitional incumbents, control the final outcome of this competition, then the transition can be called democratic.[30] The determinative moment in the transition from authoritarian to democratic rule occurs when a political actor becomes incapable of subverting the political process.[31]

Reaching that point means that most conflicts are resolved by democratic institutions, which do not determine the outcomes in advance. No group or institution subsequently can change the outcomes, and all relevant political forces comply with the decisions of the democratically elected decision makers. As Adam Przeworski observes: "Democratization is an act of subjecting all interests to competition, of institutionalizing uncertainty."[32]

The decisive step toward democracy is "the devolution of power from a group of people to a set of rules."[33] Lifting official barriers to political expression and negotiation provides extensive scope for compromise and democratic institution building. When that happens, democracy is in place, and a nation then can carry on its business under that "ingenious political arrangement for the articulation, expression, and mediation of difference."[34] Transparency and accountability of government enhance the arrangement and encourage an inclusive approach to governance rather than a winner-take-all mentality.[35]

Another significant aspect of democratization is the emergence of meaningful and autonomous local and regional governments that share power with the national government and check its whims. Local control and participation in subnational groups may provide means of further socializing citizens into the ways of democracy.

A central feature of democratic life is the separation of state from civil society. For democratization to occur in former authoritarian states, there has to be a process of "double democratization": the interdependent transformation of both state and civil society.[36] This "double whammy" of democratization is difficult and takes time to accomplish. A free flow of information and programs of citizen education are indispensable to this process.

WHAT IS AN IDEOLOGY?

An ideology is a discrete and relatively coherent system of thought or belief. The capacity of a political regime or party to mobilize support and secure some form of legitimacy depends on a continuous process of producing and renewing their systems of thought or belief. Like all belief systems, ideologies are part mythical and part inspirational. They are descriptive as well as prescriptive and provide simplified, often mythical explanations of the political world. Power is rarely exercised without some kind of symbolic attribute or support, and the study of ideology focuses on that aspect of power. Thus, the study of ideology is an indispensable part of social and political analysis.[37]

Ideologies are used to inspire the party faithful to achieve announced political goals—to explain, justify, or ratify a particular course of action. In Ethiopia, the EPRDF's ideology is called "revolutionary democracy." Critics of the EPRDF have characterized the Front's ideology as "ethnicist."[38] As we investigate the EPRDF's political and economic goals and the strategies for realizing them, the meaning of these two ideologies should become more clear.

Having set down guideposts of widely accepted definitions of "democracy," "authoritarianism," "democratization," and "ideology," let us proceed on the winding road of analysis of the record of the TGE and the EPRDF.

NOTES

1. See, Giovanni Sartori, "Constitutionalism: A Preliminary Discussion," *American Political Science Review* 56 (1962): 863.

2. Giovanni Sartori, *The Theory of Democracy Revisited* (Chatham, NJ: Chatham House, 1987), 6.

3. A. E. Housman, *The Name and Nature of Poetry* (New York: Macmillan, 1939), 31.

4. Robert A. Dahl, *Dilemmas of Pluralistic Democracy* (New Haven, CT: Yale University Press, 1983), 4. Thurber's comments should not be interpreted as sexist.

5. Joseph A. Schumpeter, *Capitalism, Socialism, and Democracy*, 3d ed., (New York: Harper, 1950), 269.

6. Aristotle, *The Politics*, trans. T. A. Sinclair, (London: Penguin, 1992), 202–206; Robert A. Dahl, *A Preface To Democratic Theory* (Chicago: University of Chicago Press, 1956), 37.

7. Dahl, *A Preface To Democratic Theory*, 6; *Democracy and Its Critics* (New Haven, CT: Yale University Press, 1989) 109–110.

8. Dahl, *A Preface To Democratic Theory*, 6; *Democracy and Its Critics*, 109.

9. Dahl, *A Preface To Democratic Theory*, 6; *Democracy and Its Critics*, 119–131.

10. Dahl, *A Preface To Democratic Theory*, 37–38; Sartori, *The Theory of Democracy Revisited*, 32–34.

11. Dahl, *A Preface To Democratic Theory*, 6; *Democracy and Its Critics*, 111–112, 338–340.

12. Anthony Lewis, *Make No Law* (New York: Random House, 1991), 61, 71.

13. Valerie Bunce, "The Struggle for Liberal Democracy in Eastern Europe," *World Policy Review* 7 (Summer 1990): 398– 401.

14. Bunce, 400; Justice Oliver Wendell Holmes, Jr., wrote of democracy as an experiment in his dissent in *Abrams v. U.S.*, 250 US 616 (1919).

15. John Rawls, *Political Liberalism* (New York: Columbia University Press, 1993), xvi.

16. Noberto Bobbio, *The Future of Democracy: A Defense of the Rules of the Game* (Minneapolis: University of Minnesota Press, 1987), 24.

17. Benjamin Ginsberg, "Elections and Voting Behavior," in *The Oxford Companion to Politics of the World* ed. Joel Krieger, (New York: Oxford University Press, 1993), 261.

18. Ibid.

19. David Held, "Democracy," in *The Oxford Companion to Politics of the World* ed. Joel Krieger, (New York: Oxford University Press, 1993), 223.

20. Jane Shapiro Zacek, "Prospects for Democratic Rule," *In Depth, A Journal for Values and Public Policy*, 3 (Winter 1993): 262.

21. Marina Ottaway, "From Political Opening to Democratization?" in *Democracy in Africa: The Hard Road Ahead* ed. Marina Ottaway, (Boulder, CO: L. Rienner, 1997), 6.

22. Bunce, 401.

23. Tamara J. Resler and Roger E. Kanet, "Democratization: The National-Subnational Linkage," *In Depth, A Journal for Values and Public Policy* 3 (Winter 1993): 18.

24. Juan L. Linz, "Authoritarianism," in *The Oxford Companion to Politics of the World* ed. Joel Krieger, (New York: Oxford University Press, 1993), 60.

25. Resler and Kanet, 18.

26. Ibid., 18–19.

27. Geoffrey Swain and Nigel Swain, *Eastern Europe Since 1945* (New York: St. Martin's Press, 1993), 101.

28. Bunce, 401.

29. Autocrats in Africa who peacefully stepped down when voted out of office include Kenneth Kaunda in Zambia, Didier Ratisiraka of Madagascar, and General Ali Saibou of Niger; see "Democracy in Africa, A Lull in the Wind," *The Economist* (4 September 1993): 42.

30. Laurence Whitehead, "Democratic Transitions," in *The Oxford Companion to Politics of the World* ed. Joel Krieger, (New York: Oxford University Press, 1993), 225; see also, Guillermo O'Donnell and Philippe Schmitter, *Transitions from Authoritarian Rule: Tentative Conclusions About Uncertain Democracies* (Baltimore: Johns Hopkins University Press, 1986).

31. Adam Przeworski, *Democracy and the Market, Political and Economic Reforms in Eastern Europe and Latin America* (New York: Cambridge University Press, 1991), 14.

32. Przeworski, 12–13.

33. Przeworski, 14.

34. Held, 224.

35. David F. Gordon, "On Promoting Democracy in Africa: The International Dimension," in *Democracy in Africa: the Hard Road Ahead* ed. Marina Ottaway, (Boulder, CO: L. Rienner, 1997), 156.

36. Held, 223.

37. John B. Thompson, "Ideology," in *The Oxford Companion to Politics of the World* ed. Joel Krieger, (New York: Oxford University Press, 1993), 409–410.

38. See, e.g., Worku Aberra, "Ethnicism: The Ideology of a *Worari* State," *Ethiopian Register* 4 (June 1997): 24.

CHAPTER 3

Squelching the UDN: Previews of Coming Attractions

In July 1991, a few days after the Transitional Charter was issued, the EPRDF was challenged to live up to its rhetorical promises about human rights and freedom of association by a newly organized multiethnic political party, the United Democratic Nationals (UDN), also known as the National Democratic Union. In responding to a peaceful challenge from an organization that took seriously the purported guarantees of the Charter encouraging citizens to organize political parties and to voice dissent, the EPRDF provided a preview of its methods of subjugation that were to become all too familiar during the following years. A full panoply of public and private sector weapons were unleashed upon the opposition.[1]

Political activists representing the three largest ethnic groups in Ethiopia, the Oromo, Amhara, and Tigrayans, founded the UDN, the first new political party established under the Charter, to oppose the ruling EPRDF and the TGE. On 5 September, some 3,000 members of the UDN elected a thirty-five person Central Committee of the party, representing many of the nation's different ethnic groups, and approved a twelve page summary of the organization's objectives.

The UDN's "Political and Economic Programmes of Action" advocated democracy, the protection of human rights, and equality, and ethnic unity for the people of Ethiopia. Several of the ideals and core values of the party were in direct opposition to those of the EPRDF. Most notably the UDN was opposed to the division of the nation along ethnic lines as prescribed by the

Transitional Charter. Objecting to the TGE's acquiescence in a referendum on Eritrean independence, the UDN maintained that "Eritreans were Ethiopians" and that the future of Eritrea was an internal question for the people of Ethiopia. The UDN pushed for requiring the Transitional Charter to be submitted to a vote of confidence by the people and for the Council of Representatives to be an elected body responsible to the people instead of being representatives of groups invited by the EPRDF. The party also supported the creation of an independent judiciary and advanced the idea of "the unrestricted right to private property which is a precondition for the economic and social progress of our people."[2] Each of these platform planks of the UDN was anathema to the Woyane.

In September 1991 the UDN began holding weekly public meetings that were attended by 8,000 or more participants. EPRDF informants infiltrated the party and reported to the TGE any UDN plans or speeches that could be interpreted as being anti-government or anti-Charter. In addition, EPRDF cadres attempted to disrupt meetings of the UDN and to harass those attending.[3] Despite these harrying tactics by the EPRDF, the UDN appeared to grow in numbers and popularity.

In response to the organization of an openly oppositional political party, the TGE-controlled mass media, especially radio, carried on a campaign vilifying the multiethnic UDN as a chauvinistic Amhara organization harboring many former members of the Derg. The government's English language newspaper, *The Ethiopian Herald*, called the UDN "a warmongering, discord-sowing and violence-advocating sadistic" group whose rank and file was comprised of "disgruntled ex-servicemen, anarchists, and hooligans."[4] To counter the government's "disinformation," the UDN published pamphlets explaining its programs, policies, and stands and distributed them widely. The leaflet campaign was effective, and on 15 September, an estimated 150,000 UDN supporters held a peaceful mass demonstration in Addis Ababa.[5]

Three days later, the EPRDF, realizing a nascent opposition party had hatched, sent a handwritten letter to "the representatives of the UDN" (the officers) accusing them of being against the TGE, the Charter, and EPRDF programs. The letter was the opening ploy of a typical scheme used by the EPRDF to infiltrate opposition parties. Wrote the EPRDF spokesman: "To defend ourselves against false accusations and to let the people know the difference between our programs, we demand that your meeting scheduled for tomorrow be conducted in a joint panel discussion between you and our representatives."[6] Officers of the UDN declined the offer to let their meeting become an EPRDF-dominated gathering.

Although the COR had passed a proclamation establishing procedures for peaceful demonstrations,[7] the TGE attempted to block a UDN mass public gathering in Addis Ababa on 24 November. The planned assemblage came in the wake of reports of widespread killings in fighting between EPRDF/TGE forces and OLF militia in Dire Dawa and of government-instigated ethnic disturbances in various parts of the country. The UDN blamed the TGE for what it viewed as a deteriorating security situation in the nation and organized a march to protest inter-ethnic fighting. Only the intercession of the embassies of the United States and other donor nations swayed the TGE to allow the Sunday demonstration.[8] More than 100,000 demonstrators turned out at Meskel Square to urge national unity and sta-bility and to call on all political groups to settle their differences peace-fully and through dialogue.[9] Throughout the rally, the EPRDF continued to harass participants. Gunfire was heard as marchers passed by what was already being called "the Eritrean Embassy." Troops along the parade route taunted demonstrators to the point that some young marchers hurled stones at the "guards." Military vehicles full of soldiers tried to drive at high speed through the mass of people assembled in the square. When UDN leaders addressed the rally with a loud-speaker system, electricity in the area suddenly was cut off. Nevertheless, according to those present, the protest was a success.[10]

The next day, the party's three top leaders were arrested, detained without charges, and imprisoned for two months—supposedly for being responsible for the rock- throwing incident under the terms of the their dem-onstration permit. Finally, on 23 January 1992 the accused were charged with making "seditious statements," cited in the record as asking how stu-dents could receive an "education in a country whose map had been frag-mented" (by ethnic divisions); and as saying "Eritrea was being sold to the Arabs" and "Ethiopia cannot be sold by individual whim." Two of the lead-ers also were charged with spreading falsifications about government offi-cials, "inciting the people's thinking with malicious thoughts," shouting slogans, and throwing stones.[11]

The charges were flimsy at best. Nevertheless, a habeas corpus order from the High Court was ignored by the TGE. Finally, upon the urging of the U.S. Embassy, a second writ of habeas corpus was brought, and the UDN leaders were released on bail.[12]

From the time of their release, the accused were under constant surveil-lance by the EPRDF. One was warned by a Western diplomat of a plot to as-sassinate him, and he escaped death only with the assistance of an United Nations official. To evade such a life-threatening situation, many of the UDN leaders have sought political asylum in other countries. Meanwhile, the UDN, though never officially banned, had its activities curtailed and its offices physically occupied by the EPRDF. The party had been infiltrated by EPRDF informants and even the founding General Secretary of the UDN, Tsegay Abiye, turned out to be a member of the EPRDF who participated in the party to bring into the open those opposed to ethnic federalism and the one-party rule of the EPRDF. Rank-and-file members of the UDN were tormented, and the party was banned from holding any further rallies and was not allowed to participate in the June 1992 regional elections.[13] In sum, a potentially popular political party standing for democracy and unity was rendered impotent by repeated harassment and intimidation of its members by the government and the EPRDF.

The UDN continues to exist but carries on its limited activities under the close scrutiny of the EPRDF. The TGE's proclamation governing political parties requires political organizations to register their members,[14] thus exposing them to annoyance, intimidation, or worse forms of coercion by the EPRDF. According to the current UDN General Secretary Mulatu Tassew, "Hundreds of our members have been forced to flee. Some are abducted by the EPRDF government and to this day their whereabouts are unknown. Still some are in jail without due process suffering torture."[15] What little opposition the UDN can offer to the government must be carried out by "underground operatives," unregistered party members who work in indirect, behind the scenes ways.

The lesson is that the ruling party would not hesitate to bring the full force of government power against those who legally oppose their policies. Human rights and due process of the law simply could not exist for non-government approved opposition. Where governmental sanctions could not be invoked, the EPRDF and its allied parties could act either subtly or blatantly against "enemies" without fear of having to answer for violating the law by denying others their human rights. The June 1992 elections afforded the EPRDF an opportunity to carry out such a strategy throughout the country and the techniques used to squelch the UDN were replicated on a larger scale.

NOTES

1. Theodore M. Vestal, "Keynote Address: Human Rights in Post-Derg Ethiopia: Atrocities and Injustices," *Unraveling Human Rights Abuses in Ethiopia, Proceedings of a Human Rights Week Observance and Electronic Mail Conference*, 3–8 March 1997 (Medford, MA: The International Solidarity Committee for Ethiopian Prisoners of Conscience, 1997) 24–37.

2. United Democratic Nationals, *Political and Economic Programmes of Action*, Addis Ababa, 1991.

3. Letter, Captain Shiferaw Kebede to Vestal, 26 September 1996.

4. Kebede Bekele, "Hooliganism or Democracy?" *Ethiopian Herald*, 1 December 1991.

5. Letter, Captain Shiferaw Kebede to Vestal, 26 September 1996.

6. Letter, Tilahoun, EPRDF Council of Committee, Addis Ababa, to Representatives of UDN, 18 September 1991.

7. Proclamation No. 3/1991.

8. Letter, Captain Shiferaw Kebede to Vestal, 1 August 1996.

9. African Regional News, "Ethiopia Demo," 25 November 1991.

10. Letter, Captain Shiferaw Kebede to Vestal, 1 August 1996.

11. Formal charges brought by Addis Ababa District Office of the Prosecutor against Tsegaye Abiy T/Haimnanot, Shiferaw Kebede, and Shenkute Kebede W/Mariam, No. 132/44/84, 23 January 1992.

12. "Release of Prisoners," Metropolitan Addis Ababa Administration, High Court, 23 January 1992.

13. "Ato Berehanu Semu was Abducted by the EPRDF Government," *Ethio-Time* (Amharic), Addis Ababa, 24 June 1996.

14. Proclamation No. 46/1993.

15. *Ethio-Time* (Amharic), Addis Ababa, 24 June 1996.

CHAPTER 4

1992 Elections

The EPRDF's methods of subjugation again were demonstrated in the district and regional elections of 1992.[1] In February 1992, the Council of Representatives appointed a ten-member National Election Commssion (NEC), purportedly representing different parties but dominated by the EPRDF and its allies, to organize and administer the elections. "Multiparty" electoral committees (with a majority of EPRDF loyalists) at each administrative level down to kebele polling stations were established by the NEC.[2] The rules of the game were written by the NEC which prepared the EPRDF for what was to come while keeping other parties and the public uninformed until shortly before the expiration of deadlines.

Official publication of "Electoral Rules of Implementation" appeared to offer all participants a level playing field. Voters had to be eighteen years of age or older and meet a two-year residency requirement. Candidates had to be twenty-one and meet a five-year residency requirement. Members of the WPE, Derg security, and Derg armed forces could not participate as voters or candidates unless they had been through a TGE rehabilitation program. COR proclamations provided for access by political parties to government-owned mass media and ensured the right of the people to demonstrate peacefully and to hold public political meetings. In reality, the high-sounding normative standards of the electoral rules were implemented to the disadvantage of non-EPRDF parties. The EPRDF had an unfair head start in knowing the rules and in possessing a preponderance of the politically relevant resources of money, communications, organization, and control of the military.

The stated goals of the elections were: 1) to empower Ethiopian national groups by decentralizing authority and by creating a federal structure of government; 2) to resolve armed conflicts among and within different contending ethnic groups; 3) to provide regional and local governments with a popular mandate and sanction the replacement of the non-elected administrators designated by the TGE; and 4) to demonstrate the TGE's commitment to pluralism. To accomplish these goals, the TGE solicited material and technical assistance from the international community in support of the electoral process.[3]

The unofficial but widely recognized goal of the elections was to demonstrate to the donor nations, the potential granters of large sums of bilateral or multilateral assistance, and especially to the United States, the good faith effort of the TGE to progress towards democratization and "governance." The granting of economic assistance appeared tied to evidence of democratic elections, respect for human rights, and structural adjustments in the management of the economy.

U.S. Assistant Secretary of State Herman J. Cohen stated the American view: "U.S. assistance to Ethiopia is dependent upon progress in democracy and human rights. We continue to closely monitor progress in these two areas and design our programs so as to promote democracy and privatization of the economy."[4] With close scrutiny as leverage, the U.S. government

expected that the elections would represent an important, incremental advance of the 1991 Transitional Charter and the coalitional politics undergirding it; that could be achieved, it was thought, if the parties simply stayed within the process and the country was thereby able to move, however short a distance, away from the previous seventeen year history of armed conflict.[5]

The TGE could easily meet the modest goals outlined by the U.S. Department of State while at the same time consolidating the power of the EPRDF and its surrogate parties.

THE SNAP ELECTIONS

The elections were conducted in two stages: first, in "snap elections" conducted in kebeles during April and May, and secondly, in national-regional elections in June. In the so-called interim, "non-partisan" snap elections, voters selected three-member election committees in each kebele by a show of hands in open meetings. The kebele officials then chose wereda committees who were entrusted with conducting the June elections within the districts and providing for their security. Well-disciplined EPRDF cadre secured a majority in the three-member election committees of most kebeles of the country and in turn chose Meles-devotees for wereda committees.

In late May there appeared to be three major contenders in the upcoming election: the EPRDF and its affiliate parties; the OLF, the only major non-EPRDF affiliated party in the government and the largest party claiming to represent the Oromo people who account for around 40 percent of the total population; and the AAPO, a national party with a name that tended incorrectly to identify it with one ethnic group. All three parties fielded candidates for most of the offices in several regions and were represented on election commissions at various levels.

Then began a campaign of what the OLF and AAPO allege was harassment and intimidation of their members and supporters by EPRDF "zealots." The OLF, AAPO, and sixteen other organizations represented in the Council of Representatives protested the abuses, especially in the snap elections, but the OLF maintained "the imprisonment and harassment of non-EPRDF activists and political candidates continued unabated."[6] Meanwhile, the Oromo People's Democratic Organization (OPDO, a member of the EPRDF) made counter claims of OLF intimidation of its supporters.[7] A few days before the scheduled elections, EPRDF security forces raided the Addis Ababa offices of the AAPO and terrorized party workers. Finally, on June 17, the OLF, AAPO, and three smaller parties, the Islamic Front for the Liberation of Oromia, the Ethiopian Democratic Alliance Group, and the Gedeo People's Democratic Organization, withdrew from the elections—hounded out by EPRDF harassment.[8]

Six days later the OLF pulled out of the Transitional Government, where it had been the second-largest party after the EPRDF. The TGE set up by the Charter was in reality an EPRDF trunk onto which a smaller OLF limb had been grafted. The trunk was composed of an EPRDF core to which were attached bogus party splinters as well as some insignificant minor parties. A few ministerial assignments were made to OLF representatives but with built-in monitoring by EPRDF faithful in strategic places. The growing tension within the government between the EPRDF trunk and its OLF branch was snapped as a result of political dirty tricks and the pinchbeck elections. After being excoriated by the EPRDF's inexorable stance and actions in the TGE and losing some rigged snap elections to the OPDO, the OLF quit the government and withdrew from the elections.

The deployment of EPRDF military units in the Oromo Region in their role as national security forces so outraged the OLF that the encampment accords were ended and some armed conflicts were reported. The tripartite commissions were powerless to prevent such violations.[9] In a short time, the outnumbered OLF military was crushed by forces of the EPRDF.

THE NATIONAL-REGIONAL ELECTIONS OF 21 JUNE 1992

In this stormy milieu, the second stage of the national-regional elections, voting by secret ballot, was held in eleven of Ethiopia's fourteen regions on 21 June 1992. Problems of security and administrative difficulties prevented voting in the Afar (Region 2), Somali (Region 5), and Harar (Region 13) Regions, and in more than half of the polling stations in the Oromo Region (Region 4) and in other areas in the south.[10]

The political parties of the nation were, with few exceptions, based on ethnicity. Some had existed for a number of years as armed insurgents opposed to Mengistu's regime. Others had been created by the EPRDF to garner support in southwestern Ethiopia. The leaders of some of the new ethnic parties were alleged to be from urbanized elites who had little local legitimacy.[11]

In the June 1992 elections, with all meaningful opposition withdrawn, the EPRDF and its surrogates garnered 96.6 percent of the vote, winning 1,108 of the 1,145 regional assembly seats.[12] Despite the one-sided results, the TGE proclaimed the election to be free and fair—an evaluation far different from that of international election observers who forcefully pointed out that Ethiopian democratization was in trouble. In this case, the presence of international election observers could not be used to legitimate fraud on the part of a governing party. Nevertheless, the June elections apparently satisfied donor governments' monitoring of Ethiopian efforts in initiating democratic transitions.

THE NATIONAL/REGIONAL ELECTIONS AS OBSERVED BY THE JIOG

Some 280 members of the Joint International Observer Group (JIOG) representing governments, NGOs, and international organizations, were dispersed throughout the country in internationally integrated teams to witness the processes in the June 1992 elections.[13] Their findings were published in reports of groups and individuals, and in the United States, observers testified before the House Foreign Relations Subcommittee on

African Affairs and participated in panel discussions sponsored by a variety of organizations.[14]

To most of the foreign observers, the elections did not live up to expectations of a democratic process and were thought to be flawed in several respects.[15] The German Observer Group reported that the election results "should not be taken as a fair and free reflection of the democratic will of the people."[16] According to the African American Institute (AAI) statement on the elections, "in very few places were there competitive, multiparty elections" and the elections "fell considerably short of [the] objective . . . to empower through the vote all of Ethiopia's nationalities within a new pluralistic system."[17]

In response to the AAI statement, President Meles acknowledged "that the election process was flawed in many ways" but represented "an important first step towards establishing a democratic political process in Ethiopia." The President affirmed that the TGE stood "firm in its commitment to discuss and address the findings of all international observer teams in Ethiopia" and reiterated the government's willingness to "redress any irregularities, even to the extent of repeating elections in some areas should that be necessary."[18] Meles' rhetoric assuaged any donor nations' concerns about the elections, but in reality, the overwhelming EPRDF victory was inviolable.

Some observers believed the JIOG had been used to build up confidence in what was essentially a single-party election.[19] The observer groups' statements were in marked contrast to the evaluation report of the NEC which held that the elections were "fair and free." The NEC dismissed JIOG criticism of the elections because "the allegations were not sufficiently supported by factual evidence and hence should not be taken into account until they have been verified."[20] With no disinterested third party present to hold the government's feet to the fire, there was no way officially to verify what competent observers had witnessed. Although details of individual reports varied depending on which regions or even which kebeles were visited, most observers rehearsed certain characteristics common to the electoral process. These features were frequently reported in a series of meetings of the JIOG and AAI observers at the completion of their assignments in Addis Ababa. Subsequently, published summary reports reiterated the deficiencies. The major problems were:

1. Voter and Civic Education

The most frequently cited issue was the widespread lack of voter understanding of the election process and the critical need for voter and civic education. While many Ethiopians were enthusiastic about participating in a democratic election, few seemed really to know for whom or what they were voting. There was a need for better understanding by the electorate of basic principles of democratic processes—representation, choice, participation, advocacy, tolerance of opposition, and a free flow of information.

Better training about what to do at the polls also would have helped. On election day, voters frequently needed instructions from polling station officials on how to vote. This slowed down the voting process and gave some officials an opportunity to assist voters in making their choices.

2. Political Participation and Intimidation

Observers found widespread allegations of intimidation, harassment, and detention of candidates, potential candidates, and party officials and supporters principally from a number of non-EPRDF parties. In many cases, observers lacked time or resources to investigate specific allegations, but it was evident that perceptions of intimidation had a harmful effect on voter confidence in the democratic processes. In some weredas, threats of violence created a climate of insecurity, fear, and suspicion that effectively terminated participation by parties and individual voters.

The dominance of the electoral process by particular parties in some areas was aided by the NEC's delivery of election materials to local political parties and interim administrations in areas where bona fide election committee infrastructures were not in place. Some political parties took partisan advantage of this situation to register voters and candidates and to exclude rival organizations from the process.

Arbitrary arrest and detention of individuals and the closing of party offices and occupation of party offices by police were also alleged. While these allegations could not always be verified by observers, the frequency with which they were raised suggests that such tactics were major factors in preventing multiparty elections.[21]

3. Campaigning, Freedom of Expression, and Dissemination of Information

The media generally gave extensive coverage to the election process, including the activities of the JIOG observers. However, political parties complained of a lack of access to the media, especially radio, and found it difficult to successfully stage press conferences. There also were allegations that the government-controlled press slanted the news in favor of the

EPRDF. Restrictions on travel in many parts of the country impeded campaigning.

Observers noted a dearth of public debate on campaign issues. This may reflect the parties' limited campaigning, resulting from a lack of resources or experience, or the shortness of the campaign period. Or it may demonstrate the EPRDF candidates' certainty of winning thus obviating any need to discuss policy questions. Competitive political parties, as contrasted to armed political movements, for the most part were absent.

4. Election Administration

In general, the administration of the elections was hampered by needed election materials not getting where they were supposed to be in a timely way.

Major problems were encountered in establishing the election committee infrastructure authorized in the Electoral Rules of Implementation.[22] In many areas, committees were not constituted far enough in advance of the June 21 election date to allow election officials to do their duty—a defect that did little to bolster voter confidence in the neutrality and fairness of the election mechanisms. In some instances, partially constituted election committees, those without multiparty participation, and election committee surrogates, such as political parties and interim administrations, created opportunities for partisan mischief in the process. The regime's control of *kebeles* and peasant associations empowered the EPRDF and its surrogates to decide the outcome of elections in most of the towns and in the countryside.

Observers met dedicated election officials personally committed to implementing fair election processes. Some of these officials were frustrated by the tardy formation of their election committees; by lack of material, such as offices, typewriters, telephones, and even pens and pencils, and of staff and financing; and by the absence of directives, training, and communication from higher election authorities. The ingenuity of certain election officials in solving administrative problems was especially noteworthy.

Training programs were provided for zonal, wereda, and kebele officials in a number of areas. Unfortunately, most of these "seminars" were held the week before elections—much too late in the process to enable election officials to effectively carry out their responsibilities or to communicate uniform, accurate information to the electorate. The absence of written training materials and directives from the NEC probably contributed to the confusion of local election officials and exacerbated communication of inaccurate information and inconsistent implementation of electoral rules. It also was noted that news of late changes in election procedures by the NEC and the COR did not reach some local officials in time to be implemented.

Observers expressed concern about the lack of control the by NEC and Regional and Zonal Committees over election materials, particularly registration cards and books, which were not numbered. There were deficiencies both in the physical control of materials and in administrative accountability in monitoring and tracking their distribution. Claims were frequently heard that particular political parties had obtained registration cards and distributed them to their supporters. In some cases observers saw individuals with several registration cards.

Voter registration was flawed in many instances because kebele election committees were not constituted enough in advance of election day and there were not enough registration materials. The extension of the deadline for registration until the day before voting effectively made a dead letter of the appeal process set out in the Electoral Rules of Implementation.[23] The requirement that voters specify their ethnic identity (e.g., "Oromo," "Amhara," "Tigrayan," etc.) antagonized a number of people during registration. Many resented being enrolled in a prescribed procrustean dormitory. In a few cases, voters obtained court rulings allowing them to register as "Ethiopians." In other cases they were refused registration for failing to state their ethnic origin.

The climate of intimidation and fear discouraged the nomination and registration of candidates in some areas. Partisan control of the registration process prevented some from acquiring the requisite signatures to qualify for candidacy. The late arrival of voter registration materials after original deadlines for candidate registration had passed also caused problems. The extension of registration deadlines and eventual elimination of the signature requirement for candidates supported by organizations came too late for many of those excluded earlier from the process. In some areas, news of these changes never reached local election officials or potential candidates previously excluded from participation. The extensions of the deadline also reduced the possibility of recourse to the appeal process. In most races EPRDF candidates did not have competition from rival parties for each position to be filled.

5. Secrecy of the Vote

Observers reported frequent infringements of secrecy in voting booths. Voters were sometimes accompanied by election assistants while they cast their ballots. In some instances, the assistant merely instructed the voter on procedures; in others, the assistant would indicate where to mark the ballot, press illiterate voters' inked fingers on the ballot, write in a candidate's name for the voter, or instruct the voters to write their names next to the symbols of particular candidates. There also were reports of two or more voters entering the voting booth at the same time with ensuing consultation on whom to vote for. The consensus of observers was that many of these problems resulted from voters' unfamiliarity with voting procedures rather than an intent at fraud.

LESSONS LEARNED?

In the wake of the June 21 elections, the EPRDF leadership was severely criticized by diplomats, election observers, and the international press for not holding democratic, multiparty contests.[24] The AAI-National Democratic Institute for International Affairs evaluation bluntly declared that the elections were premature, especially for the southern half of the country, ill-conceived, dubious, and counter productive in their contribution to the democratization of Ethiopia. The evaluation further charged that the elections intensified ethnic tensions, reinforced the hegemonic power of the EPRDF while marginalizing other fledgling parties, and were a central factor in the withdrawal of the OLF from the TGE and the return to war in the Oromo Region.[25]

The patina of fair elections sought by EPRDF leaders was scraped off by their unrestrained forces in the field. The ensuing muddle embarrassed Meles and lowered the nation's stock in the eyes of foreign analysts who had hoped for some demonstration that democratization was on track. To mollify critics, on 27 July the COR approved a proclamation establishing an Election Review Board "to see into grievances and complaints in order to correct irregularities."[26] A month later, the COR selected the twenty-one member Board from candidates representing some ten specifically designated governmental groups and NGOs, almost all of which were safely dominated by EPRDF cadre or their associates. The Board received only six minor complaints, none from major parties. The AAPO and OLF and other southern parties refused to bring allegations of abuse before the Board insisting instead that the June polling results be nullified and new elections scheduled.[27] The Board concluded its work at the end of the year without bringing about a reconciliation between the EPRDF and the parties that had withdrawn from the elections.

In September the NEC published an evaluation report of the elections, an apologia primarily responding to election observer concerns. The evaluation emphasized the necessity of political groups learning "to survive and thrive under the new democratic conditions."[28] The spin given the meaning of "new democratic conditions" by the government was to shape the future of Ethiopia under EPRDF dominance. The new democratic conditions were geared for one-party rule.

The national/regional elections were a great disappointment to many of Ethiopia's strongest well-wishers in foreign countries. Numerous friends had admired the democratic rhetoric of President Meles and other leaders, and they were distressed by what they observed or read about the elections.

Nevertheless, the 1992 elections apparently satisfied donor governments' vetting of Ethiopian efforts in initiating democratic transitions. Subsequent showcase improvements in human rights, exemplified by releasing on bail some 400 prisoners who were former officials of the Derg regime, and structural adjustments in the economy, factored in with the TGE's repentant attitude toward the electoral process, apparently established a level of trust sufficient to justify both bilateral and multilateral development projects of the international community. The now you see it, now you don't, one-step forward, two-steps back rhythm of policies for the democratization of Ethiopia by the *isist* or chameleon government seemed to beguile the myopic grantors of aid.

In October the United States agreed to spend $161 million over three years to develop competitive markets and to supply wheat and food oil for urban entrepreneurs and cotton for the country's textile industry. This was the first major United States–Ethiopian bilateral agreement since early in the Derg era. The U.S. action was in line with a $1.2 billion World Bank-led initiative to jump-start the Ethiopian economy.[29]

Thus the TGE accomplished its principal goal with the bogus election. Furthermore, the TGE made good use of what the Japanese call *gaiatsu*, which means "waiting for foreign pressure and using it to overcome domestic resistance to needed policies."[30] The June elections, held in haste at the behest of the donor community, had provided the EPRDF with an opportunity to shore up its power while cozening critics with spurious democratic voting.

The political opposition was in disarray—all grist for Meles' mills. Since the concept of a loyal opposition and an open society are alien to the Marxist-Leninist mind set, it followed that, once they had broken with the OLF, their erstwhile coalition partners, the EPRDF would try to preclude any possibility of a freely competitive political system reversing their "democratic" victories. Their successful management of the elections left the EPRDF and its allies confident that they could then win or successfully rig parliamentary elections and the subsequent ratification of a new constitution.

THE FATE OF "COOPERATING" NON-EPRDF PARTIES

For non-EPRDF political parties that remained in the government after 1992, the cooperative road to "Revolutionary Democracy" was far from smooth. Those who went along with the Front did so on its terms. The Ethiopian Democratic Union (EDU), a national party with a strong base of support in Tigray, had difficulty holding public meetings or renting office space. Would-be landlords received threats about what would happen to them or their families if they rented to such "undesirable tenants" as the EDU. If property owners did not heed such warnings there were other ways to change their minds.

In one instance EDU representatives, following TGE procedures, had letters from the central and regional governments authorizing their establishing an office in a provincial town. On the day of their arrival, citizens of the town were asked by a government official to come to a meeting to discuss some matter of civic concern. The crowd was infiltrated by a few TPLF cadre, assisted by baksheesh-induced minions, who turned the assembly into a "spontaneous demonstration" against the EDU. Eyewitnesses say that most of the crowd did not know what was going on when anti-EDU maledictions were shouted by the infiltrators. The landlord understood the meaning of the gathering, however, and the EDU could not rent office space in that town. When EDU officials protested the proceedings and their outcome, they were told that the citizens were exercising their democratic rights. No mention was made of a constitutional right of association.

Extrajudicial punishment was meted out by the TPLF/EPRDF to supporters of the EDU: some were jailed on trumped-up charges; others lost their jobs; many were socially ostracized. Businessmen could make financial contributions to the EDU only at the peril of losing their business. Most poignantly, EDU supporters from a traditionally devout part of the country were denied sacraments of the Ethiopian Orthodox Church, including baptism, marriage, and burial in a Christian cemetery.[31]

In spite of the obstacles it faced in trying to participate in the government, the EDU continued to be represented in the COR. In late 1993, however, the EDU, along with five other small parties, was tossed out of the COR for attending a Peace and Reconciliation Conference that the government opposed. By the time the Transition Period concluded in 1995, ten of the original political parties represented in the COR were dismissed or forced to resign from the TGE. The EDU still exists, but its members are subject to harassment by local officials and armed members of the ruling party.[32]

THE AAPO: TRYING TO PARTICIPATE

In 1991, when many political groups were organizing on ethnic lines, a pan-Ethiopian, non-ethnic political movement was started by Professor Asrat Woldeyes and others. While the movement's program was being developed, Amharas were being killed in several regions and many fled to Addis Ababa. At that time, Amharas had no organization to plead their case before the TGE, and they were directed to Asrat and his colleagues. To appeal the Amhara's case to the government, the movement was required to be registered as an organization and to hold a permit. To have a pan-Ethiopian organizational name while appealing the plight of the Amharas and not that of others as well, posed a problem for the movement. To stop the pogrom aimed only at Amharas, the movement formally organized as the AAPO. Asrat believes that the major achievement of the AAPO at that time was to lessen the unnecessary killing of Amharas.[33]

The difficulties experienced by the AAPO in attempting to work within the political system after withdrawing from the *soi-disant* elections of 1992 provide further evidence of the EPRDF's crushing of political opposition. Members of the AAPO were divided over whether to register as a political party or to continue operating as a private organization dedicated to exposing atrocities of the regime. Finally, in April 1994, several months after registration of most other political parties, the AAPO agreed that its own status should be so formally recognized.

In preparing to take part in the 1995 elections to select members of the legislature of the FDRE, the AAPO had spunk, leadership, organizational skills, and a considerable number of followers that might pose a serious challenge to EPRDF dominance in a fair election. To prevent such an event from happening, forces of the TPLF/EPRDF closed down some forty regional offices of the AAPO, confiscated vast numbers of party documents, and arrested AAPO president Dr. Asrat Woldeyes and other officers. The AAPO headquarters in Addis Ababa were occupied for several days by government forces who removed truck-loads of documents that were never returned. Members or sympathizers of the AAPO were subjected to arbitrary arrests and beatings for aiding and abetting opposition forces; other members were imprisoned or killed.[34]

The AAPO also was denied permits for staging public meetings or demonstrations. In Addis Ababa, killil officials refused to rent assembly halls to the AAPO or to allow the group to pitch tents in open spaces in the area.[35] According to law, it is not necessary to get permission from the government to stage a peaceful demonstration or to hold a public political meeting. The only requirement is that organizers inform the appropriate government office about an event forty-eight hours in advance.[36] In practice, it is impossible to stage a demonstration without first securing permission from a killil's "Permit Section." Furthermore, the AAPO has been required to apply for permits no earlier than forty-eight hours before a planned event while other, "politically correct" organizations are granted permission a month or more in advance of planned events. The uncertainty in scheduling makes it difficult to publicize meetings that are allowed.

Such is the fate of opposition groups that attempt to play on Ethiopia's less than level political playing field. Without the imprimatur of the EPRDF, opposition political parties are considered to be the enemy and fair game for suppression by "revolutionary democratic forces." On the other hand, lilliputian, inchoate ethnic political parties that are subservient to the EPRDF coalition or pose no threat to it are encouraged and their participation in elections is cited as evidence of pluralism by government officials. This is all part of an EPRDF strategy that, as we shall see, was aimed at winning elections without interruption and holding power without let up.

NOTES

1. See, e.g., Theodore M. Vestal, "Perspectives on the Ethiopian Elections of 21 June 1992: The View From the Center," in *Proceedings of the 35th Annual Meeting of the African Studies Association*, Seattle, WA, 20–23 November 1992. The Charter authorized local/regional elections to be held within three months of the establishment of the TGE, but the June elections were eight months behind schedule.

2. Proclamation 11/92.

3. National Democratic Institute for International Affairs and the African American Institute, *An Evaluation of the June 21, 1992 Elections in Ethiopia*, Washington, DC, November 1992 (hereafter, NDI Report), 1–2. The United States committed $1.6 million to the elections, of which $1.1 million was for observation and $.5 million for the NEC. Altogether, the NEC received more than $12 million in financial and material support from the donor community for the elections.

4. "Testimony of Assistant Secretary Herman J. Cohen Before the House Foreign Affairs Committee Africa Subcommittee on September 17, 1992," 7.

5. Memo, Steve Morrison, USAID/ADDIS, "Reflections on the International Community's Observation of Ethiopia's June 21 1992 Local/Regional Elections," October, 1992; 1–2.

6. "June 4 Manifesto," Statement of Various Member Organizations of the Council of Representatives Objecting to NEC Plans for June 21, 1992 Election; National Election Commission Response to the June 4 Manifesto, 9 June 1992; "Statement of the Oromo Liberation Front Delegation Testifying Before the U.S. House Foreign Affairs Subcommittee on Africa," 17 September 1992, 10. See

also, "Resolution Passed by the 1st Congress of Southern Ethiopia Peoples Democratic Coalition," Addis Ababa, 11 July 1992; OLF Central Committee, "Statement on the Current Situation in Ethiopia and a Proposal for a Political Solution," 23 September 1992; letter, Taman A. Youssouf, OLF North America Representative to James Bishop, Director: International Relief and Development, U.S. Department of State, 6 October 1992. In the Oromo Region, military forces of the EPRDF quickly and with relative ease defeated the divided and poorly equipped OLF. Jennifer Parmelee, "Ethiopia's Democratic Test," *Washington Post*, 6 October 1992, A16. About 20,000 POWs were captured by the EPRDF during the post-election battles. After six months of orientation, 17,000 POWs were released from rehabilitation centers at Hurso and Dedessa. "Seventeen Thousand OLF POWs Released; Pledges Made to Spur Peace, Development," *News from Ethiopia*, Embassy of Ethiopia, Washington, DC, 11 March 1993.

7. See, e.g., "Peoples for Elections Despite Acts of Disruption by OLF," *Ethiopian Herald*, 30 June 1992.

8. Oromo Liberation Front, "Statement Announcing Withdrawal from the Election Process," 17 June 1992.

9. Marina Ottaway, "Of Elections, Democracy, and Holy Water: Reflections on the Ethiopian Experience," in *Proceedings of the 35th Annual Meeting of the African Studies Association*, Seattle, WA, 20–23 November 1992.

10. Elections eventually were held in Region 2 (Afar) in September 1992.

11. Terrence Lyons, "The Transition Toward Democracy in Ethiopia: Observations on the Elections in Welega, June 1992," Testimony before the House Foreign Relations Subcommittee on African Affairs, 17 September 1992, 6.

12. The breakdown among EPRDF parties was: OPDO 433 seats (38.8 percent); Ethiopian People's Democratic Movement (EPDM) 279 seats (24.3 percent); TPLF 243 seats (21.2 percent); EPRDF 81 seats (7.1 percent); Sidamo People's Democratic Organization (SPDO) 36 seats (3.1 percent); Keffa People's Revolutionary Democratic Organization (KPRDO) 27 seats (2.3 percent); and Gedio People's Revolutionary Democratic Front (GPRDF) 9 seats (0.3 percent). Non-EPRDF affiliated parties or individuals that won seats included the Bench People's Revolutionary Democratic Movement (BPRDM) 17 seats (1.5 percent); independent candidates 14 seats (1.2 percent); and four small parties 8 seats (0.8 percent). See also, Editorial, "Event of Historic Significance," *Ethiopian Herald*, 23 June 1992, 2.

13. The role played by international election observers in Ethiopia is a subject of debate. One observer noted that "the lack of clarity about the purpose of their presence seriously undermined the success of the exercise. . . . They supposedly built confidence in the process—without asking whether the process was worthy of confidence." Ottaway, 7–10. AAI field director, Dr. Edmund Keller, contends that the TGE was unprepared for such thorough work by the observers.

14. The report by United Nations staff based on the findings of the JIOG, "Ethiopian Regional Elections June 1992, Summary of Observer Findings," has not been released publicly. "An Evaluation of the June 21, 1992 Elections in

Ethiopia," the report of the National Democratic Institute for International Affairs and the African American Institute, Washington, DC, was published in November 1992. See also, "Statement of the African American Institute," 25 June 1992; "Statement of the German Observer Group," Cologne, 26 June 1992; *Friends of Ethiopia Newsletter*, Special Edition on Ethiopian Elections, August 1992. Among panel discussions by JIOG observers were those sponsored by the Ethiopian Community Center in Washington, DC, on 31 July 1992, and by the Friends of Ethiopia and the Ethiopian Community Development Council in Crystal City, VA, on 6 August 1992.

15. "Testimony of Assistant Secretary Herman J. Cohen Before the House Foreign Affairs Committee Africa Subcommittee on September 17, 1992," 3. Citing reports of international election observers, the European Parliament passed a resolution condemning the arrests and intimidation of opposition candidates. Resolution B3–1032 and 1042/92, reported in *Ethiopian Review* 2 (August 1992).

16. "Statement of the German Observer Group," Cologne, 26 June 1992. The German observer group was sponsored by the Heinrich Boll Foundation. See also Siegfried Pausewang, "Local Democracy and Central Control," in *Ethiopia in Change: Peasantry, Nationalism and Democracy* eds. Abebe Zegeye and Siegfried Pausewang, (London: British Academic Press, 1994), 220–222.

17. "Statement of the African American Institute," 25 June 1992.

18. "Ethiopian President's Response to AAI Statement," 25 June 1992.

19. Marina Ottaway, "Should Elections Be the Criterion of Democratization in Africa?" *CSIS Africa Notes*, 4.

20. Transitional Government of Ethiopia, *Election Commission Bulletin*, Issue Nos. 7 and 8, September 1992, Foreword, 1, 18–22.

21. For a description of harassment, intimidation, and violence against opposition parties, see Annette C. Sheckler's unpublished paper, "District and Regional Elections in Ethiopia: An Exercise in 'Anticipatory' Democracy," 5–6.

22. Transitional Government of Ethiopia, *Election Commission Bulletin*, Issue Nos. 4 and 5, "Electoral Rules of Implementation (Supplement)," June 1992.

23. Any person refused the right to be registered was to present his grievance to the Polling State Electoral Committee within two days of the receipt of said refusal. "Electoral Rules of Implementation (Supplement)," Chapter Two, Procedures on Registration of Voters, 29. Presenting Grievances and Objections.

24. See, e.g., "Ethiopia: Africa's Balkans," *The Economist*, 27 June 1992; "Ethiopia's Endangered Dream," *Newsweek* (International Edition), 6 July 1992, 19.

25. NDI Report, 7.

26. Proclamation No. 21/1992, Election Review Board Establishment Proclamation, 27 July 1992. "Election Review Board Members Elected," *Ethiopian Herald*, 29 August 1992, 1.

27. NDI Report, 34.

28. Transitional Government of Ethiopia, *Election Commission Bulletin*, Issue No. 7 and 8, September 1992, 31–32.

29. "World Bank Official Commends Ethiopian Reform," *News from Ethiopia*, Embassy of Ethiopia, Washington, DC, 11 March 1993. For background on the Ethiopian economy before structural adjustments were made, see J. Stephen Morrison, "Ethiopia Charts a New Course," *Journal of Democracy*, Summer 1992, 133–137.

30. See Leslie H. Gelb, "Japan, Or So It Seems," *New York Times*, 28 March 1993, E15.

31. Information on the EDU is based on interviews with party members conducted in May 1993.

32. "Mengesha Seyoum's EDU Complains of Harassment of its Members," *Ethiopian Register* 4 (October 1997): 9.

33. "An Interview with Professor Asrat Woldeyes," (Amharic) *Reporter*, 8 October 1998.

34. For reports of harassment of AAPO, see *Moresh* 2, 3, 4 especially (Apr/May, July/Aug, Aug/Sep, Dec 1994; Aug, Oct/Nov 1995); Neka Tibeb, "Speech," *Andinet* 3 (1 February 1997). One of the AAPO's original principal concerns was the physical protection of Amharas who are a minority in areas dominated by other ethnic groups. For a description of "tribal politics" and the Amharic speaking people, see "An Interview with Mesfin Wolde-Mariam," *Ethiopian Review* 2 (December 1992): 23–28.

35. Neka Tibeb, "Interview," *Moresh* 3 (Oct/Nov 1995).

36. EHRCO, "Violence Does Not Solve Problems," Special Report No. 13, Addis Ababa, 2 May 1997.

CHAPTER 5

Early Signs of Autocracy in the TGE

Believe then, if you please, that I can do strange things.
                                                —*As You Like It*

There are formidable obstacles, historic and contemporary, against creating a viable participatory system that is constitutional and liberal in Ethiopia. To begin with, there never has been a democratic culture nor prior experience of genuine multiparty elections to fall back on. During most of the twentieth century, Ethiopia has had a legacy of the imperious rule of "big men," the emperors Menelik and Haile Selassie and the dictator Mengistu. Traditional patrimonial forms of administration dominate economic and political life, and the socioeconomic bases for civilized coexistence have all too often been blocked or destroyed by those accustomed to wield absolute power. This heritage of authoritarianism has spawned an apathetic populace psychically numbed and basically unschooled in participatory politics.[1]

The people also have been taught to hate. The war against the Derg and the removal of its totalitarian rule promoted the eruption of hitherto-suppressed ethnic antagonisms. These centrifugal forces have worked to the detriment of extremely fragile national political communities.

In face of these liabilities, the TGE, at best, fostered a discontinuous evolution of democracy. While the U.S. State Department and other TGE apologists proclaimed that the winds of freedom blew in the highlands of

Ethiopia, the EPRDF was getting its breath in preparation for the big blow-out that was to follow.

It became clear that the new EPRDF-directed government had no intention of sharing political power. Whatever distinction existed between party and state soon blurred, and observers of the new regime were confused by the murky similarity between the TGE and the EPRDF and its front organizations. Meles and his comrades controlled both and adroitly used them in a two-track system. Publicly and in diplomatic circles, the TGE said and did what was needed to mollify donor nations and garner developmental aid. At the same time, the government or the party, sometimes openly but often times covertly, would carry out authoritarian crackdowns on human rights and the political opposition. For neutral observers, TGE's attempts at explaining their abuses of democratic processes became so much sophistry when pitted against the accounts of those who were abraded by the harshness of the Woyane and their allies.

The EPRDF brought to governance its history as an insurgent group. For its leaders, conducting domestic politics was viewed not as an exercise in compromise and consensus building among fellow citizens, but as a model of warfare against enemies. The EPRDF used battlefield skills in leadership, discipline, and control of resources to divide and conquer political foes. Central to the plan of battle was the down playing of nationalism and the fostering of social fragmentation by emphasizing horizontal divisions of institutions and organizations and vertical divisions of ethnicity.

THE TGE'S CREDO OF ETHNICITY

The credo of the TGE was the right of nations, nationalities, and peoples to self-determination, the Charter's obfuscated declaration of governance based on ethnicity. The high-sounding principle was more Machiavellian than Wilsonian however. If the outnumbered Tigrayans who directed the EPRDF/TGE could keep other ethnic groups divided and roiled against each other in ethnoxenophobias or content to manage affairs only in their own limited bailiwicks, then larger matters could be subsumed by the one governing party. Thus, what the TGE viewed as the false ideology of nationalism for a "Greater Ethiopia" could be kept in check and its proponents divided and conquered, *ex uno plura*.

Under the TGE blueprint, both government and civil society were fragmentized on the basis of ethnicity. "Ethnic" refers to characteristics of groups that may be, in different proportions, physical, national, cultural, linguistic, religious, or ideological in character. In the post-Derg setting, "ethnicity" seems to refer to "tribal" origins. Foisted on the country was the

Marxist-Leninist "fable of rapport" in order to establish a "presumption of connectedness" between people of the same ethnic background[2] in contrast to their being "Ethiopians." This was no small task since, in Ethiopia, races and ethnic groups had for centuries been inextricably mixed and blended in unity.

The national legislature, the Council of Representatives (COR), was composed of members of ethnic parties and liberation fronts. The state was administered by newly drawn, decentralized, ethnically-based regions or *killils*. The governmental bureaucracy was purged of unwanted elements, labeled as enemies of the people or remnants of Mengistu's government. Ministries were "downsized" under the pretext of pressure from the International Monetary Fund and other multilateral financial institutions. As the TGE completely vitiated the civil service system, dismissed government workers were frequently replaced by poorly qualified TPLF/EPRDF loyalists. A significant number of Eritreans superseded top level bureaucrats in the Ethiopian Telecommunications Authority, commercial and national banks, the Urban Housing Authority, and other agencies.[3] The nation's corporate pride, Ethiopian Airlines, was restructured with most top executives being fired and their places taken by EPRDF-selected managers.[4] Social organizations too were reorganized where feasible, along ethnic lines, with new rival associations, subtly directed by EPRDF regulars, created to challenge and displace existing ones. Among the largest prey caught in this web of ethnic rivalries were the Ethiopian Teachers Association (ETA), the Confederation of Ethiopian Trade Unions (CETU), and even the Ethiopian Orthodox Church and Islamic religious institutions. The proliferation of minor political parties, of which the TGE boasted, also was attributable to this strategy of ethnicity run riot. The *killil* or ethnic region, the TGE's version of the politics of apartheid, became the dominant factor in society.

The TGE's restructuring of the economy was permeated with ethnic and partisan preferences. The Tigray Development Agency (TDA) received a disproportionate share of government subsidies and loans for local investors and entrepreneurs. Statistics indicate that the EPRDF's Privatization Agency Board favored the TDA in auctions of state owned business and industrial enterprises. Eritrean contractors, meanwhile, took over many construction ministry subsidiaries. Both the TDA and Eritrean investors were prime recipients of projects and investments funded by foreign capital.[5]

Economic reform by the TGE produced short term results or at least government generated statistics about growth of Gross Domestic Product (GDP) sufficient to satisfy donor nations. Some of Ethiopia's leading economists, however, questioned the authenticity of the TGE's figures on GDP.[6] Economic development was hindered by lingering problems of land tenure and government ownership of property left over from earlier re-gimes. Nevertheless, two principles of the Marxist-Leninist philosophy as interpreted by the TGE, state ownership of land and the equal distribution of wealth, were at the heart of the country's economic activities. But the results of TGE reform were not encouraging. During the TGE's governance, both rural and urban Ethiopians were among the poorest in the world, and the World Bank reported that the purchasing power of the average Ethiopian in-come was the lowest of the twenty poorest countries monitored by the Bank. Revolutionary democracy appeared to be a revolution of rising frus-trations.[7]

THE PARTY IN ASSOCIATIONS

The technique of control by the EPRDF is a textbook example of Marxist-Leninist strategy—an epilogue to lessons from the communist takeover of Eastern Europe in the 1940s. The EPRDF would monopolize political power and transform the country's socioeconomic substructure into a web of ideologically "correct" alliances subservient to the party.

In the chaotic times following the fall of the Derg, the EPRDF/TGE went about destroying or modifying the bulk of social organizations that had ex-isted prior to the Charter. The ruling party encouraged people to join asso-ciations carefully vetted by the EPRDF. At the same time, the Front made life miserable for other organizations that lacked enthusiasm for the new re-gime. Tightly organized and firmly disciplined EPRDF cadres infiltrated and eventually manipulated many of the institutions and mass organizations of public and collective life, such as grass-roots "action committees," work-ers grievance committees, and local government. Almost all social activity takes place in the context of these front organizations that project an image of "pluralism" in Ethiopia without disturbing the real EPRDF power rela-tions. When party dominance of an institution or organization was chal-lenged, the EPRDF had the means to harass and intimidate opposition until it withdrew—using force if necessary. Conveniently, the EPRDF armed forces had been designated by the Charter as the State Defense Army, and the internal security apparatus was tightly monopolized by the party.

The penumbras of terror spread from the shadow of a framework of gov-ernment modeled on that of the Albanian communist Hoxha. From its Marxist-Leninist mentors, the EPRDF had learned well the lessons of con-trol epitomized by the Soviet system in which everything is related to some-thing else. The entire population could be disciplined by an Ethiopian security leviathan untrammeled by legal, ethical, or religious norms.

Organizations monitored by the EPRDF ensured party dominance on official boards and commissions constituted by the COR. For example, the Constitution Drafting Commission and the Election Review Board were composed of representatives of groups, organizations, and associations—an innocuous, power to the people-sounding arrangement. The hidden agenda was that a comfortable majority of representatives on each board would come from social organizations under the EPRDF umbrella. The work of such boards, while rationalized as broadly democratic, was actually party-controlled. Form purposefully triumphed over substance.

THE OPPOSITION DURING THE TGE

During the time of the transition, the political opposition parties of Ethiopia played the role of a badly divided Greek chorus.[8] That appellation perhaps was overly optimistic in implying that chorus members were at least united in purpose in commenting on the main action in the tragedy of Ethiopia. Given the lack of unity and harmony in the feckless opposition at that time, a better designation for them might have been an array of unaccompanied soloists. They had not yet learned to sing together.

The opposition was composed of individuals and groups with widely differing self-understandings and conceptions of personal fulfillment. During the reign of the TGE, these groups squandered time and resource in endless political bickering and indeterminate internecine warfare. When the opposition gathered, it was like the lively junction of tectonic plates—the earth shifted and shuttered, but when things settled down, there was nothing but destruction to behold. Criticism of everyone else was *de rigueur*, but it was not constructive. The more the division, the greater grew the contentions, and the greater the flow of words, the less the importance of what was said. The notion of compromise had little utility to wily strongmen leaders of personality cults, intent on maintaining their personal power, or to ethnic chauvinists who fostered distrust of all except the chosen few of their own kind. Many harbored hoary grudges against those who wronged their group—regardless of how long ago the crime had been committed. The clash of groups over questions which elicited radical disagreement engendered paralysis, squandered everyone's time, and exacerbated animosities. By magnifying such disagreements among themselves and failing to concede that there were ties that bound them together, the opposition was easy prey for the divide and conquer tactics of the EPRDF.[9] Critics of the TGE sadly dwelt in the valley of despond and disrepute.

The cacophony of opposition voices, with its noise level too high to allow clear reception of worthwhile ideas, gave the United States and other donor nations an excuse to ignore them. Indeed, the meaninglessness of the constantly carping opposition became a catechism of supporters of the TGE. The result was that even when the opposition offered plausible policy alternatives, the donors refused to hear them—or at least they acted audibly challenged.

Making sense of that Tower of Babel of dissent was a formidable task but through the tumult there were two dominant voices. Major players of the opposition were basically divided over two issues: 1) national self-determination, and 2) Ethiopian unity.[10] Advocates of the two sides repelled each other like opposite poles of a magnet. Rational and calm analysis and argument seemed to bounce off those two polar views.

Those who favored national self-determination emphasized the ethnic differences between the people of Ethiopia. Those "ethnic-firsters" were unforgiving of the old imperial state dominated by the Amhara and Tigrayans, that was hostile to their group's language, religion, culture, and development. They saw themselves as grievously injured by events of the twentieth century and vowed that never again would they accept discrimination and second class citizenship at the hands of other ethnic groups. They demanded proportional representation in any new government or else looked to secession to satisfy their sense of justice.

Groups favoring unity saw a Greater Ethiopia as the best hope for the nation's future. They espoused common factors of language, religion, and culture as unifying forces. The accommodationists viewed national self-determination as a secessionist movement—a threat to Ethiopian unity. They feared a fragmented Ethiopia of nonviable states "balkanized" into warring tribes—as in post-Cold War Yugoslavia.

The opposition parties finally made some efforts to present a united front by holding Peace and Reconciliation Conferences in Paris and in Addis Ababa in 1993. The Council of Alternative Forces for Peace and Democracy in Ethiopia (CAFPDE), was organized and sought entry into the transition process.[11] Under strong pressure from the international community, the TGE reluctantly assented to a conference being held in Addis Ababa in December. A special government welcoming committee escorted by tanks and armored vehicles met some of the delegates as they stepped off their airplanes, and seven opposition party members were arrested at the airport. One of those arrested, Aberra Yemane Ab of the Coalition of Ethiopian Democratic Forces, was imprisoned without being charged for four years and is still incarcerated.

At the conference, CAFPDE called upon the TGE to desist from hindering the democratization process and to join in another round of transition with the full participation of all political groups and parties operating within and outside of Ethiopia. The TGE boycotted the meeting and denied the need for such a gathering since, from the perspective of the government, Ethiopia was at peace and democracy reigned throughout the land. The government-controlled media denounced the gathering and gave little coverage to the activities of participants. Nevertheless, members of CAFPDE stated that the conference had been successful in raising the political consciousness of the people. Some who participated in the meetings were punished by the government. Several non-EPRDF political parties, including five southern groups, the Agew People's Democratic Movement (APDM) and the Ethiopian Democratic Union (EDU), were expelled from the TGE for their participation in the conference.[12]

OUTSIDERS' ATTEMPTS AT RECONCILIATION

Representatives of the United States made two attempts at bringing together the TGE and the opposition for constructive talks. In December 1993 former United States President Jimmy Carter, who had some success in bringing to the negotiating table seemingly irreconcilable groups in several fractious nations, met with representatives of opposition groups and negotiated a proposal for the formation of a new broad-based transitional government, the restructuring of the police and the military, and the postponement of June 1994 elections. Carter attempted to persuade the TGE to meet with representatives of opposition groups to discuss mutual concerns in March 1994. The proposed peace talks were rejected by President Meles who declared that the TGE would not yield to efforts to reverse the transitional process or change its programs and structure.[13]

In light of that failed attempt at reconciliation, the success of the Task Force on Ethiopia of the U.S. House Subcommittee on Africa to bring together representatives of some opposition groups with a special envoy from the TGE on 6–9 February 1995 came as a surprise. The Task Force, headed by Congressman Harry Johnston (D-FL), sought to facilitate the return of the opposition groups to the political process in Ethiopia. There was dialogue between the TGE and the OLF, the AAPO, the Coalition of Ethiopian Democratic Forces (COEDF), and the Southern Ethiopia People's Democratic Coalition (SEPDC). Members of the Council of Alternative Forces for Peace and Democracy in Ethiopia (CAFPDE), the umbrella group that many hoped would represent an united opposition, could not agree upon a common strategy and was not represented at the talks, although the group subsequently attempted, unsuccessfully, to enter into a dialogue with the TGE. The Medhin Party was excluded from participating by the Task Force. According to the Task Force, the discussions, the first of their kind since the

London peace talks of 1991, were conducted in an open and serious manner and reflected the strong desire of all parties to resolve their differences.[14] Four bilateral communiqués from the TGE and each of the participating groups were published.

Johnston was pleased with the discussions and asserted that "this initial coming together was a significant step toward opening the democratic process in Ethiopia."[15] Others were less sanguine about the chanting of the *chœur mystique* that basically only agreed to consider further discussions in Ethiopia in the future. The one immediate possibility of talks, that of the SEPDC and the TGE in Addis Ababa in March, was aborted by the government's intransigence in meeting the party's clearly stated preconditions for dialogue.[16]

The TGE was purported to have agreed to provide security and access to the media for opposition parties so long as they agreed to abide by the rule of law. President Meles assured Johnston that there would not be a repeat of human rights abuses. In reply, Johnston told the president that future aid might depend on progress in the protection of human rights in Ethiopia.[17]

Johnston maintained that opposition parties could endorse the proceedings by participating or become "footnotes" in Ethiopia's history. He presented the opposition with a Hobson's choice, a lose-lose situation: either to take part in a flawed-before-it-began election and thus lend their bona fides to a Marxist-Leninist authoritarian regime or to sit down and shut up. This charade was a far cry from structured discussions between the TGE and the opposition to reason fairly and honestly about the proper reconstruction of the constitutional order. Instead, an opportunity for peaceful change was lost. Cynics might have considered the failure of the effort a victory for America's "Africanists," the clique inside and outside of government, who "have a vested interest in perpetuating the hodgepodge of misunderstanding, ignorance, and indifference that passes for policy."[18]

The Task Force exercise was the end game for hope that the United States somehow would use its moral suasion or developmental aid clout to broaden the base of governance in Ethiopia during the transition. Ambassador-to-be David Shinn, then U.S. Department of State's Director of East African Affairs and a member of the Task Force, indicated that the EPRDF government coming to power in 1995 would have America's support.[19]

NOTES

1. There were parliamentary elections during the reign of Haile Selassie. See, Bahru Zewde, *A History of Modern Ethiopia 1855–1974* (Athens: Ohio University Press, 1991), 141, 207.

2. Laurel Richardson, "Narrative and Sociology," *Journal of Contemporary Ethnography* 19.1 (1990): 116–135.

3. Wassy Tesffa, "EPRDF's Quest for Legitimacy," *Ethiopian Register* 2 (March 1995): 33, 35–37, 39.

4. W. M. Akalou, "Ethiopian Airlines Under Siege," *Ethiopian Review* 4 (April 1994): 19–23; Donald E. Paradise, Victor H. Harrell, Jr., Jack Asire, Joseph Brumit, and Norm Dargie, Open Letter "Ethiopian Airlines," *Ethiopian Review* 4 (June 1994): 26–29.

5. Wassy, 37.

6. Eshetu Chole, "A Preliminary Appraisal of Ethiopia's Economic Reforms 1991–1993," in *New Trends in Ethiopian Studies*, ed. Harold G. Marcus, Vol. 2, (Lawrenceville, NJ: Red Sea Press, 1994): 311–333; Daniel Teferra, "Ethiopia: Restrictive Behavior and Continued Poverty," in *Proceedings of the 38th Annual Meeting of the African Studies Association*, Orlando, Florida, 3–6 November 1995; Selamawit Gerimu, "What is the Economic Situation in Ethiopia?" *Ethiopian Register* 2 (September 1995): 24–25.

7. World Bank, *The World Development Report 1994: Infrastructure for Development* (New York: Oxford University Press, 1994), Table 30, 220–221. The idea of a revolution of "rising frustrations" is from Robert L. Hardgrave, Jr. and Stanley A. Kochanek, *India: Government and Politics in a Developing Nation* (San Diego: Harcourt Brace Jovanovich, 1986): 22–23. For analysis of frustrations arising under the TGE, see Dawit Abate, "The End of Crises? Or Crises Without End? The Evolving Dynamics of Post-Derg Ethiopia," in *Ethiopia in Change: Peasantry, Nationalism and Democracy* eds. Abebe Zegeye and Siegfried Pausewang, (London: British Academic Press, 1994), 280–308.

8. Theodore M. Vestal, "Deficits of Democracy in the Transitional Government of Ethiopia Since 1991," in *New Trends in Ethiopian Studies*, ed. Harold G. Marcus, Vol. 2, (Lawrenceville, NJ: Red Sea Press, 1994): 188–204.

9. Ibid.

10. Ethiopian Research Service, "Ethiopia: The Questions of Nationality and Unity and the Need for a National Coalition," Washington, D.C., November, 1994, No. 12.

11. Mankelklot Haile Sellassie, "The Peace and Reconciliation Conference of December, 1993," *Ethiopian Examiner* (February 1994): 12–13.

12. See, Getachew Mekosha, "Peace and Reconciliation," *Ethiopian Review* 4 (February 1994): 12.

13. "Carter Peace Effort Suffered Setback," *Ethiopian Review* 4 (April 1994): 10.

14. "Task Force Pleased with Outcome," *Ethiopian Tribune*, 1 March 1995, 1, 10.

15. Ibid.

16. Ibid.

17. "Harry Johnston Speaks His Mind," *Ethiopian Tribune*, 16 March 1995, 1, 10.

18. James M. Haley, "The Abandonment of Our Africa Policy," *Geographia*, 26 February 1995, 4.

19. Adugnaw Worku, "Interview: David H. Shinn, Director, East African Affairs U.S. Department of State," *Ethiopian Review* 5 (March 1995): 29, 32–33.

CHAPTER 6

Human Rights Abuses by the TGE

Upon taking power, leaders of the Transitional Government promised the people a new era for civil rights and civil liberties for the country. The protection of human rights, that is, governmental respect for freedom of expression and association, for due process of law, for equality before the law, and for the rights of citizens not to be subjected to cruel and degrading punishment,[1] would have been a welcomed attainment for Ethiopia recuperating from the oppression of the Derg. The Transitional Charter specifically stated that every individual should have:

a. The freedom of conscience, expression, association, and peaceful assembly;
b. The right to engage in unrestricted political activity and to organize political parties, provided the exercise of such right does not infringe upon the rights of others.[2]

In addition, proclamations by the COR codified a variety of civil liberties protections.

But even as the TGE was proclaiming its devotion to protecting individual and associational freedom, members of the EPRDF and its government agents were engaged in blatant violations of human rights. Everyday offenses against human dignity were legion. According to Africa Watch, Amnesty International, and the Ethiopian Human Rights Council (EHRCO), thousands of individuals were imprisoned without due process. The most flagrant abuses in the EPRDF/TGE's catalogue of calamities involved the military and the police.

While procedures for peaceful demonstrations were codified in a COR proclamation,[3] the government kept a close reign over those brave enough to publicly step out against TGE policies. The military's killing and wounding of student protestors at an anti-government demonstration at Addis Ababa University (AAU) in January 1993, firing into a gathering of Christian worshipers and murdering several in Gondar in September 1993, and shooting into a crowd and slaying and wounding many at the Great Anwar Mosque and in the Markato in Addis Ababa in 21 February 1995 had a chilling effect on those who would challenge *en masse* the acts of the apostles of Meles.[4] These notorious massacres showed the continuing problem of maintaining the army of the EPRDF, seen in urban areas as "irksome liberators," as the principal law enforcement body even after regional police forces were established.[5]

In addition, freedom of association, one of the bedrocks of human rights, was abrogated by the EPRDF/TGE as part of its monopoly of power. Central to the party's suppression of political opposition was control of the country's socioeconomic substructure of social organizations such as professional associations and trade unions. Peaceful demonstrations by such groups could be denied by government fiat. Freedom of assembly was controlled by a myriad of non-transparent, unpublished rules and regulations that euphemistically could be called "administrative guidance."

A few high-quality, internationally recognized institutions of the nation did not waffle before governmental pressures to conform to the party line, and the independence of these bodies was especially vexing for the EPRDF. Addis Ababa University, which had maintained a remarkable degree of academic freedom even under the Derg, was a hotbed of democratic, anti-authoritarian ideas, and outspoken critics of the TGE. Weeding out the professorial opposition *tout ensemble*, the government summarily dismissed the university president, two vice-presidents, and thirty-nine other faculty and administrators in early 1993. The TGE's justification for the action was to quell on-campus political activities which authorities said had gotten out of hand and threatened the institution's academic integrity. More likely, TPLF leaders, who first became political activists while students in the 1970s, did not want similar seeds of discontent nurtured in a latter-day garden of learning. They erred badly, however, in their choice of professors selected for dismissal. Many of those fired had advanced degrees from prestigious foreign universities and were known for their contributions to AAU's academic renown. The government's squelching of highly regarded scholars accomplished its objective: student and faculty will to resist was broken.[6] But the *bona fides* of the TGE abroad was severely eroded.[7]

Ethiopian Airlines (EAL), reputed to be the best and most reliable airline in Africa, also was targeted for restructuring by the TGE. The generally profitable EAL enjoyed strong traffic demands and recently had purchased new Boeing and McDonnell Douglas aircraft as part of a fleet renewal plan. The soundness of the enterprise made incredulous the announcement of the EAL Board of Directors, headed by the TGE's minister of defense, that the airline was being reorganized to save it from "apparent collapse." *Tout de suite*, EAL's top thirty-eight executives, accused by the board of "corrupt and inefficient management," were replaced by EPRDF-selected managers. The restructuring plan called for EAL to be owned and operated jointly by the governments of Ethiopia, Eritrea, and Djibouti.[8] The corporate pride of the nation, the airline that was "bringing Africa together," had a new flight plan. The new "Near Abroad Airlines" flew the corporation into previously unchartered nether regions of deficits and reduced quality of services.

The bridling of the country's most independent institutions by the TGE sent a clear message to other groups: toe the party line or face TGE-enforced restructuring, loss of jobs, and further harassment. The TGE could get away with its institutional intimidation because the fragmented Ethiopian civil society was incapable of generating legitimate opposition or social consensus. The citizenry, ill-informed or disinformed, was kept guessing about the government's next move.

A STIFLED PRESS

Meanwhile, the flame of press freedom that had flared briefly following Mengistu's departure was extinguished by the TGE. Although the Council of Representatives had passed a Proclamation on Freedom of the Press on 21 October 1992, newspapers and magazines critical of the government were shut down and news distributors harassed into carrying only politically correct publications. The law, supposedly passed to guarantee a free press, was principally a negative set of restrictions on the media with criminal penalties for violations. Specifically, the proclamation listed taboo subjects for publication that included: "any criminal offence against the safety of the State or of the administration" or of the national defense force; any defamation or false accusation against any individual, nation/nationality (ethnic group), people or organization; or any criminal instigation of one nationality against another or incitement of conflict between people.[9]

With the EPRDF/TGE or its non-independent courts determining the meaning of "criminal offence," "defamation or false accusation," or "criminal instigation," journalists and publishers soon found that almost any criticism of the TGE or the EPRDF or its front organizations or their policies could be punished. A lively free press, so essential in developing an informed public and in holding the government's feet to the fire, was castigated as "an anti-government lobby." The free market of ideas was replaced by the EPRDF company store that peddled the official line.

News distributors and publishers conformed to EPRDF/TGE pressures or went out of business. By 1994 some twenty editors and journalists of privately owned newspapers had been arrested by the TGE. Ethiopia was well on its way to surpassing such totalitarian regimes as the Peoples Republic of China and Syria in its willingness to throw journalists in jail.[10]

Without the safeguard of a free and uncensored press, the fawning government-controlled media informed the public of only what the EPRDF thought appropriate. Government policies and activities were routinely praised rather than being questioned by the mass media. The EPRDF/TGE effectively cut off the "breathing space" for criticisms of public officials or government institutions or policies and stifled any "commitment to the principle that debate on public issues should be uninhibited, robust, and wide-open" and "may well include vehement, caustic, and sometimes unpleasantly sharp attacks on government and public officials."[11] Instead, party line propaganda passed for "news." The watch dog press had been neutered into a lap dog media yapping only on command.

VIOLATIONS OF DUE PROCESS

Other human rights violations scarred the record of the TGE. The government held 1,700 prisoners for their alleged crimes under the Derg, but the Special Prosecutor's Office was overly slow in charging the former government officials and bringing them to trial.[12]

The official number of other security prisoners was unknown, but EHRCO estimated that thousands of OLF activists had been detained since 1992 when that organization deserted the TGE and carried on guerrilla warfare that was crushed by the Army of the EPRDF. According to Mesfin Wolde Mariam, chairman of EHRCO, by 1994 more than 2,000 individuals had been imprisoned without due process,[13] and there were at least 8,000 state security prisoners whom he regarded as "politicals."[14]

The imprisonment of Dr. Asrat Woldeyes, the distinguished surgeon, professor, and president of the AAPO was the most infamous case of TGE persecution of a political opponent. Under Dr. Asrat's leadership, the AAPO was gaining popular momentum and was positioning itself to politically challenge the EPRDF in mid-1994. Dr. Asrat, called by some "Ethiopia's Mandela" for his fight against the ethnic fragmentation of his country, was arrested on bogus charges of conspiring to incite armed rebellion against the state.[15] His "conviction" by the Central High Court, dominated by members of the TPLF, and imprisonment were condemned worldwide as an attempt to cripple the AAPO's leadership and destroy the organization. Amnesty International found that Dr. Asrat had been arrested "on the basis of slender and dubious evidence and without direct proof of the alleged conspiracy." The same can be said of all the spurious criminal cases brought against him.[16] In September 1994, when peaceful demonstrators attempted to protest the imprisonment of Professor Asrat at the Central High Court in Addis Ababa, they were beaten, jailed, and humiliated by representatives of the EPRDF/TGE.[17]

The example made of Professor Asrat gave clear warning. The EPRDF would brook no meaningful opposition—even from those attempting to operate within the confined political milieu of the TGE. For speaking out strongly for democracy, Ethiopian unity and territorial integrity and against the ethnic policies of the EPRDF, Dr. Asrat languished in prison for more than five years. He was not the only Ethiopian suffering for his beliefs, speech, and writing. Thousands of other prisoners of conscience from all walks of life—political activists, teachers, businessmen, workers, peasants, and members of professional and trade associations—have endured torture, imprisonment, and even worse punishment for opposing the EPRDF regime.[18]

Further, the treatment of prisoners of conscience is reported to be reprehensible. Many are incarcerated in what have been described as dirty prison cells unfit for human habitation. At least twenty-eight of those detained by the government have died in prison, mainly for lack of adequate medical treatment and due to poor sanitary conditions. Professor Asrat and members of the AAPO central committee were allowed visitors only on Saturday and Sunday afternoons and only for a period of thirty minutes. When Negatu Tesfaye, defense counsel for the AAPO, complained to the Central High Court about inhuman prison conditions, he was charged with defamation of "the good name and reputation" of the Central Prison.[19]

THE NEED FOR OPPOSITION IN A DEMOCRACY

What the TGE did not want was opposition as understood in parliamentary democracies. Public disagreement is an essential instrument of popular government. Democracy, to a great extent, is government by public discussion, not simply the enforcement of the will of the majority. Not any "will," but only a will formed in vigorous and wide-open debate should be given sovereign authority. By confusing opposition with rebellion, the TGE prevented key players from participating in deliberations. Without being threatened or deprived of their livelihood by the TGE, Ethiopians were unable to articulate and publicly defend nonconformist political views. Consent was meaningless without institutional guarantees of unpunished dissent.[20] The popular sovereignty claimed by the TGE was pointless without rules organizing and protecting public debate. The rhetorical commitment of the TGE to protection of rights of expression, assembly, and association vital to political opposition were shams in practice. The legally protected right of opposition provides an essential precondition for the formation of a democratic public opinion—something that was not allowed to develop in Ethiopia. A political system that limits government can prevent rulers from insulating their decisions from future criticism and revision.[21] Rules forbidding punishment of dissenters might compensate for a lack of better motives by EPRDF leaders.

The TGE had no difficulty with one fundamental norm of democratic government: after a decision is made, the outvoted minority must submit to the will of the majority. But the rules of the game of democracy allow losers to mount aggressive campaigns of public sarcasm and to focus public opinion irritatingly on the unforeseen consequences of the decision reached—a situation the EPRDF will not tolerate. In the long run, such momentarily annoying arrangements make for better decisions. In other words, rights are not designed merely for the protection of the minority but also for the correction and instruction of the majority.[22] Thus, the restraints of constitutionalism tend to make government more intelligent—a condition badly needed in Ethiopia.

PARTY STRATEGY FOR SUPPRESSING HUMAN RIGHTS

The suppression of human rights in Ethiopia was not an *ad hoc* occurrence, however. It was part of the long-range strategy of the EPRDF. The party's plans for gaining and maintaining political control of Ethiopia, including "materializing the peoples' political and human rights," were spelled out in a secret document that was distributed to EPRDF cadre in June 1993. To better understand the actions of the EPRDF and its front parties during the transition period and afterwards, it will be necessary to examine this detailed strategy document.

NOTES

1. Aryeh Neier, "Human Rights," in *The Oxford Companion to Politics of the World* ed. Joel Krieger, (New York: Oxford University Press, 1993), 401–403.

2. Transitional Government of Ethiopia, *Transitional Charter of Ethiopia*, Part One, Article One, Addis Ababa, 22 July 1991.

3. Proclamation No. 3/1991.

4. In Adebabay Iyesus Church in Gondar, seventeen were killed and sixteen wounded by security forces on 7 September 1994; at the Anwar Mosque in Addis Ababa, nine were killed and 129 wounded by security forces on 21 February 1995. "U.F.E.R.'s Report to the UN," *Ethiopian Register* 4 (June 1997): 20.

5. Jean Helene, "Defiant Ethiopian Leader Boycotts Peace Conference," *Le Monde* in *Guardian Weekly* (2 January 1994).

6. Robin Lubbock, "A Campus Subdued," *Chronicle of Higher Education*, (10 November 1993): A39; Donald N. Levine, "Is Ethiopia Cutting Off Its Head Again?" *Ethiopian Review* 3 (August 1993): 25–29, 31.

7. The Council of the American Association for the Advancement of Science on 16 February 1997 passed a resolution against the Ethiopian government's violation of the human rights of AAU professors. The AAUP did the same.

8. W. M. Akalou, "Ethiopian Airlines Under Siege," *Ethiopian Review* 4 (April 1994): 19–23.

9. Proclamation No. 34/1992.

10. "Renewed Crackdown on the Free Press," *Ethiopian Register* 2 (September 1995): 15; "Harassment on Free Press Continues," *Ethiopian Review* 4 (March 1994): 10–11; "Press Freedom in Question," (April 1994): 10.

11. *New York Times v. Sullivan*, 376 US 254 (1964).

12. "Trial of Derg Members," *Ethiopian Register* 2 (February 1995): 13–14.

13. "EHRCO Released its 6th Report," *Ethiopian Review* 4 (February 1994): 11.

14. Nicholas Kotch, "Human Rights an Issue in Strategic Ethiopia," Reuters World Service, 20 June 1996.

15. "The Case of Professor Asrat Woldeyes," *Ethiopian Register* 3 (August 1996): 32–34.

16. "Free Asrat! The Cry of Many," *Ethiopian Review* 4 (August 1994): 15; Lisanua Fitihaye, "Professor Asrat Woldeyes—Victim of TPLF's Political Conspiracy," *Ethiopian Register* 5 (July 1998): 20–29.

17. "A Communique Issued by the Head Office of the AAPO," *Ethiopian Register* 1 (October 1994): 9. According to government media, "Police asked and were granted by court to take action against the crowd of about 500 demonstrators who violated the peace of the court on September 20." "AAPO Confirms Arrest of Supporters, Proposes Measure," *Ethiopian Herald*, 27 September 1994.

18. See, e.g., Getachew Haile, "Violation of Human Rights of Ethiopians by the Tigray People's Liberation Front," *Unraveling Human Rights Abuses in Ethiopia: Ways and Means of Alleviating the Problem*, Proceedings of a Human

Rights Week Observance and Electronic Mail Conference, 3–8 March 1997 (Medford, MA: ISCEPC, 1997), 38–43.

19. "AAPO Leaders' Defense Lawyer Charged with Defamation of AA Central Prison," *Ethiopian Register* 5 (February 1998): 7–8.

20. See Stephen Holmes, "Precommitment and the Paradox of Democracy," in *Constitutionalism and Democracy* eds. Jon Elster and Rune Slagstad, (Cambridge, UK: Cambridge University Press, 1988), 233.

21. Ibid.

22. Ibid.

CHAPTER 7

The Strategy of the EPRDF

In June 1993 (Sene 1985 Ethiopian Calendar) at the time the EPRDF was transforming itself from a revolutionary front into the governing body of the nation, the Front published a sixty-eight-page Amharic document, "Our Revolutionary Democratic Goals and the Next Steps." The document, written to define in detail the party's goals, was distributed to party cadre but was kept secret from the public. In 1996 the *Ethiopian Register*, an American journal, obtained a copy and published an abridged English translation.[1] This translation provided non-EPRDF cadre for the first time with a clear statement of the political and economic goals of the Front and the strategies and tactics to be used in attaining them. With the document as guide, the actions of the EPRDF/TGE can be seen as part of the party's plan for gaining and maintaining political control of Ethiopia. A review of some of the details of the strategy document explains many of the EPRDF's actions and will help inform the formulation of a political theory of the Front. The content of the document is presented here with the same headings and subheadings used in the original version.

REVOLUTIONARY DEMOCRACY

The EPRDF strategists, heirs of the Marxist-Leninist League of Tigray, retreated from their communist roots and wartime strategies of the early 1990s. Major changes around the world and in Ethiopia forced the EPRDF to adjust its approach and to proclaim "Revolutionary Democracy" in place of Marxist socialism as the party's ideology. The contents of revolutionary democracy are expounded in the political and economic goals of the strategy document. At the heart of the concept of revolutionary democracy is the old communist idea that leaders of the Marxist-Leninist party at the center of public life should direct all aspects of society on the basis of a supposedly superior knowledge of the nature of social development conferred on them by the party ideology. Explicit in the document is the division of society into traditional communist classes: the peasantry, the bourgeoisie, the proletariat, and the comprador class. The enemy of revolutionary democracy is "imperialism," a euphemism for nations that practice free market capitalism—a paradoxical view since development aid from "imperialist" countries to a large extent keeps the EPRDF in power. Strawmen called "chauvinists," "narrow nationalists," or "secessionists" are alluded to in the document to denigrate opposition and to contrast their wanton ways with those of the Front.

The document began optimistically by noting that in general, conditions in 1993 were conducive for the EPRDF to realize its goals. Nevertheless, the party would be able to fulfill only such limited objectives as conditions allowed during the Transition Period. Once the Transition Phase was "successfully completed," however, the party could begin fully to implement its program. Thus, revolutionary democracy could be realized only after a new constitution was ratified and the Federal Democratic Republic of Ethiopia (FDRE) came into being.

POLITICAL GOALS

The organization's first political goal was listed as "Materializing the peoples' political and human rights completely." According to the document, Revolutionary Democracy is based on a polarized society composed of the people and the ruling classes. By "the people," the document alludes to "the great majority of the population," also called "the great oppressed majority," while "the ruling classes," or "oppressors" refers to those who were in power during the regimes of the Emperor Haile Selassie or the Derg—or more correctly to any who oppose the EPRDF. The party program quite bluntly does not equally stand for the rights of both the people and the ruling classes. The democratic rights of the masses are listed and include a roster of such human rights and due process protections as freedom of expression, the right to organize at any level and in any form, the right to strike in accordance with the law, and the right to express one's opposition even to the revolutionary democratic government which serves the people's interest. In light of rights actually denied to the general public by the TGE, it is instructive to see the rights of the people enumerated in the strategy document, including guarantees against imprisonment without due process and protections from beatings, confiscating of people's property, searching people's property, searching people's houses, or restricting their freedom of movement or belief. All of these civil liberty protections were denied various opponents of the government by the TGE. But even this anomaly was explained in the document.

Whether the rights of "the ruling classes" will be protected depends upon the relevance that this will have to protecting the rights of the masses. If the rights of mass clash with those of ruling class, then the rights of the oppressors will have to be suppressed and the rights of the oppressed will have to be respected.

This party line of support for the rights and interests of the oppressed masses vis-à-vis those of the oppressors will have to be soft-pedaled, however, for two reasons. One is that such blatant partisanship would "be unacceptable in the eyes of Western democracy and would invite the fierce opposition of imperialism." The strategy document notes that "the two imperialist camps" (the Cold War protagonists) "have crumbled and given way to the hegemony of the imperial power led by the United States" This reduction in world powers has narrowed the chances for the EPRDF to realize its goals by shifting allegiance from one camp to the other. United States hegemony has increased the chances of the Front offending the American government which could mobilize imperialist forces against the EPRDF—that is, they could cut off development aid vital to Ethiopia's economy.

The second reason is that it is possible to ensure human and democratic rights of the masses without suppressing all the rights of the oppressors. There also are two reasons for this. The first is that historically the enemies of Revolutionary Democracy in Ethiopia—"feudal, anti-people bureaucratic forces"—are poor. Although imperialism has global hegemony, it can only fulfill its interests in Ethiopia through what the EPRDF perceives as "the enemy within." But Ethiopian supporters of capitalism lack the political, economic, and military power to be of service to imperialists, and their organized representatives are "paralyzed by internal contradictions and cannot offer a viable alternative to the people."

The other factor is the superior power of the EPRDF in comparison to that of its enemies or of "vacillating" forces such as the national bourgeoisie. The Front enjoys greater support from the people, especially the peasantry, and thus the EPRDF can protect the rights of the masses without openly suppressing the rights of the oppressors.

The strategy document describes several techniques for protecting rights of the masses. First, the country's new constitution "should be formulated in such a way that it guarantees the rights of the masses." Laws made in pursuance of the constitution would be used to protect the rights of the people and outlaw "obstructionist activities of the enemies." Institutions to protect the constitution and EPRDF-made laws would be established. When the ruling classes attempt "to obstruct the exercise of the rights of the masses," any relevant legal article can be cited to punish them. Should the oppressors rebel against the constitution, the EPRDF would "mobilize the people and crush them."

The Front's stand on human rights is clearly stated:

When we say that all citizens' democratic rights will be respected in the future socio-political system, it doesn't mean that Revolutionary Democracy will stand equally for the rights of the masses and the ruling classes. Our support is always for the rights of the masses only.

In spite of what guarantees of rights are written into the constitution or in future legislation, the strategy document implies that equal protection of the law for all citizens will not be a feature of an EPRDF government.

Political parties likewise will be treated differently depending on their sponsorship. The First Congress of the EPRDF had passed a resolution stating that the political system to be established would be multi-party. Under the interpretation given "multi-party" by the strategy document, "the masses will have many parties" and the ruling classes "will have the opportunity to organize." These parties can compete for political power, but if the ruling classes try to "obstruct the masses from exercising their rights, Revolutionary Democracy will use the constitution and other laws to punish them and bring under control their illegal activities." The meaning of "obstructing the masses" or "illegal activities" is not explained, but the interpretation of these phrases by the EPRDF does not bode well for any who might compete against the Front for political power.

Under the TGE, the Defense Force was composed of the armies of the EPRDF's member organizations. As long as the military belonged to one political force, it could legitimately work in behalf of that political organization. Under a multi-party system, however, the Defense Force would become the army of the state, and it could not continue as the army of the EPRDF. Unless the army severed its direct organizational link with the EPRDF and its division into TPLF, EPDM, and OPDO units, it would "invite the opposition of imperialism." To avoid this, the liberation front armies would have to be restructured and integrated into a unified defense force.

According to the strategy document, cutting the army's direct ties to the EPRDF does not mean abandoning its revolutionary democratic character. The Defense Force could be free and neutral in appearance but in reality be organized "to carry out the required revolutionary democratic tasks through indirect ties" to the EPRDF.

The second political goal enumerated in the strategy document was the setting up of a government which ensures the all-round participation of the masses. A power structure will be established to "enable people to decide on local issues at Kebele, Woreda, zone, regional, and central level" and to recall elected representatives who fail to serve constituents' interests. The masses also will be organized on the basis of gender, trades, and professions to bring pressure on parties and actions of the central government and other power structures. The brevity of this section of the strategy document compared to that concerned with political and human rights probably indicates the pro forma nature of "participation of the masses" in a communist-inspired government.

The third political goal of the document was the ensuring of peoples' right to self-determination and building Ethiopia's unity based on equality and free choice. This goal reiterates the often repeated EPRDF mantra of the right of nations, nationalities, and peoples to secede—but with a caveat: Revolutionary Democracy believes that people benefit from staying together rather than seceding; but unity must be based on voluntary association and equal partnership. Such voluntary unity would provide people with the option to opt out when they so wish.

Opponents of the secessionist doctrine are deprecated as "chauvinists" or "narrow nationalists." Chauvinists, champions of "Greater Ethiopia," aspire to national unity with power concentrated at the center. On the other hand, narrow nationalists, such as the OLF, support the right to secession but do not stand for a strong union of peoples. They prefer "either a powerless central government and an all powerful regional government or the disintegration of the country so that they can rule over their region in the name of their nationality."

The strategy document notes that imperialism and the ruling classes oppose the peoples' right to self-determinism because they misperceive the relationship between the individual's rights and the peoples' rights. According to the EPRDF, ensuring the peoples' rights, i.e., the rights of ethnic groups, is the basis for ensuring the individual's rights. From such a perspective, the rights of the individual cannot be separated from the peoples'. Enemies of the Front have a misconception of these rights and "try to drive a wedge" between them.

ECONOMIC GOALS

Using the hackneyed vocabulary of Marxist-Leninism, the strategy document advocates building an economy that promotes self-sufficiency and speedy growth while maintaining a balance between the economic sectors and geographic regions. The characterization of the beneficiaries of the EPRDF goals reveals much about the attitude of the Front towards various sectors of society. The document also immodestly proclaims that "our revolutionary democratic goals are the only guarantee for the survival of the country." In the language of the true believer, the implementation of EPRDF goals is described as "the only means of bringing about fast growth and transforming our backward country . . . the only option for improving the livelihood of our people and effecting social justice." According to the document there are no other options to improve living standards and survival of Ethiopia as a nation.

A relatively independent economy based on a large local market is central to the EPRDF's scheme. Such an economy is preferable to one based on foreign markets and dependent on imperialism with its varying needs for raw materials. In the EPRDF economy, the government's revenue and fiscal policy will be used to promote social justice by taxing the wealthy and allocating a higher budget to the sectors representative of the "oppressed masses."

The main beneficiary of the Front's economic policy is the peasantry, the largest sector of society with 85 percent of the country's productive manpower. The goal of government policy should be to develop human resources of peasants and improve their living standards. This can be accomplished by creating a climate which enables peasants to produce more and thus benefit from development of agriculture and growth of the local market.

The EPRDF is less trusting of the urban sectors. The Proletariat, although relatively small in number, is the Front's most reliable supporter among urban groups. The achievement of revolutionary democratic goals should improve workers' job opportunities and living standards.

Among urban groups, the Urban Petty Bourgeoisie, involved in small-scale production and petty trade in goods and services, will benefit the most from the EPRDF's economic goals. Progress in rural-based development will expand the sphere of the bourgeoisie's activities. The intelligentsia is included in the EPRDF's categorization of the Urban Petty Bourgeoisie and is seen as a vacillating group that could align itself with enemy forces. The intelligentsia favors a multiparty system that protects the privileges of the ruling classes. Furthermore, they advocate the rights of the individual at the expense of the rights of the people and are antagonistic to the Front's political goals.

The National Bourgeoisie also stand to benefit from the goals of revolutionary democracy, but the group's vacillating nature prevents it from becoming a firm supporter of the Front. According to the strategy document, the national bourgeoisie seek economic autonomy from imperialism but want to promote its interests at the expense of those of the people. The lower stratum of this section probably can be won over by the Front. The upper stratum should be neutralized so that it will not obstruct the realization of EPRDF goals.

Imperialists and the comprador class are the declared enemies of revolutionary democracy. These groups seek to impose a dependent economy on the country, and their political interests are incompatible with the Front's political goals.

ECONOMIC STRATEGIES

In enunciating the Front's economic strategies for implementing its goals and describing the main economic forces that play a role in this process, the EPRDF wandered farthest from its Marxism-Leninism roots. In the post-Cold war world, the Ethiopian economy would no longer be largely or entirely in public ownership. Creative communists in the name of "revolutionary democracy" have established variations of "private ownership" under EPRDF control to further party goals. Regardless of the ownership of the dominant sectors of the economy—whether industry, finance, or transport—all their activities were organized under a national economic plan and for the primary benefit of the party.

To achieve the objectives of agricultural and industrial development, the country must produce the necessary manpower. To accomplish this, the strategy document proposes changing the present education system which emphasizes academic studies to one with a "production-oriented" curriculum.

Heading the list of economic activities are those benefiting the peasantry and centered on the land. To guarantee that peasants have access to land, the EPRDF follows the principle that land should never be sold or exchanged. Such a scheme guards against peasants selling land during hard times and thus getting mired in landless poverty. Land redistribution will be undertaken "over a long period of time" and when the local people believe it essential. Peasants will be provided with fertilizer, improved tools and seeds, and training to increase their production. An infrastructure of feeder roads, primary schools, health, and other services will be developed.

The motive forces of the Front's economic strategy include the government, investors, and revolutionary democratic forces. The role of government has changed considerably since the First EPRDF Congress. At that time, government was the principal actor regulating the economy by running state enterprises in finance, energy, mines, and industry while private investors played little role.

According to the strategy document, in current global economic thinking governments are not expected to be involved in production activities and when they are involved they should be guided by the profit motive. Yet without being widely involved, the Ethiopian government could play a decisive role in the economy by controlling, among other things, the distribution of foreign currency, the import of fuel, the export of coffee, and the regulation of transport. The State also could remain in control of key industrial and agricultural enterprises that affect export earnings or the livelihood of large numbers of people. In the EPRDF plan, these include rail, air, and sea transport, electricity, telephone, and water supply services, the textile industry, engineering works, the chemical industry, metal foundries, and mining. If such enterprises cannot be kept under State monopoly, then joint ventures might be created with the State having a higher share. The State also can use fiscal policies, including taxes, budget allocations, and regulation of interest rates to influence economic activities. But the Government's involvement in economic activities is opposed in Ethiopia by representatives of imperialism, the comprador class, and the vacillating national bourgeoisie.

The Role of Investors

In the Front's plan, revolutionary democratic associations, organizations, and individuals will join the national bourgeoisie as major forces in investments. In certain economic sectors where the State cannot directly be involved, these revolutionary forces can play "a special and irreplaceable role." To redirect the economy in the direction of revolutionary democracy, action by such forces, envisioned "as a self-sufficient force," is necessary.

The Role of Revolutionary Democratic Forces

The objectives of investments by this force are: 1) to supplement or carry out the role of the state; 2) to regulate and influence the activities of private capitalists; and 3) to serve as a source of income for revolutionary democracy.

In areas where financial and administrative restraints or external economic factors prevent the state from directly regulating the economy, "revolutionary democratic forces should take over the role of the State and invest as one individual in those economic sectors which have no direct State influence."

Revolutionary democratic forces can regulate and influence the activities of private capitalists by acting as a powerful private investor. In this role, they can demonstrate modern business practices to small businessmen while putting pressure on larger businesses so as to strengthen the State's leadership role.

The EPRDF needs large amounts of money to carry out its programs, and investors under the banner of revolutionary democracy can be a source of income. In the countryside where the Front is strongest, such forces should monopolize rural credit services and their resources. Wherever possible, they should become involved in rural trade, transport, imports and exports, rural banking services, production of agricultural raw material, the manufacture of fertilizer and other modern agricultural inputs, and invest in mining. In urban areas, investment forces should establish wholesale trade, transport, banks, insurance companies, small-scale industries, and service cooperatives.

To achieve these objectives, revolutionary democratic forces should select economic spheres outside the direct purview of the government that play a crucial role in development and strive to control them or to hold an upper hand in their processes. EPRDF investors should strengthen ties with petty producers and seek ways to guide their development. In the work place the forces should create an environment to facilitate participation of individuals with a strong revolutionary democratic outlook. The overarching goal is for the forces to become "absolutely profitable."

The Role of Local Investors

Local investors also can play an important role in the economy. They should be encouraged more than foreign investors to develop their assets, but they "should be directed by and disciplined to follow the direction of Revolutionary Democracy." Priority should be given to what the strategy document calls the "lower stratum" of this section, those involved in small-scale production and services. The lower stratum gets its resources locally and easily can be guided by revolutionary democratic forces. To enhance their role in the development process, lower stratum investors should be supported with credit facilities and favorable governmental policies and services.

The Role of Foreign Investors

The strategy document declares that prevailing global economic conditions require the EPRDF "to give more access to foreign capital." The document makes clear, however, that certain spheres of the economy are off limits to foreign capital. Basic services, such as telephone, electricity, and train transportation; financial services, including banking and insurance; and small-scale industry are specifically mentioned as not being open to foreign involvement. The document warns that "if the major international financial institutions or banks are allowed access to the economic sector, they will twist the state's arms and those of Revolutionary Democracy."

Foreign investors would be allowed access to investment spheres where they could bring in more hard currency than the amount they take out, and they would be encouraged to invest in joint ventures with the State. If foreign investors adhere to government policies, they will provide the Front with access to expanded international markets and enable the EPRDF to build local capacity with which eventually to replace foreign capital.

The government's fiscal policies would be used to direct the involvement of investors in the economy. State incentives would encourage the growth of targeted economic spheres and forces. Conversely, the state's fiscal instruments would be used to "destroy those that are not in line with the goals of Revolutionary Democracy." For example, the power to tax could be used as the power to destroy. As the strategy document indicates, the government "will reduce or write off for some years the taxes due from those forces or economic spheres" which the Front supports and "pile up the tax burden" of those the EPRDF does not support.

POLITICAL STRATEGIES ENSURING PERMANENT HEGEMONY

The EPRDF is determined to make its official ideology the dominant political theory of the nation. Led by cadres of revolutionary democracy, the party planned to win the first elections under the TGE and to perpetuate itself in power by winning all subsequent elections. The strategy document is straightforward about how the Front will establish its "permanent" hegemony:

We can attain our objectives and goals only if Revolutionary Democracy becomes the governing outlook in our society, and only by winning the elections successively and holding power without letup can we securely establish the hegemony of Revolutionary Democracy. If we lose in the elections even once, we will encounter a great danger. So, in order to permanently establish this hegemony, we should win in the initial elections and then create a conducive situation that will ensure the establishment of this hegemony. In the subsequent elections, too, we should be able to win without interruption.

Revolutionary Democracy is to be made the governing ideology of the society, and the people should be made to reject the outlook and views of the enemy and vacillators.

The Front's theorists believed that in 1993 objective and subjective conditions were favorable to Revolutionary Democracy attaining hegemony and staying in power "continuously." They modestly thought that the interest of the majority of the population would be fulfilled only through the EPRDF's Revolutionary Democratic lines. The ideologues contended that objective condition required the establishment and continuity of the Front's hegemony.

In reviewing subjective conditions, the EPRDF's theorists found that the opponents of Revolutionary Democracy "had not taken root in the society." The opposition lacked organization and material resources. In contrast, the forces of Revolutionary Democracy were properly organized and embraced by the people. The EPRDF had military and political superiority and material resources. Thus, the subjective conditions also were conducive for the hegemony of the Front.

The gaining of hegemony by the enemy and the vacillators would be impossible because such a situation would hurl the country into "an endless crisis" and Ethiopia would not survive as a nation. Front apologists reason that although imperialism has massive political and economic power, these cannot be used to establish hegemony in Ethiopia. The local ruling classes that serve imperialism have been weakened and cannot create a strong army or bureaucracy through which to rule. Likewise, the national bourgeoisie lacks economic and political power and is too weak to stand as an independent political force.

MOTIVE FORCES OF REVOLUTIONARY DEMOCRACY

Each class or sector of society in the Marxist-Leninist scheme of things is analyzed as a motive force of party ideology. The peasantry is considered the pillar of Revolutionary Democracy, the center of economic development, and the focus of political work. To ensure the support and massive involvement of the peasant class in the Front's revolutionary activities, its members were to be mobilized through social, political, and economic organizations. The EPRDF would lead these peasant associations through loose organizational ties. Prominent peasants who have earned the respect of their communities would be recruited as cadres. The number of rural cadre would be enlarged with the aim of increasing the influence of EPRDF member organizations. On the basis of their wartime experience, the Front thought it best not to bring in "outsiders" to lead the peasants.

In rural areas the increasing number of development workers from Government Organizations (GOs) and Non-Governmental Organizations (NGOs) pose a problem. EPRDF theorists feared that these "lower-level members of the intelligentsia" could undermine the Front's influence and development program if they opposed the party's political line. The counter-propaganda of representatives of GOs and NGOs might persuade peasants to deny support to the EPRDF and obstruct the hegemony of revolutionary democracy. Therefore, the strategy document concludes, the GO and NGO development workers must be brought over to the side of the Front.

The Urban Petty Bourgeoisie

Next to the peasantry, the Urban Petty Bourgeoisie could be a major beneficiary of EPRDF development programs. The majority of this sector, however, are not supporters of the Front. They tend to be vacillaters who can be infected by narrow nationalism or by chauvinism. In addition, the EPRDF has not yet created the condition which proves to the bourgeoisie that only the Front's approach can fulfill its interests. According to the strategy document, the EPRDF has not done enough political and organizational work in relation to the Petty Bourgeoisie. Because of this sector's strong political and ideological influence and its growth potential in an expanding economy, the Front will mount a special effort to win over the Bourgeoisie to Revolutionary Democracy.

The intelligentsia and their associations receive serious attention in the strategy document. The EPRDF plans to encourage the associations of the intelligentsia while infiltrating them with members and sympathizers, who can direct these organizations into the camp of Revolutionary Democracy. As the Front's political influence increases, so will the EPRDF's ability to control indirectly the intellectuals.

The strategy document prescribes another means of persuading the intellectuals: "by filling their bellies and pockets." Because many of the intellectuals are in the civil service or involved in economic activities that can be affected by government incentives or denial of support, "the combined strength of the State and Revolutionary Democracy's economic institutions should be used to attract their support or to neutralize opposition of the intelligentsia." The Front should demonstrate to the intellectuals that the

EPRDF's economic strength could serve their interests, and if they oppose Revolutionary Democracy, the party should make empty their "belly and pocket." More attention is to be given to the large number of lower level intelligentsia in rural areas who are easily amenable to EPRDF influence.

The Proletariat

The workers comprise another large sector of the urban population that could benefit from the Front's development program and also become firm supporters of the EPRDF. The Front should encourage trade unions, but without compromising their organizational independence, try to control and lead them through indirect organizational links. Workers employed in Revolutionary Democratic business companies should be given better pay and training than those in other enterprises at the same levels. Thus, the Front could use its workers to infiltrate national trade unions and play a leading role in drawing the rest of the proletariat into the EPRDF's orbit.

The Local Investor

It will be difficult for the EPRDF to win the support of the upper stratum of investors so the Front must force this sector to be neutral. On the other hand, the lower stratum, "despite its suspicions and anxieties," can be made firm supporters of the party with the proper care and handling.

The Front should demonstrate in practice and through analysis that its programs can fulfill the interests of local investors. Through representatives of EPRDF firms, the Front should penetrate and lead the organizations which investors form. If the Front is unable to direct such organizations, it sould neutralize them so that they will not be adversaries of the EPRDF. The strategy of the Front will be to ensure that the livelihood and profit of investors are dependent on the goodwill and support of the state as well as EPRDF economic institutions and restrain local investors "from taking extreme positions" by filling their bellies and pockets.

TACTICS USED TO IMPLEMENT POLITICAL STRATEGY

In the strategy document, "tactics" are instruments used to mobilize the people for the fulfillment of the goals of Revolutionary Democracy and for concerted action against enemies of the EPRDF.

The major slogans of the party read in light of the Front's strategy take on added meaning and reflect the priorities assigned to the motive forces or sectors of society by the EPRDF. The main slogans are:

Protect all the political and human rights of the masses! Establish a government that ensures the all-round participation of the people! Respect the right to self-determination as a basis for permanent peace and unity! Speed up the peasant-based and rural-centered development process! Strengthen the free trade unions of the proletariat! Develop the human and natural resources of our country! Establish a just system in which the masses can benefit from the national development!

The Propaganda Machinery

Key propaganda tools of the EPRDF include the mass media, schools, religious organizations, and various mass organizations. These tools should be exploited directly or indirectly in carrying out propaganda activities.

The most important of the mass media are controlled by the State and include newspapers, radio, and television. They can be used by the party to popularize government policies and activities, bring grievances of the people to the attention of the government, and strengthen the relation between the government and the people. The organizational and manpower skills of this sector should be improved so that it can more effectively promote the goals of Revolutionary Democracy. News reports, articles, and entertainment programs should be of such quality as to attract larger audiences. Theater and motion picture houses controlled by the State should be reorganized and their practices reoriented to serve as useful propaganda tools.

Media owned by forces of Revolutionary Democracy will compete with others under private control. The Force's media should mobilize their financial and organizational resources and assume a key position in the private sector. The EPRDF plans to strengthen and modernize its existing media, set up new ones, and control the market. The media of revolutionary democracy must work with all their resources to publicize the Front and government's activities and policies, facilitate the people's active participation, and influence the masses to fully support the government. In order for the media to carry out these duties, the EPRDF plans to improve the professional quality of journalists through training and the strengthening of their association.

The Schools (Indirect Propaganda)

In the nation's schools, the curriculum can be used to disseminate scientific knowledge and teach respect for the histories and cultures of various ethnic groups. The study of the country's constitution provides an opportunity for the Front to inculcate the basic goals of revolutionary democracy. Because such study is not openly presented as propaganda, it will effectively serve the purposes of the EPRDF.

The Front also will attempt to persuade teachers, key figures in education as propaganda, to stand for Revolutionary Democracy. The EPRDF will involve teachers in curriculum design and convince them of the need for changing the educational system. By involving teachers in social and developmental activities and subjecting them to party-line explanations provided on such occasions, the Front hopes to "bring them to the fold of Revolutionary Democracy."

Students, too, should be involved in party developmental and political activities. The EPRDF will utilize sports activities, associations such as boy scouts, clubs, and various seminars to mold the views of young people.

The Religious Organizations

Religious organizations are characterized in the strategy document as always being propaganda tools and frequently aligned with reactionary forces in society. Such organizations can be used to disseminate the revolutionary view within certain limits. If such a strategy is impossible, the Front should attempt to curtail organized religion's obstructionist activities.

Rather than focusing on the leadership of religious groups, the EPRDF will direct its effort at village level religious organizations closer to people. Without denying the religious the respect due them, the Front will attempt to mold their views, curtail their propaganda against Revolutionary Democracy, and even use them to serve the party's end. The EPRDF also will forge a close relationship with the leadership echelon of religious bodies, exploit "their internal contradictions," and prevent them from coordinating propaganda against the Front. If possible, the EPRDF will use religious leaders to disseminate the propaganda of Revolutionary Democracy.

Mass Organizations

The Front's strategy is to use mass organizations as forums for political and propaganda work to ensure the hegemony of Revolutionary Democracy. The party would try to influence mass organizations through indirect means rather than imposing its leadership on them by disregarding their internal organizational autonomy. Seminars and panel discussions will be organized by the EPRDF to draw members of mass organizations to the camp of Revolutionary Democracy.

The Question of Organization

To establish the system envisioned by the Front, "the masses have to be organized in various social and political associations" which connect them and lead them in the direction of Revolutionary Democracy. While maintaining the relative autonomy of such associations as a means of promoting popular initiatives and as a check on corrupt tendencies in party cadres, the EPRDF plans to influence the activities of organizations and to recruit their members.

The masses will be organized by sectors including the peasantry, the bourgeoisie, the proletariat, government workers, and ethnic groups.

Organizations of peasantry will include peasant associations, women's and youth associations, cooperatives, and local militia.

Democratic Petty Bourgeoisie's Urban Organizations will include professional associations in education, medicine, and journalism; peace organizations, human rights organizations, and development organizations.

The most desirable form of workers' associations are trade unions organized as industrial organizations rather than on the basis of ethnicity or region. The various sectors of the proletariat should then be united in a single umbrella organization.

The Government Organizations

The EPRDF feels secure about its control of organizations in lower levels of government because they are formed mainly with the involvement of the peasants. Middle and upper levels of government, where there are no elected officials and where intellectuals are involved, are more problematic to the party. Included in this sector are the army, security forces, and the judiciary which will not be under the direct control of political organizations as such. However, according to the strategy document, since these groups are there to promote and indirectly implement the goals of Revolutionary Democracy, they form part of its strength. The mission of government agencies, as seen by the Front, is to protect the political and human rights of the masses, contribute their share in the implementation of EPRDF development strategies, widen the political influence of Revolutionary Democracy through their activities, and act as its key instrument in combating the illegal activities of the enemy.

At the apex of associations of nations, nationalities, and peoples will be a nationwide organization formed from democratic nationality (ethnic) organizations. This nation-wide political organization will be formed, not by multi-national organizations (in the EPRDF sense of the term), but by a union of ethnic-based organizations.

The mission of these nationality-based organizations is two-fold. On the one hand, they are to disseminate in various languages the same revolutionary democratic (party line) substance; to translate this substance into practice by adapting it to local conditions; and to rally peasants and other progressive forces around the goals of Revolutionary Democracy. On the other hand, the ethnic organizations are "to promote the common interests of all the people."

The strategy document takes a final swing at the strawmen chauvinists, ruling classes, secessionists, and narrow nationalists by pointing out why they are adverse to a nationwide organization of nationality-based organizations. The chauvinist ruling classes, who back the idea of "*Itiopiawinnet*" (Ethiopianness), would prefer a multi-national organization composed of individuals from various ethnic groups "that have betrayed the causes of their people and bowed to these chauvinists." Narrow nationalists and secessionists "do not want the fulfillment of the peoples' common interests," so they also oppose the proposed nation-wide organization.

CONCLUSION

The document concludes with self-assured assertions of the rightness and rectitude of the EPRDF cause. The ideologues contend that the Front's Revolutionary Democratic goals can liberate the majority of Ethiopian society from poverty and backwardness and that they can assure the widest democratic rights and participation in the political system. For the party faithful, the EPRDF's political and economic strategies and tactics "ensure the realization of these goals and the victory of Revolutionary Democracy."

The document dogmatically states that if the Front's goals do not materialize, "the people will suffer from endless poverty and crises and there will be no single and united country called Ethiopia." Therefore, in order to fulfill the peoples' interests and to ensure the survival of the nation, the victory of EPRDF goals is imperative. The cadres and other participants in the struggle, called "*tagays*" or "combatants," should proudly stand for such "an honorable cause," and they "must do everything possible in order to courageously and successfully carry out this popular and national responsibility."

THE HIDDEN AGENDAS OF THE STRATEGY DOCUMENT

Behind the facile Marxist-Leninist ideas of the document are the concerns of ideologues under stress. In a world where communism and

Marxist-Leninist regimes, with a few exceptions, have faded away, how can EPRDF theorists be true to their Marxist principles and at the same time appease donor nations? In the face of "people power" that said "No!" to authoritarian regimes in so many Marxist states during the past decade, how can a small elite of former guerrilla fighters follow the old communist pattern and boldly proclaim that they know what is best for Ethiopia and its people?

To answer these questions, the strategy document provides techniques for avoiding conflict with "the imperialists" while creating a facade of democracy, the protection of human rights, and free market capitalism. New "masters of deceit" give instructions in how to beguile donor nations and international bodies with what the party appears to do even as the Front follows a very different agenda in its actions.

At the top of the agenda is the party's goal of permanently establishing hegemony. Lacking confidence that the people would accept its self-proclaimed legitimacy, the EPRDF feared "losing the elections even once." Thus, the Front will do whatever it takes to win all elections and to destroy effective political opposition. Backed by an army that is "free and neutral in appearance" but really the EPRDF military, the Front will not hesitate to cite "any relevant legal article" to punish its detractors.

Following Lenin's advice, the EPRDF seeks to "control the commanding heights of the economy." To scale the heights, the Front will get a boost from its two-track public and private powers. Government fiscal policy will reduce taxes on EPRDF-backed forces while "piling up" taxes on others. Front workers will receive "pay and training far better" than others. Trade unions will be infiltrated by party loyalists. Economic "Revolutionary Democratic" forces, euphemistically companies affiliated with the Front, will "invest as one individual in those economic sectors which have no direct state influence." This use of "party capitalists" is a clever ploy that allows the EPRDF indirectly to play an economic role that the Front knows the West would not let it play directly.

As described in the strategy document, the use to the fullest extent possible of "key propaganda tools," including schools, religious organizations, and mass media is a shrewd scheme to present the Front in the best possible light. The document also cunningly recommends propaganda that "is not openly presented as propaganda" as effective in the party's use.

The strategy document gives instructions in the latest version of the Lenin two-step, a dance for the Front artiste featuring far more than two steps backward to avoid bumping into the forces of imperialism while doing one step forward to demonstrate ideological adroitness for the comrades. The EPRDF has well learned the choreography and, as we shall see, has skirted around Western nations and international bodies on the main dance floor. Meanwhile, the Front continues to affront fellow citizens who refuse to cheer its performance with a crude stomp dance.

NOTE

1. TPLF/EPRDF, "TPLF/EPRDF's Strategies for Establishing its Hegemony & Perpetuating its Rule," English translation of TPLF/EPRDF document originally published in June 1993, *Ethiopian Register* 3 (June 1996): 20–29. All of the quotations in this chapter are taken from this translation.

CHAPTER 8

Drafting and Approving a New Constitution

Under the Transition Charter, the transitional period was to culminate in the drafting of a democratic constitution to be ratified by a newly elected National Assembly. A twenty-nine member Constitution Drafting Commission (CDC) was established by COR proclamation on 18 August 1992. Members of the Commission were elected by the COR "from among the various sections of the population" and the members of the COR—a licence for domination by the EPRDF or its front organizations. Former Foreign Minister and ambassador, Kifle Wodajo, one of seven members from the COR, was named chairman, and the commission was organized into panels on: 1) human rights; 2) government structure and division of powers; and 3) special issues, including official languages and citizenship.

The work of the commission was financed in part by the Carter Center and USAID and was carried out, if not in secret, at least in sporadic, frequently non-publicized meetings. The CDC "invited international experts to address members of the commission and the public on different aspects of constitutional law."[1] The most meritorious of these efforts was the showplace "Symposium on the Making of the New Ethiopian Constitution" held in Addis Ababa from 17–21 May 1993 under the sponsorship of the InterAfrica Group, a non-governmental organization with close ties to the TGE.[2] Several distinguished international scholars, lawyers, and jurists joined Ethiopian government officials, legal experts, and invited participants in "lively and thought provoking discussions" and presentations.[3]

Six months later, in November 1993, the CDC published the booklet "About Basic Concepts of Constitutions: Presented for Public Discussion" (in Amharic) as part of a nationwide civic education program. The TGE explained that the booklet included "all ideas that might be contained in a constitution" without advocating "any particular style of government or political ideology."[4] The work was permeated, however, with the EPRDF's ethnic ethic. Sections of chapters dealing with "basic concepts" of democracy and constitutionalism and "tribal and ethnic human rights" delivered a strong civics lesson in the primacy of ethnic groups in the proposed constitution.

In theory the concept paper was to serve as the basis of discussion of what the people wanted in the constitution. Recommendations were solicited from party-approved "community elders, religious leaders, representatives of women's groups, and various sectors of the society."

More widely publicized were two-day meetings held in January 1994 to discuss constitutional issues at regional, district, and kebele levels. In arranging these gatherings, the TGE followed the example of St. Augustine when he decided to dragoon reluctant people into the Christian camp by using a scriptural phrase taken from the parable about the man whose guests did not come to his wedding feast: *Coge intrare*—"Compel them to come in." Government offices were closed for the occasion and workers were cajoled to appear at the kebeles. Citizen participation was encouraged by threats to the recalcitrant of cessation of sales of sugar, edible oils, soap, and salt at kebele shops—an especially effective inducement in the countryside. Similar subtle suasions discouraged the hesitant in urban areas. Despite the pressure of hype, firsthand observers estimate no more than 30 percent of the citizenry participated throughout the nation. The government, on the other hand, reported "high turnouts in all the kebeles."[5] According to Meles, 16 million Ethiopians took part in democratic forums throughout the country to voice opinions on a proposed constitution.[6]

"Discussions" at these gatherings were dominated by party liners of the EPRDF. Party pulpiteers preached to docile kebele choirs, while the best soloists did not show up for rehearsals or were not allowed to sing. The ethnic leitmotif of the EPRDF was well rehearsed. On the basis of the predictable recommendations of participants in these meetings, the CDC was to draft the constitution.

Their handiwork was delivered to the COR on 8 April 1994. In sessions of the COR broadcast on radio and television, Chairman Meles conducted a *weyiyet* (a one-way confessional) on the proposed document. The proceedings were described by Mesfin Wolde Mariam as neither a debate nor a discussion.[7] The lecturer-chairman harangued the members and so cowed them that few spoke in other than solicitous agreement with Meles. The legislative body then unanimously approved "The Draft Constitution of Ethiopia" with alternate texts in only two articles supported by a minority of the COR.[8]

This action set the stage for the election of a Constituent Assembly (CA) on 5 June 1994. Having learned in 1992 how to run elections with effective opposition shut out and with a focus on the mechanics of voting, for the satisfaction of astigmatic election observers, the TGE directed its perfected version of national elections. To no one's surprise, the EPRDF and its surrogate parties won 484 out of 547 contested seats.[9] According to the National Election Commission, 508 party candidates and 848 independent candidates competed in the elections. "Independents" provided verisimilitude for the occasion, but many of such candidates were thought to be EPRDF stand-ins. The Front, having established hegemony, was demonstrating how to win elections without interruption.

The National Election Commission (NEC) announced a high voter turnout and headlines of the government-controlled *Ethiopian Herald* vaunted "Addis Ababans demonstrate impressive voter enthusiasm."[10] Unannounced were the all-stops-out, force- them-to-turn-out EPRDF tactics that included, according to an Ethiopian on the scene, "harassment, intimidation, threat, physical violence, arbitrary arrest, and detention." Civic responsibility was encouraged by heads of families being summoned to kebele offices for a recitation, by EPRDF stalwarts, of the riot act for failure to have all eligible family members show up at the polls on election day. The fruits of hostility and fear propagated participation.

As in previous elections, many at the polls did not know what they were voting for, and there were some irregularities in official assistance in ballot marking and in the lack of secret voting.[11] But election day passed without violence or major flaws and some 600 domestic and international observers and journalists could find little to fault in election mechanics. With few exceptions, the international press joined in the TGE's mantra of "free and fair elections."[12] Journalists more significantly might have noticed that the elections carried little persuasive force among Ethiopians because few of the participants felt any responsibility for the action taken.

The CA was convened on 28 October 1994 to begin work on the approval of the draft constitution or, less likely, on the writing and approval of a new one.[13] The proceedings of this faux *shengo* (assembly) were a foregone conclusion. *Non placet* was unacceptable. The new EPRDF constitution reflecting "respect for and faith in the decisions of the people" was ratified by the CA on 8 December 1994 and prescribed parliamentary elections were scheduled in the spring to choose a National Assembly and to establish the Federal Democratic Republic of Ethiopia (FDRE).[14]

Suspense over the outcome of the EPRDF/TGE-controlled elections in May 1995 was impalpable. Although the TGE could boast of fifty-nine political parties registered with the Election Board, most were miniscule ethnic front organizations of the EPRDF. Voters elected state parliaments and members of the Council of Peoples' Representatives (CPR), the "lower" house of the national legislature. Election observers representing eighteen Western nations reported that overall voter interest was low, especially in urban areas and uncontested constituencies. In contrast, the *Ethiopian Herald's* headline proclaimed: "Massive Turn-out Marks First Multi-party Election."[15] The EPRDF, the only major political organization participating, won 483 seats, over 90 percent of the votes. The Organization of African Unity (OAU), in the role of election observer, expressed "satisfaction with the general conduct of the electors and the electorate at the polling centers which facilitated voting and counting without any significant irregularities."[16] The OAU did not mention that the non-participation of major opposition parties reduced the significance of the choices available to many voters—a point made by the donor nations election unit.[17]

The alleged multiparty and authentic nature of the elections was spurious. The principal political opposition parties boycotted the elections knowing from bitter experience that the Front and its epigones would not allow a fair competition for votes. Opponents in exile, categorized as "oppressors," or worse, were aware that any of their representatives who dared to return to Ethiopia did so at their own jeopardy. EPRDF leaders seem satisfied with the merely ritualistic, symbolic gestures of ratification of the policies of a one-party government. They view such orchestrated shows for the glorification of the Front as the active incarnation of revolutionary democratic consciousness whose strength is fed by the trust of the spontaneously oppressed masses and their feeling that the party is the objectification of their will (obscure though this may be to themselves).

The modes of mass political participation in Ethiopia are really a kind of depoliticization of public life. The real decision-making process remains just as remote from the fallacious mass electorate, just as much a monopoly of a small, self-selected political elite as it was under the Derg.

In mid-August 1995 the Council of Representatives of the TGE held its last session and on 21 August in ceremonies in the old parliament building, the FDRE officially came into being.[18] The leaders of the new government were not new faces; most of them came from the inner circle of the ruling party, and there was a substantial carry over of personnel from the TGE.[19] The former President, Meles Zenawi, was elected Prime Minister.

According to the government press "the peaceful power transfer (from the TGE) to the popularly elected government was the highest achievement in the history of the country."[20] Opponents of the EPRDF, however, saw the entire activity as just another chapter in the Front's carefully planned strategy for staying in power.

THE MEANING OF "CONSTITUTION" AND "CONSTITUTIONALISM"

For observers of the drafting and ratification of the final document of the TGE, precise definitions of such critical terms as "constitution" and "constitutionalism" were missing from debate. Also involuntarily absent were Ethiopian political scientists who in particular among academicians are responsible for ruling out insincere or faulty language in political discourse. This responsibility takes on added significance when the language of the observer is required to improve, if necessary, the language of the observed, or when the observer is confronted with distortions of terms that are intentionally raised with a view to hoodwinking the audience. The EPRDF had harassed or intimidated most of the academy into silence and those brave enough to speak had limited means of communicating with a mass audience. Had they been able to make known their ideas, debate on the new constitution might have been enlivened with language gleaned from contemporary scholarly usage. To facilitate analysis of the new constitution, let us look at two significant definitions.

The term "constitution" refers both to: 1) institutions, practices, and principles that define and structure a system of government; and 2) the written document that establishes or articulates such a system.[21] A constitution has been described as "the autobiography of a power relationship."[22] Most constitutions are a melange of affirmative commitments as well as procedures and proscriptions.

Under a constitution, government institutions are established, and their functions, power, and interrelationships are defined. A constitution sets forth directives determining the manner in which policy shall be formulated and implemented within the area of jurisdiction of the state. If these arrangements are short-circuited or contravened, the government's action is not legitimate. The constitution, then, imposes on the governors an obligation to adhere to prescribed procedures that make it possible "for opponents of proposed action, whether they be within the governmental structure or outside it, to manifest their opposition systematically and as effectively as their abilities and the merits of their case permit."[23]

A written constitution is almost a prerequisite to international recognition for new nations. In the post-colonial era, virtually every nation-state has devised a constitution to suit the political power structure of its society. Constitutions are the ecumenical common denominator of all forms of government from liberal democracies to totalitarian dictatorships on the political spectrum. The content of these documents ranges from sublime to ridiculous in the attempt of those empowered to draft justifications of the allocation of functions, powers and duties among the various agencies and offices of government, and to define the relationships between rulers and the ruled.

A constitution also reinforces the *sine qua non* of democracy, the wide sharing of power. As a procedural document, the constitution of a liberal democracy secures the "preconditions for rational consent and dissent, public debate, conflict-resolution without violence and the thoughtful and cumulative revision of the constitutional framework itself."[24]

While all nations may ascribe to constitutions, only a few are committed to "constitutionalism." The concept of constitutionalism denotes not merely the existence of a written or unwritten constitution, but also a *commitment to limited government*.[25] Constitutions can limit government by regularizing governmental processes and prohibiting capricious action or by establishing policies or procedures that cannot be modified by ordinary legislative action (procedural limitations). Limitations also can be imposed by specific constitutional provisions, such as a bill of rights (limitations on the area within which government may make decisions or the withholding of authority to take certain actions regarding the members of the community) or the separation of powers.[26]

Constitutionalism is a hallmark of liberal democracies in the post-Cold War world. For such regimes, a constitution is "a fundamental law or a fundamental set of principles, and a correlative institutional arrangement which would restrict arbitrary power and ensure a limited government." Such an institutional arrangement would provide a frame for political society, organized through and by the law for the purpose of restraining arbitrary power.[27] Thus, a constitution enables the people to develop the needed confinements of discretionary power through standards, principles, and rules and helps enforce a desired "role performance" upon the government officials designated by citizens to temporarily rule in their behalf.

Using the constitutionalism of a liberal democracy as a normative standard, it is obvious that not every nation with a constitution is committed to constitutionalism. History abounds with examples of sham, fictive, or facade constitutions whose provisions do not correspond to actual governmental practice. Classic examples of shams were the 1987 "Ethiopia

Tikdem" Constitution of the People's Democratic Republic of Ethiopia and the Soviet constitutions of 1937 and 1977 that set forth operative principles of government that had little relationship to the actual business of governing and which certainly did not limit or restrain governmental power.

Under such circumstances, a government publicly professes its commitment to constitutionalism in a written document in order to deflect attention from arbitrary exercises of power that characterize the nation's "unwritten constitution."[28] A facade of this type allows unscrupulous officials to make a discretionary use of power under the camouflage of a good work.

In contrast to the "sham," a "nominal" constitution is a written document that describes but does not limit governmental behavior. In other words, such a document articulates the nation's unwritten constitution but does not subscribe to principles of constitutionalism. The Ethiopian constitutions that Emperor Haile Selassie propounded in 1931 and 1955 were of this nominal type.

Forearmed with normative definitions of "constitutions," legitimate, sham and nominal, and of "constitutionalism," let us now examine the new constitution of Ethiopia.

NOTES

1. "Lively Debate on Draft Constitution," *News from Ethiopia*, Embassy of Ethiopia, Washington, DC, 30 April 1994, 1–2.

2. InterAfrica Group, *Proceedings of the Symposium on the Making of the New Ethiopian Constitution, 17–21 May 1993*, Addis Ababa, 1994.

3. Transitional Government of Ethiopia, *Constitutional Commission Newsletter*, No. 1 (March 1994), 1; special discussion meetings of the CDC are listed in John M. Cohen, "Transition Toward Democracy and Governance in Post Mengistu Ethiopia," Harvard Institute for International Development, Cambridge, MA, 1994, 7.

4. "Ethiopians Participate in Constitutional Discussion," *News from Ethiopia*, Embassy of Ethiopia, Washington, DC, 26 January 1994, 1–2.

5. Ibid.

6. *News from Ethiopia*. Embassy of Ethiopia, Washington, DC, 28 March 1994, 1–2.

7. Mesfin Wolde Mariam, "Constitution Proposed by the Council," (Amharic) *Ethiopian Register* 1 (June 1994). Cf. Getachew Kejela, "Lively Debate on Draft Constitution," *Ethiopian Herald*, 20 April 1994, 6.

8. "Council Ends Deliberation on Constitution," *Ethiopian Herald*, 4 May 1994, 1.

9. "EPRDF Wins Elections," *Ethiopian Review* 4 (August 1994): 10; Gobena Ibssa, "The Skeletons Crowing EPRDF's Election 'Victory'," *Ethiopian Register* 1 (August 1994): 20– 21.

10. 7 June 1994.

11. Norwegian Institute of Human Rights, *The 1994 Elections and Democracy in Ethiopia: Report of the Norwegian Observer Group*, Human Rights Report, Bergen, Norway, August 1994, 1. Foreign elections observers critical of the 1992 elections were conspicuously absent in 1994.

12. "There was a consensus among both local and international observers that, for the first time, a truly democratic election was conducted." Editorial, "Towards a Representative Government," *Ethiopian Herald*, 8 June 1994, 2.

13. "Constituent Assembly Begins Deliberations Today;" Editorial, "Basic Law Under Scrutiny," *Ethiopian Herald*, 28 October 1994, 1.

14. "Assembly Ratifies Ethiopia's New Federal Democratic Constitution, *Ethiopian Herald*, 9 December 1994, 1. See also, "Pivotal Role of New Constitution in Fostering Civil Society," Interview with Ato Kifle Wodajo, *Ethiopian Herald*, 13 December 1994, 2.

15. 9 May 1995; Seifu Mahifere, "Millions Go to the Polls Today," *Ethiopian Herald*, 7 May 1995, 1.

16. See Girma Abebe, "The Eyes Have It," *Ethiopian Register* 2 (September 1995): 27–30.

17. Donor Election Unit, "Final Analytical Summary of Donor Election Unit Reports, The 7 May 1995 Ethiopian Elections," Addis Ababa, 30 May 1995.

18. "New Democratically Elected Government Assumes Power," *Ethiopian Herald*, 22 August 1995, 1.

19. "Ethiopia: Looking Federal," *Africa Confidential* 36 (22 September 1995), reprinted in *Ethiopian Register* 2 (November 1995): 43–44.

20. "Council of Representatives Ends Mission," *Ethiopian Herald*, 19 August 1995, 1.

21. Suzette Hemberger, "Constitution," in *The Oxford Companion to Politics of the World* ed. Joel Krieger, (New York: Oxford University Press, 1993), 189. Great Britain, New Zealand, and Israel are major states that do not have written constitutions.

22. Herman Finer, *Theory and Practice of Modern Government* (New York: H. Holt, 1949), 116.

23. Albert P. Blaustein, *Constitutions That Made History* (New York: Paragon House, 1988), xi.

24. Stephen Holmes, "Precommitment and the Paradox of Democracy," in *Constitutionalism and Democracy* eds. Jon Elster and Rune Slagstad, (Cambridge, UK: Cambridge University Press, 1988), 233.

25. Hemberger, 189.

26. S. E. Finer, "Notes Towards a History of Constitutions," in *Constitutions in Democratic Politics* ed. Vernon Bogdanor, (Aldershot, UK: Gower, 1988), 18.

27. Giovanni Sartori, "Constitutionalism: A Preliminary Discussion," *American Political Science Review* 56 (1962): 853–864.

28. Ibid.

CHAPTER 9

An Analysis of the Constitution of the FDRE

In the process of drafting, debating, and ratifying the new constitution, the EPRDF/TGE lacked the most basic agreement necessary—the agreement to disagree. In order to make the constitutional decision genuine, the decision must be reached after the mature deliberation of all parties who should participate in the decision. By confusing opposition with rebellion, the TGE prevented key players from participating in deliberations. If the Ethiopian people were to act collectively, there needed to be an exchange of views on the issues involved in the constitutional decision. If that opportunity was not available, there could be no agreement on fundamentals. Nothing valid or lasting could be decided.[1]

Uninformed and uncritical deliberation, exemplified by meetings supposedly to discuss constitutional principles at the regional, district, and kebele levels, was a mutilation of the thinking process of the community, a perversion of education into propaganda. From uninhibited, robust, and wide-open democratic debate[2] on such issues would come legitimate popular consent, informed by reason, for empowerment of government under a constitution. Without it, the TGE's efforts were simply an intolerable wrestle with words and meaning, a triumph of an unacceptable ideology.

The drafting and approving of the new constitution in late 1994 was sharply criticized by non-EPRDF-beholden commentators.[3] Most found that a flawed process of constitution-making produced a sham and fictive document that did not express political reality but instead was a facade behind which the true actuality of the ethnic-Marxist-Leninist political order was hidden.

The constitution does not restrain government because it is not an expression of a firm belief in the importance of doing so.[4] Exercise of power in such a system is not subject to review by someone other than the holder of the power—the antithesis of constitutionalism.

The framers of a constitution founding a new nation should seek to secure through compromise the cooperation necessary for national unity and economic prosperity. Such a founding document should establish law-making and law-enforcing bodies and guarantee human rights by limiting governmental power. The security of such rights requires a commitment to individual autonomy and a judicial remedy responsive to individual complaint. The Constitution of the FDRE with its fictive and nominal shortcomings fails to meet these requirements.

A central function of a constitution is to make the business of governing publicly accountable. A government should function under prospective, publicly articulated rules that enable a citizen to evaluate the justification for "whatever laws and policies are directed to him."[5] And the individual must have a reasonable opportunity to register objections and to argue for whatever changes he believes ought to be made. These are constitutional rules of the game, and unless played by these rules, the game is "fixed" from the start.

The constitution should be an authoritative device for signaling when and how the fundamental rules of the game have been broken by government and what sanctions will punish such a break. Exercise of power in a constitutional system also must be subject to review by a body independent of the power holders.[6] Experience under the TGE made it a foregone conclusion that under the new constitution the maintenance of governance in contradistinction to these standards would continue. By denying political opposition groups meaningful participation in the drafting of the new constitution and in the process of its adoption, the EPRDF/TGE missed an opportunity to broaden, by peaceful means, the political base of governance.

PRE-CONSTITUTIONAL ASSUMPTIONS

A constitution cannot be understood without looking at what lies behind it—the political processes that gave it birth and the historical experience that conditioned the thinking of its founders. The constitution itself is an expression of these concerns rather than a generator of constitutional values.[7]

Nominally, the constitution of the Federal Democratic Republic of Ethiopia (FDRE) is a deliberate revolutionary break from that of the Derg (the 1987 PDRE model), in order to reflect the new political and social situation and to create new ground rules. The preamble lays open the pre-constitutional suppositions of the EPRDF founders: the New Order, won by struggles and sacrifices on the battlefield was to be based on socialism and ethnic divisions and with an unforgiving disdain for the past ("historically unjust relationships"). These controversial sentiments interpret events through the prism of the founders' own concerns. They are propounded at the beginning of the document lest any literate citizen forget the New Order.

The historical experience of the TPLF was shaped in war and guided by Marxist-Leninist theories. Party leaders were Hoxhaphiles, admirers of Albanian Stalinists, who eschewed democratic principles and encouraged ethnic hatred in an all- out effort to defeat the Derg. The TPLF-turned-EPRDF used martial skills in leadership, discipline, and control of resources to divide and conquer military or political foes. Unwilling to compromise and lacking in magnanimity in peace as well as war, the liberation front as government brooked no meaningful opposition. Backed by the United States and other donor nations, the TGE foisted its values upon all of Ethiopia. In incorporating its ideology in the new constitution, the EPRDF sought to consolidate its vision of the future for the nation—even if that vision conflicted with that of a majority of the people.

A constitution will succeed if it reflects "fixed principles of reason" directed to certain fixed objects of public good. These fixed principles of reason bind because the "community hath agreed" to be bound by them.[8] Ethiopian society has been unstable and disharmonious under the principles expounded by the TGE and that is evidence that those principles do not express what a majority of the community believe about governance and social justice. A constitution should embody basic legal conceptions of the community, their outlook on life or *Weltanschauung*, insofar as it can be embodied in general legal rules.[9] The TGE's constitution was based on principles that differ from those of the community, dooming the document from the start.

In articulating its principles, the TGE turned its back on pre-existing Ethiopian law which was the essence of constitutionalism. Actions of the government under the Transitional Charter were out of keeping with the "way of life" of the country—contrary to norms of Ethiopia. The new constitution did not take into account the people's tacit understandings—certain norms and standards which lie beyond the document itself and which cannot easily be inferred from it by someone not steeped in the history and culture of the country. Pre-constitutional norms shape the people's idea about regulating government, and it is upon these norms that the health and viability of a governing system will depend. Ethiopia's pre-constitutional norms came from both sacred and secular sources. Some were traditional and had been passed down through generations in the oral tradition and in grass roots practices. Others were written down as in the *Kibre Negest* and *Fetha Negest*. These half remembered documents are important politically not in themselves but for the ideals which they were held to encapsulate and which came to be so widely diffused among members of the society.

Historically, most societies in Ethiopia have practiced self-governance with some form of village and community democracy in which issues are openly discussed, compromises are made, and the majority's decisions are accepted.[10] Such systems are based on duties and responsibilities, not on rank and privilege. Frequently they encompass term limits on office holders and institutional checks and balances. Disputes are settled in open hearings by judges chosen by the community for their wisdom. By whatever name these self-governing democracies are known, whether *Shengo* or *Gada* or *Sabunnet*, they embody pre-constitutional values of common sense justice, fairness, cooperation, and mutual assistance.

Respect for law and justice is inherent in the Judeo-Christian-Islamic traditions in Ethiopia and in their scriptures. Widespread adherence to natural law is evinced by the sayings: *Hig* (law) belongs to God; God is God of law; and Right is done according to God's law. The *Fetha Negest*, the Law of Kings, recorded, in its two parts, the traditional civil and ecclesiastical codes. For Muslims, the *Shariah* is the basis of political, moral, and social life for the *Ummah*. Ethiopia, as the "Land of the First Migration" or *Dar Al-Hijrat-Al-Ula*, has a long history of tolerance based on mutual respect among religious groups. Religion permeates the daily life of the individual Ethiopian by reinforcing the concepts of duty and discipline. Social responsibility epitomized in compassion, charity, and alms giving is endemic in all the traditions.

The *Kibre Negest* describes the respect given King Solomon, a wise and just king, prior to the journey of the Queen of Sheba, Makeda, to Jerusalem. The story also is told of Menilek, the son of Solomon and Makeda, bringing the law and lawyers from Israel to Ethiopia. From that time on, Ethiopia was ruled by law and Solomon was the role model for those that would lead. Indeed, the highest praise bestowed upon an Ethiopian king was to be called "the Solomon of Ethiopia."

Also in the *Kibre Negest* is the narrative of Ardamis, the third son of Solomon and King of Rome (Constantinople), that emphasizes the notions of justice and fairness in his "fruit and leaves" decision in the *shepherd v. gardener* dispute. Likewise, King Amde Siyon, the Christian empire builder of the "Solomonic dynasty," who ruled from 1314–1344, is admired for his integrity in insisting upon uncompromising punishment for his son in a capital case. In more recent times, the chronicles of Menelik II relate how his son attempted to be like his father, a just ruler. For ages, the Ethiopian Christian saints, when deemed consummately truthful, were honored as "those who do justice," the *tsadiq*, the righteous.

From the mysterious sentiment of religion come "principles of justice and pity," pre-constitutional values of Ethiopians that cannot be ignored by those who would define a system of governance for the nation. For believers and non-believers alike, this religious background is the ultimate source of individual morality.

This is significant because the constitutional liberal state can only thrive if the moral conscience of the individual citizens is in harmony with the moral principles that underlie it. Political organizations which reject their moral commandments lose, as a result, their right to command. Legal legitimacy is based on "a belief in the legality of patterns of normative rules and the right of those elevated to authority under such rules to issue orders."[11] By rejecting the values of justice, fairness, compromise, cooperation, tolerance, benevolence, and respect for the law in their actions, the leaders of the EPRDF/TGE irreparably damaged their credibility to rule in the name of the people, much less to write a constitution for the nation.

CONTENT OF THE NEW CONSTITUTION

The constitution of the FDRE is both nominal and fictive. Its provisions describe but do not limit governmental behavior and they do not correspond to actual governmental practice. There is no commitment to constitutionalism, and the pre-constitutional principles of the mass of the people are not reflected in the document. Inspection of several of the articles reveal constitutional values that many Ethiopians find troubling.

For example, Chapter Two, The Fundamental Principles, begins with the credo of the EPRDF: *all* sovereign power emanates from ethnic groups. This predisposition to "nations, nationalities, and peoples" is stated forthrightly as the first principle and its echoes are explicit and implicit throughout the remainder of the document. The terms "nation, nationality, or people" refer to a "group of people" who "share a large measure of common culture, or similar customs, mutual intelligibility of language, belief in a common or related identities, and who predominantly inhabit an identifiable, contiguous territory"[12]—in other words, ethnic groups or tribes.

Fasil Nahum, one of the drafters of the constitution, maintains that an emphasis on ethnic background is in the psychological make-up of the Ethiopian people. He states that "in a free political process aiming at a democratic society, ethnicity seems the inevitable stepping-stone to political maturity. Therefore, the issue is how to maintain a state of stable equilibrium between centripetal and centrifugal forces in the state and hence the federal experimentation."[13]

In light of events in Rwanda and Bosnia-Herzegovina during the life of the TGE, such an experiment is a daring principle from which to operate. Further, events in Ethiopia during the TGE era raise serious doubts about ethnicity being a significant pre-constitutional principle of most Ethiopians. There is little evidence that the Ethiopian people are dedicated to the idea of government of the ethnics, by the ethnics, and for the ethnics.

Chapter Three contains a formidable list of Fundamental Rights and Freedoms subdivided into Human Rights and Democratic Rights. Fifteen articles spell out human rights including protections of life, liberty and security of the person, rights of prisoners and the accused before the bar of justice, and privacy rights, as well as religious freedom. Democratic rights are a more eclectic grouping of sixteen rights including those of thought, opinion, expression, assembly, association, and movement and a description of rights of citizenship, family, women, children, labor, and, of course, "nations, nationalities, and peoples." Also included as democratic rights are access to justice and economic, social, cultural, political, developmental, property, and environmental rights.

Nominally, this "bill of rights" chapter imposes limitations on the power of government by political and legal procedures. Unfortunately, in many instances, there is a stark contrast between the rights declared and the exact opposite that actually obtained under the TGE and later, the FDRE. There are numerous examples of the contradiction between ideal and practice.

For instance, many Ethiopians would welcome a meaningful Right to Privacy with an implied protection of an individual in his personal sphere of genuine autonomy from interference by the political community, as proclaimed by Article 26. The reality of life under the TGE with subtle restraints and coercions of individuals belies the article's noble aspirations. Worshipers in Gondar who were attacked by the military in September 1993 would be pleased to know that their rights will be protected by Article 27, Freedom of Religion, Belief and Opinion. Article 29's safeguard of the Right of Thought, Opinion and Expression (including press freedoms) would be reassuring to the Addis Ababa University faculty and administrators summarily dismissed by the TGE and the journalists imprisoned and fined by the government. The demonstrators protesting the imprisonment of Professor Asrat Woldeyes at the Central High Court in Addis Ababa in September 1994 who were beaten, jailed, and humiliated by EPRDF troops, or the AAU student demonstrators fired upon by the police in January 1993 can take comfort in Article 30's protection of The Right of Assembly, Demonstration, and Petition. Article 31, Freedom of Association, will be good news to members of the ETA and CETU whose organizations were taken over by the EPRDF. Article 38, The Right to Vote and to be Elected, should provide solace to supporters of the OLF, AAPO, and other political organizations and independent candidates who were harassed out of participating in the elections of 1992, 1994, and 1995.

In sum, the chapter on Fundamental Rights and Freedoms purports to chronicle the avoidance of oppression in certain areas of life. Bitter experience during the rule of the EPRDF suggests the false nature of such protections under the TGE and FDRE.

The idea of rights implies the availability of remedies to vindicate them. Such remedies as democratic processes and respect for due process of law ought to be implicit in the theory and structure of government.[14] Even so, fundamental rights and freedoms will have meaning only if a fearless and impartial interpretation of the law by a free and independent judiciary defends against insidious encroachments of despotism.

One fundamental remedy lies in the right of self-government and the right to vote, to select one's representatives, and to replace them if they abuse rights. The essential feature of authoritarian systems is that some groups have an effective capacity to prevent political outcomes that would be highly adverse to their interests. There exists, in other words, some power apparatus capable of preventing meaningful participation in the institutionalized political process.[15] An authoritarian stranglehold on democratic processes makes a mockery of proclaimed rights and freedoms.

The second fundamental remedy, due process of law requires that government regulation be by law, not by official fiat, and that it be rational with the means reasonably directed to a public end. Due process also requires that when official actions impinge on one's private interests, the individual be provided a fair hearing.

Under due process there are certain things no government should be permitted to do. Government officials should never punish a person for something that had not been publicly declared punishable when the act was committed. Nor should representatives of the state act in an arbitrary manner by treating like cases differently or by treating some persons more or less favorably than others without justification. By these standards, due process has frequently been abrogated by official actions of the TGE and FDRE. But as documented in the EPRDF strategy document, due process and other basic rights are not available to all citizens but only to those chosen by the Front as "the oppressed."

In addition to effective regularized restraints on government action, extralegal restraints are needed too. Regular and effective criticism and possible opposition by political parties, the press, and interest groups, none of which are squelched by or beholden to the government, help to uphold human rights. Such meaningful extralegal restraints exist only to a limited extent in Ethiopia.

Included among rights of the individual and groups is Article 39, Rights of Nations, Nationalities, and Peoples, which carries over the Transitional Charter's provision for ethnic self-determination including the right to secession— an invitation to national self-destruction. This right is founded on memories of what members of the EPRDF perceive as painful past discriminations inflamed by ethnic hatreds fostered by the Derg.

To proponents of Article 39, some of the world's most intractable problems arise when ethnic divisions are politicized by attempts at national integration. Communal loyalties, tinged with sectorial xenophobia, are in tension with membership in the state as a whole. By allaying fears of ethnic subgroups, Article 39 attempts to contain the country's diversity through ethnic confederations rather than through the integration of all people into a Greater Ethiopia. Ethnic differences are highlighted while principles and goals shared in common by the various groups are played down. From this perspective, minority security is a common good, and primordial attachments and conflicts are emphasized instead of being informally and realistically adjusted through cross-cutting political parties and interest groups.[16]

Critics of Article 39 contend that by authorizing secession, the state is inviting a series of separations that could become endless. Smaller and smaller groups could claim the right of self-determination, and the politics that result would be "noisy, incoherent, unstable, and deadly."[17]

In a liberal democracy, allegiance to the state need not conflict with, but can, on the contrary, accommodate subordinate loyalties to sub-national communities—whether those communities are defined in terms of ethnicity, language, or territory.[18] Such accommodationist ideas, competent to contain the country's diversity, are the opposite of the intent of Article 39.

Article 40, The Right to Property, implies that property means whatever the state says it means. Under the Derg, the legal concept of property—a symbol of stability and security —underwent changes that amounted to disintegration. With the end of the Mengistu dictatorship, most property owners assumed a return to the well-established legal tradition of protection: the right to acquire, own, use, and transfer property, generally by means and within limits recognized under Ethiopian law. Property owners accepted generally the authority of government to regulate these rights for the health, safety, or welfare of the community. While many Ethiopians owned only small amounts of land, they had a fierce pride in possession.

According to Article 40, "private property" refers to products "produced by the labor, creativity, enterprise or capital of an individual citizen." Private property does not include land and natural resources, the ownership of which is "exclusively vested in the State." Although Ethiopians may be granted the use of land, constitutionally, they have been rendered tenants of the State.[19] Had the EPRDF drafters of the constitution been influenced by Machiavelli rather than the Soviet Constitution of 1977, they might have been more concerned that "when neither their property nor their honor is touched, the majority of men live content."[20]

Changes in the law of property fostered by the TGE and consolidated under Article 40 attack a central Ethiopian value and an integral part of the social system. Property retains its symbolic, almost mythic, force as the foundation of Ethiopian freedoms and as the bulwark of individualism. The right to hold and to have the exclusive use of personal property allows a sufficient material basis for a sense of personal independence and self-respect, both of which are essential for the development and exercise of the moral powers.[21] By challenging the bases of the concept, Article 40 threatens this mythic quality. Most Ethiopians, having once traversed "the golden bridge to the paradise of socialism," with its concomitant landless ethos, have no desire to do it again.

Chapter Four establishes the state structure with a federal system composed of nine ethnic states derived from the administrative districts established by the TGE. The states are based on the "settlement patterns, identity, language, and consent of the people concerned" and are bounded by what the EPRDF believes to be homeland areas of major ethnic groups. Further subdivisions of the tribal homelands are possible under Article 47 which borders on the ludicrous with its replete list of some fifty-one ethnic groups, each with its own right to statehood, irrespective of whether such an entity would in any way be viable.

Chapters Five through Eight spell out the structure and powers of the federal state and the legislative and executive branches. Chapter Five, The Structure and Division of Powers, sets up a federalist state and defines the powers of the central government (the Federal State) in Article 51 and those of the states in Article 52. A preponderance of power resides in the central government. Legislative power in each state is vested in a State Council.

Chapters Six through Eight rejig the "parliamentary system" of the Transition Charter into a semi-presidential system similar to that of the Republic of India. Chapter Six establishes a two-house parliament with the Council of Peoples' Representatives (CPR), directly elected by the people as "the highest authority of the Federal Government," and a Federal Council (FC), representing the ubiquitous "nations, nationalities, and peoples," elected by the State Councils. Executive and legislative powers are merged in a British-like parliamentary system rather than being separated as in the U.S. model.

Chapter Seven, The Presidency, provides for "the Head of State," a ceremonial figurehead, elected by the Councils. Real executive power lies in the hands of the Prime Minister (PM) and Council of Ministers, selected by the PM, as described in Chapter Eight, The Executive. A full panoply of unrestrained executive power is asserted. Since the PM can be removed only by the loss of a majority in the CPR, a long tenure is guaranteed to the PM in a one-party state.

Chapter Nine, Structure of the Courts, is vital to the creation of an independent judiciary as part of the separation of powers and as the defender of fundamental rights and liberties. Regrettably, the chapter is a classic example of the "box within a box" tactic whereby ruling party-controlled local organizations elect intermediate organizations, which elect national organizations, which appoint executives, boards, commissions, and other public bodies from social organizations dominated by the party. In this world within a world composed entirely of a nest of boxes sits Meles and the TPLF leadership in the innermost box.

At the apex of the judicial system is the Constitutional Court composed of eleven justices basically chosen or confirmed by the two houses of the national legislature. In addition to the Chief Justice and Vice Chief Justice of the Federal Supreme Court (nominated by the PM on the basis of selections made by the Federal Commission for Judicial Administration, a party-dominated organization, and approved by the CPR), the Constitutional Court also includes three legal experts appointed by the President on nominations by the CPR and six persons selected by State Councils, which are elected by party fronts. The decisions of the Constitutional Court are not final until approved by the Federal Council which is elected by State Councils which are elected by party fronts. In short, the judiciary is very much controlled by the party in power through the unseparated legislative and executive branches.

Judges are removed by the Judicial Administration Commission (JAC), whose creation and composition are not explained in the constitution. If the JAC established by the TGE continued to function under the constitution, it would do so under a cloud of suspicion. The report on the Ethiopian judiciary by the International Human Rights Law Group criticized the JAC as not being able to stand up to the TGE. If an independent judiciary is to exist, it must be insulated and separated from executive interference, and the JAC must be free from the executive in terms of composition and accountability.[22]

Chapter Ten, National Policy Directives, provides affirmative governmental prescriptions on ethnicity in Article 88 and on state ownership of land and on the "equal distribution of wealth" in Article 89. Special Provisions of Chapter Eleven include a disturbing emergency proclamation of Article 95. This detailed article takes up more space than does the description of the structure, powers, and function of the Constitutional Court. Is this elaborate rehearsing of a worse case scenario including the suspension of democratic and political rights an invitation to a self-fulfilling prophecy?

In summary, the constitution embodied essentially what the EPRDF/TGE wished the world outside and its own people to believe about the political order. A sham and fictive constitution presented a respectable front to outsiders and provided satisfaction to party-loyalists. Other Ethiopians would experience the disquiet caused by a government unrestrained in power. The EPRDF, having "successfully completed" the Transition Phase with the ratification of a new constitution, could begin fully to implement its program of revolutionary democracy as described in the Front's strategy document. But first, the EPRDF issued its order of march, a document providing a blueprint of the organization of party and government to establish and maintain hegemony in the newly established Federal Democratic Republic of Ethiopia.

NOTES

1. See Carl J. Friedrich, *Constitutional Government and Democracy: Theory and Practice in Europe and America* (Boston: Little, Brown, 1941), 127; Alemante G. Selassie, "Constitution-Making," *Ethiopian Review* 3 (October 1993): 24–28.

2. *New York Times v. Sullivan*, 376 US 254 (1964).

3. Tecola Hagos, "EPRDF's Constitution," *Ethiopian Register* 2 (March 1995): 41–47; Theodore M. Vestal, "An Analysis of the New Constitution of Ethiopia and the Process of its Adoption," *Northeast African Studies* 3 (1996): 21–38; Minasse Haile, "The New Ethiopian Constitution: Its Impact upon Unity, Human Rights and Development," *Suffolk Transnational Law Review* 20 (Winter 1996): 1–84.

4. Minasse, 5. See generally, Carl J. Friedrich, "Constitutions and Constitutionalism," *International Encyclopedia of the Social Sciences* (New York: Macmillan, 1968).

5. Arthur Kuflick, "The Inalienability of Autonomy," *Philosophy and Public Affairs* 13 (1984): 271, 297.

6. John E. Finn, *Constitutions in Crisis: Political Violence and the Rule of Law* (New York: Oxford University Press, 1991), 39–40.

7. Vernon Bogdanor, "Introduction," in *Constitutions in Democratic Politics* ed. Vernon Bogdanor, (Aldershot, UK: Gower, 1988), 10.

8. Lord Bolingbroke, *Historical Writings*, ed. Isaac Kremnick, 4 vols. (Chicago: University of Chicago Press, 1972) 2: 88.

9. Friedrich, *Constitutional Government and Democracy*, 120.

10. Hailu Fulass, "Democracy in Ethiopian Polities," *Ethiopian Register* 1 (March 1994): 21–23; for analysis of the interaction of spirituality and governance during the reign of the "Solomonic" dynasty, see, Taddesse Tamrat, *Church and State in Ethiopia 1270–1527* (Oxford: Clarendon Press, 1972).

11. Ghita Ionescu, "The Theory of Liberal Constitutionalism," in *Constitutions in Democratic Politics* ed. Vernon Bogdanor, (Aldershot, UK: Gower, 1988), 39–48.

12. Ethiopian Constitution Article 8(1).

13. Fasil Nahum, *Constitution for a Nation of Nations: the Ethiopian Prospect* (Lawrenceville, NJ: Red Sea Press, 1997), 45. Fasil's book provides a thorough review of the constitution from the Front's perspective. Fasil is one of Ethiopia's leading technocrats of constitution writing. He helped draft: 1) a constitution in 1972 proposing a constitutional monarchy for the Emperor; 2) the constitution of the People's Democratic Republic of Ethiopia during the Derg's regime in 1987; and 3) the constitution for the FDRE in 1994.

14. Louis Henkin, "Introduction," in *Constitutionalism and Rights: The Influence of the United States Constitution Abroad* eds. Henkin and Albert J. Rosenthal, (NY: Columbia University Press, 1990), 9; George Kateb, "Remarks on the Procedures of Constitutional Democracy," in *Constitutionalism*, eds. J. Roland Pennock and John W. Chapman, NOMOS XX (New York: New York University Press, 1979), 216–219.

15. Adam Przeworski, "Democracy as a Contingent Outcome of Conflicts," in *Constitutionalism and Democracy* eds. Jon Elster and Rune Slagstad, (Cambridge, UK: Cambridge University Press, 1988), 59–61.

16. See Stephen Holmes, "Gag Rules or the Politics of Omission," in *Constitutionalism and Democracy* eds. Jon Elster and Rune Slagstad, (Cambridge, UK: Cambridge University Press, 1988), 27–31.

17. See Michael Walzer, *Thick and Thin: Moral Argument at Home and Abroad* (Notre Dame, IN: Notre Dame University Press, 1994), 70.

18. See Vernon Bogdanor, "Britain: The Political Constitution," in *Constitutions in Democratic Politics* ed. Vernon Bogdanor, (Aldershot, UK: Gower, 1988), 53–72.

19. Minasse, 68.

20. *The Prince*, Ch. 19. Machiavelli might agree that there will be no contentment over property rights in Ethiopia until people can enjoy *rist* without risk and *gult* without guilt.

21. John Rawls, *Political Liberalism* (New York: Columbia University Press, 1993), 298.

22. International Human Rights Law Group, *Ethiopia in Transition: A Report on the Judiciary and the Legal Profession*, Washington, DC, January 1994, 9–10.

CHAPTER 10

Organizing Revolutionary Democracy

A short time after the May 1995 elections, the Front published its *Guideline for EPRDF's Organizational Structure and Operation* (in Amharic), another secret document available only to party leaders and cadre. The *Guideline* was written, in the vocabulary of Marxism, by the Organizational Center of the EPRDF Central Committee "to secure the highest unity between the thoughts and action of the Front" and its members. The document is a blueprint for implementing the EPRDF's "struggle" for Revolutionary Democratic goals and for extending its control over the political, economic, and social activities of the country. It describes the organizational configuration of the centralized and secretive revolutionary party that works primarily through its cadres, "professional revolutionaries," whose occupation consists largely or entirely of political activity. Once again, it was the *Ethiopian Register* that translated and made public the Front's secret document.[1]

The *Guideline* reveals a complete fusion of the EPRDF organizational structure with that of its ethnic member organizations, including the founding TPLF. Organized on principles of bureaucratic rationality, the EPRDF's organizational ladder descends from the highest rungs of the government to the lowest steps of the rural locality, the *gott*. The offices of the Prime Minister and the President, the parliament, the central government ministries and agencies, including public enterprises are all part of the Front's vast network. In the states, EPRDF organizational units control activities in the killil, zonal, woreda, sub-woreda, and kebele administrations, down to departments and the smallest sections. Universities, high schools, hospital and non-governmental organizations, and profit-for-the-party companies are included in the scheme. To make this system operate, the Front must rely on public resources—manpower, money, facilities, and time—because the executives in almost all public offices are party cadres assigned specific organizational responsibilities to maintain EPRDF hegemony.

A major responsibility of cadres is "monitoring" (a euphemism for "spying on") the people in general and the opposition forces in particular. Party cadre in organizational branches at various levels infiltrate independent associations, such as trade unions, professional organizations, or any other civic associations, and attempt to take over positions of leadership. Any organization that is not controlled from the top by EPRDF cadres or units is considered dangerous by the Front and is to be opposed vehemently.

The EPRDF's organizational structure encourages ethnic divisions within society and strictly limits any associational activity that may transcend ethnic boundaries. The *Guideline* prescribes Lenin's "democratic centralism" as the lodestar of the EPRDF's organizational philosophy. The Front stresses the importance of an authoritarian command structure and of strict discipline. Party members carry out EPRDF political and organizational activities on "platforms of struggle" that range "from country-wide to the lowest sector of the society." The party's structure is so centralized that even action plans to be implemented by the lowest bodies are commanded from the top leadership. Quotidian activities such as setting dates and venues of meetings of study cells have to be set in advance and reported to higher bodies. The entire operation is geared to reinforce the command structure with a speedy exchange of information between the units at various levels. The party directs its diverse wings through caucuses of activists within them, and it regulates appointment to leading positions at all levels through the EPRDF version of the Soviet's *nomenklatura*, a list of positions that could be filled only by party approval.

The common program of the EPRDF is approved by a Congress of its member organizations. The Front's Congress elects a sixty-person Council for the Front and a twenty-man Executive Committee, composed of five representatives from each of the Big-Four ethnic components of the Front, the TPLF, OPDO, ANDM, and Southern Ethiopian Peoples Democratic Front (SEPDF). The Executive Committee in turn elects the General Secretary and a Deputy Secretary. Each member "national" organization has its own parallel leadership structure, but following the principles of "democratic centralism," command of the ethnic fronts effectively remains with the leadership of the EPRDF, which is dominated by the TPLF.

Following the model of Lenin and the Bolsheviks, the Front uses two means—organization and propaganda—to mobilize the masses. The powerful Propaganda and Organizational Committee (POC) of the EPRDF's Central Committee leads this effort. Members of POC are selected from the Front's Executive Committee. The POC formulates the party's plan of action and assures its implementation by the Front and its member organizations. It harmonizes decisions and plans of each of the organizations with those of the EPRDF, approves the basic content of propaganda for all member organizations, oversees the assignment of cadres, responds to financial requests of member organizations, and determines the sources of finance and the utilization of funds.

The POC is divided into two operating units, the propaganda and organizational centers. The mission of the Propaganda Center (PC) is to "mold the outlook of the rank and file members and the public at large by firmly indoctrinating them with the outlook of revolutionary democracy." This the PC does by using mass media to communicate party views and "the activities that the EPRDF undertakes through the government to benefit the people," as well as the programs carried out by development associations (state enterprises and EPRDF companies) and other organizations closely affiliated with the party. The "destructive method of struggle and political stand of the opposition forces" are to be exposed on government media. Private sector newspapers and magazines that have attained "public acceptance" will be encouraged to publicize the party's views. Moreover, the PC will set up its own "private" newspapers and magazines to further the party line. The Center also compiles information necessary for propaganda work inside and outside the country.

The training of cadres is a special function of the PC which "monitors and manages" their political education. The PC prepares manuals, teaching materials, and discussion papers for seminars and conducts courses and study cells "to strengthen the political maturity and revolutionary resolve" of party members." Like Orwell's Big Brother, the Center ambitiously "formulates and implements the steps for shaping the day-to-day political life of the members." In addition, it monitors "higher and middle intellectuals" in trade unions, professional associations, and development associations, as well as in Federal and killil government agencies. Through party members, the PC "strives to lead activities of intellectuals in the direction of revolutionary democracy without yet violating their professional freedom."

The other major center of the POC, the Organizational Center (OC), monitors civic associations. It organizes the various sectors of society into independent associations and strives to win them over to the viewpoint of revolutionary democracy without undermining their autonomy. "Capable members within these associations" are recruited by the OC and boosted into leadership positions "on the basis of the maturity of their views" or party fervor. The OC attempts to dominate the labor movement through the efforts of specially selected EPRDF members of trade unions. Even Ethiopians living abroad fall under the scrutiny of the OC, which tries to organize them into associations based on ethnicity. Working with the Front's branches at various levels, the OC "finds out details of the specific identity of the leaders of the opposition organizations within and outside the country" and monitors the tactics these groups employ, "their internal conditions as well as the relationships among them." The importance of the OC within the EPRDF organizational scheme is underscored by its being entrusted with the writing of the *Guideline*.

At state and local levels, there is a similar structure of organizational and propaganda subcommittees in a parallel chain of command extending from the killil to the woreda. Within the organizational structure, every member of the EPRDF is assigned to a Primary Organization, a clone of the old Soviet Union's "Primary Party Organization." A Primary Organization is composed of up to twenty party members. In the ethnic homelands of the *killil,* as might be expected, organization is by "national" affiliation.

At the Regional and Zonal levels, Institutional and Propaganda Subcommittees ensure the quality and effectiveness of the activities of party operatives. They monitor mass organizations, government workers, and the intelligentsia and carry on propaganda work within all groups. At the kebele level, in government agencies and offices, Primary Organizations and Study Cells spearhead propaganda and organizational efforts by inculcating the general public with the ethos of Revolutionary Democracy. Mass organizations are used as "popular democratic forums" for the protection of party interests.

Study Cells of from three to seven members reinforce "the political maturity and revolutionary ethics of members" at the *gott* level. In development institutions (state enterprises and Front companies), managers of head offices chair EPRDF branch committees to assure that members play "an organized vanguard role" in making the institutions successfully fulfill their objectives—especially in making a profit.

EPRDF branches are organized in agencies and institutions of the Central Government including the offices of the Prime Minister and the President; the House of Peoples' Representatives; ministries, commissions, authorities, and other country-wide agencies; universities; and the Addis Ababa Administration. Their work is overseen by a Central Leadership Committee. All party members in the Central Government are organized on the basis of ethnicity. The Front's Parliamentary Committee manages the day-to-day activities of the members of parliament, while the party's Parliamentary Leadership Committee provides "overall leadership which the Parliament should get from EPRDF."

Party branches in higher education seek to bring faculty and students under the sway of the EPRDF. "Democratic views" are to be developed among teachers and students, who are to be inculcated with "a healthy patriotic feeling" and an appreciation of the equality of ethnic groups. Party loyalists must combat the academics' tendencies toward chauvinism and narrow nationalism by helping them understand EPRDF's positions and views. "Legal" associations of students and teachers are to be encouraged, led by those "imbued with democratic views and attitudes." Student and faculty party members are formed into separate Primary Organizations on the basis of "nationality" at the departmental and faculty (e.g., arts and sciences, law, engineering) levels. Students in the same year are organized into Study Cells. EPRDF student members "will be made to be elected" as members of the Student Council and form their own Study Cell. The Primary Organizations and Study Cells will do their political study according to the propaganda plan regularly passed on to them from above. Although the *Guideline* advocates universities producing "the skilled manpower the country needs," there is no mention of their seeking the truth or teaching students to think for themselves, activities traditionally associated with higher education in Ethiopia.

The proletariat with its class struggle also receives special attention in the *Guideline*. Workers can become members of the EPRDF only if they are organized under one of the ethnic member organizations. Because labor unions are not under the direct control of the government or a political party, the Front must win the support of workers by propounding ideas that serve "the interests of the proletariat." The EPRDF's Labor Branches seek to enable workers to acquire short-term and long-term benefits without disturbing the industrial peace—an intriguing project given the party's direct or indirect ownership of industries. The Front's Country-Wide Labor Leadership Committee provides overall and day-to-day direction to the labor movement. Its work is enhanced by party members being assigned or planted in the leadership of labor federations and the national confederation. Proletarian EPRDF members are organized under Primary Organizations in their factories and service organizations and lead party activities in their specific trade unions as well as among unorganized factory workers.

The *Guideline* states that it is increasingly difficult for the Front regularly to call public meetings to keep members and cadres informed about events in their locality and country. Although the EPRDF still may call meetings on special topics, other means are needed to augment regular communications. Propaganda work is thus to be divided into three categories focusing on the people, the associations and labor unions, and the intelligentsia.

Party cadres will set up study cells for political indoctrination at various levels throughout the government. The political commitment and loyalty of cadres will be evaluated on the basis of their participation in the Study Cell. The EPRDF prepares study materials in Front magazines and newspapers that serve as discussion topics for the cells. The EPRDF magazine, *Hizbawi Adera* (*Popular Cause* or *Mission*) is published every three months in three languages, and each of the ethnic member organizations has its own publications in the language of its linguistic killil. The weekly newspaper of the EPRDF is disingenuously titled *Abyotawi* (*Democracy*).

A cadre assigned to an administrative body or to Propaganda and Organizational Committees may be sent to cadre school for training. Those who complete this training are subjected to a gauntlet of regular monitoring by the party. A cadre will be judged by: how he performs the assigned tasks; his leadership ability and "revolutionary vigor" in implementing plans; his buying and reading the organization's newspapers at his own initiative; his participation in Study Cells; his commitment and loyalty to the EPRDF goals and political line; his efforts to rid himself of "erroneous views" and his determination to "struggle against reactionary outlooks and forces;" and his relation with the people and other members and his efforts to know and solve their problems. The cadre is appraised on these and other criteria every three months. In addition, the cadre must submit to criticism and self-criticism focusing on his political commitment and the maintenance of a "revolutionary personality." Cadres who repeatedly fail to show improvement will be purged from the party during appraisal sessions. The Front also relies on *Tagays*, former members of the EPRDF military, who carry out the same duties as cadres.

In its political work with the general public, the party instigates propaganda activities aimed at molding the outlook and raising the "consciousness" of the people. "Consciousness" was Lenin's term for the awareness needed to guide the revolution into political effectiveness. The *Guideline* recommends that party members "do agitation work to persuade the people to come out in large numbers" to public meetings. Churches and other meeting places are to be used for informally communicating the Front's views while still agitating strongly for the public's acceptance and implementation of the party's key development plan. According to the *Guideline*, as long as the people are aligned with the EPRDF, the Front does not need to call meetings for the sake of refuting what the enemy says.

By the time the FDRE came into existence, the Front's organizational structure was in place. The EPRDF now was ready to "fully implement" its "struggle" for Revolutionary Democratic goals. If past were prologue, the nation could look forward to continuing contentious strife as the EPRDF went about exerting its control over virtually all aspects of the people's lives.

NOTE

1. EPRDF Central Committee, *Dirijitawi Ma'ekel, Guideline for EPRDF's Organizational Structure and Operation*, English translation of TPLF/EPRDF Amharic language document, published in six parts, *Ethiopian Register* 4 (September 1997): 16–19; (October 1997): 18–22; (November 1997): 18–21; (December 1997): 22–27; *Ethiopian Register* 5 (February 1998): 20–24; (March 1998): 18, 20–22, 24. All quotations from the *Guideline* are taken from this translation.

CHAPTER 11

The Kitab of the TGE: Final Reckoning

The *kitab* or magic scroll of the Transitional Government of Ethiopia was completed in 1995. The traditional Ethiopian magic scroll is a long narrow band of parchment on which a calligraphy narrative is illustrated with the images of saints and angels alternating with astral shapes, diabolic masks, and interlaced patterns. As prepared by *debteras* (unordained priests) of the EPRDF, the top of the TGE *kitab* is crowned by a painting of St. Meles Zenawi on a white horse spearing the evil dragon Mengistu Haile Mariam while the wide-eyed angel of the United States looks on approvingly from above. In the upper left corner of the icon is the figure of Issayas Afeworki, the President of Eritrea, slipping away with spoils of war, the sacred soil of Ethiopia, under his arm. The narrative of the scroll tells the history of the TGE from the time of its founding in 1991 until its termination with the election of the new government of the FDRE in August 1995.

The scroll is a talisman or amulet to protect the wearer, the TGE, from the evil eye—i.e., from the discerning eyes of critics who recognized the faults of the government in its efforts at "democratization"—or to be used in magic rites for exorcising those possessed by evil spirits (those who opposed TGE policies). The entire length of the scroll equals the height of the beneficiary—short in many respects. The unordained priests-artisans of the EPRDF had intended the kitab to literally protect the TGE from head to foot. Their design was foiled, however, by art and literary critics at home and abroad who understood the meaning of the paintings and who could read between the lines of the narrative and were thus able to sear the conscience of the public and to call attention to deficits of democracy in the TGE.

GOVERNANCE UNDER THE TRANSITIONAL CHARTER

The main features of the TGE's *kitab* have been described in previous chapters. From wartime insurgent group, the EPRDF was transformed into transitional government by the magic wand of the U.S. State Department. Anointed with donor nation dollars on the collateral of promised good behavior in democratic ways, the EPRDF got to choose the players and make up the rules for a TGE. While most of the world breathed sighs of relief that Mengistu and the Derg were gone, few attended to the mischief the TPLF-dominated EPRDF was about. Indeed, many friends of Ethiopia cheered the democratic shibboleths and the freedom that was promised throughout the country.

Ethiopia's new leaders generated high expectations and faced formidable demands in moulding an intermediate social and political order. EPRDF leaders committed themselves to politically correct democratic ideas—multiparty elections, protection of human rights, a free press, the rule of law, and a pluralist society with equal status for all people. Their rhetoric was laced with the vocabulary of Jefferson and Locke as well as Marxist-Leninist doggerel.

The TGE's initial progress was encouraging. The political, economic, and human rights situation started improving immediately after the EPRDF took over. Free expression and criticism of government policies were tolerated as never before. Nascent political parties were hatched. A large number of new newspapers and magazines were published and openly sold in Addis Ababa and elsewhere. President Meles held long discussions with intellectuals on prime-time evening television. Political exiles returned home without the threat of arrest, and citizens generally moved freely throughout the country. Members of the Derg regime accused of human rights violations were arrested but not executed, and a Special Prosecutor was named to bring offenders to justice. The field hands of the EPRDF cleared the Augean stables of the residues left by the excesses of the Derg, and most of Mengistu's livestock was put out to pasture.

The new government speeded up the process of economic reform and made, what donor nations thought, satisfactory progress in a short time.[1] According to TGE figures, Gross Domestic Product (GDP) grew substantially, varying from 5 percent to 8 percent per annum during the Transition

Period. Economic development was hindered, however, by lingering problems of land tenure left over from earlier regimes.

Less than a year after the adoption of the Charter, the TGE's promising beginnings were compromised as governmental actions caused concern that the environment of limited political tolerance was eroding. From that time on, it became increasingly difficult for the TGE to convince outside observers that a transition to democracy was indeed taking place. Although Meles and the EPRDF leaders continued to speak in the language of freedom and democracy, their performance was sharply condemned as authoritarian by Ethiopian and foreign critics. Friends of Ethiopia, many of whom had been willing to give the benefit of the doubt to the TGE, became concerned that the democratization process was off track and doomed to failure unless some corrective actions were taken.

What friends and critics alike were seeing was the manifestation of the true nature of the symbiotic Marxist-Leninist EPRDF/TGE. The anti-Mengistu alliance entered a second phase during which the weaker members were purged and a new authoritarian system was established. Ethnicity became the basis of rule, opposition was snuffed out, and basic human rights were denied by the arbitrary rule of unreachable authorities. A glaring public relations error marred the TGE's previous beguilement of foreigners: the invitation to international observers to sprinkle holy water on the carefully orchestrated fake elections of 1992. Instead, the observers declared the proceedings to be all wet. Nevertheless, the TGE got away with continually manipulating the rules of the governance game. Donor nations, including the United States, with its "African policy lite,"[2] were quite content to rock along with cosmetic changes for the TGE but with nothing fundamental being done to democratize the country. In the courts of public morality and common sense, the United States was indicted for having empowered an oppressive regime in Ethiopia.

As the transition period came to a *de jure* if not *de facto* end, the wiles of the TGE became more blatant. The nuanced soft killing of opposition changed to the brazen thuggery unleashed at peaceful demonstrators protesting the incarceration of Professor Asrat Woldeyes at the Central High Court in Addis Ababa in September 1994. This *Walpurgisnacht* frenzy showed that the EPRDF/TGE now felt immunized against "rule of anticipated reaction," the expectation by those in power that there are certain types of action which the public or organized groups within it would not tolerate. In reaction to such barbarity, the United States, the principal financier of the TGE, languished in gormless stupor admitting only that the situation was "complex."[3]

These events in the *kitab* of the TGE are recorded as the establishment of a "government based on freedom, equal representation, and democracy."[4] Profuse examples illustrate each magic formula and democratic incantation. Realists, however, find other meanings in these benign artifices.

The *debteras* had recorded a premature closure of the process of democratic transformation through the TGE's establishment of formal procedures and institutions before a real change in the nature of power had taken place. This premature closure was brought about through laws that imposed difficult requirements on disorganized parties and voluntary associations, through regulations that purportedly guaranteed "the responsible behavior of the independent media" but in reality muzzled them while they were barely getting off the ground, and through elections that sidelined the opposition before it got organized. Couched in the trappings of democracy, the TGE's insidious premature closure was as detrimental to democratization as repression.[5]

THE BALANCE SHEET

Deficits of democracy were apparent when one compared the significant steps of transition with normative standards: "Between the idea/And the reality/Between the motion/And the act/Falls the Shadow."[6]

The shadowy party-as-government under the TGE failed to meet the criterion of a "liberal democracy." Power was not widely shared but was concentrated in the hands of EPRDF party leaders. Citizens did not have ready access to positions of decision making either in the sense of contacting policy makers to attempt to influence their decisions nor in the citizen's capability to compete for decision-making positions in an election. The rule of law was not dominant. Guarantees of civil liberties were meaningless and insufficient to ensure the integrity of political competition and participation. Government was neither representative nor accountable. The bureaucracy was not rule-bound nor merit-based. And economic resources were concentrated in the hands of the government.

The TGE's rule more correctly fit the gauge of authoritarianism.[7] The EPRDF controlled the military to provide security for the regime and control of society. The government created a pervasive bureaucracy staffed by the Front. Internal opposition and dissent were controlled by the party-in-government. And various means of socialization were utilized by the EPRDF in an attempt to create allegiance to the TGE.

Democratization failed because there was no transition from the authoritarian Derg to a form of government that in meaningful ways guaranteed civil liberties and provided citizens with a means to attempt to influence policy outcomes. The transitional incumbents rather than the people determined the results of contests for public office. Official barriers to political expression and negotiation were erected by the TGE making compromise and democratic institution building impossible. There was no separation of state from civil society.

In terms of power, having *established* power through military expediency blessed by the high priests of the donor nations diplomatic corps, the TGE consolidated its power in the government and in society through its highly disciplined cadres. The government's roots in Marxist-Leninist ideology came to the fore in the *exercise* of power that was *maintained* by stifling political opposition and bridling dissent. The *"transfer"* of power amounted to a rearranging of the EPRDF deck chairs on the Ethiopian ship of state with donor nations assisting with fictive "democratic" trappings. The FDRE was to be the TGE continued, afloat on the Sea of Hostility.

As the transition ran out, so did the statute of limitations on the rule of lenity. Those who had hoped for a successful transition to democracy were disappointed.

A NEW CONSTITUTION AND THE FDRE

The penultimate image of the *kitab* is a scroll representing the new constitution reflecting "respect for and faith in the decisions of the people." Under the Transition Charter, the transitional period culminated in the drafting of a "democratic constitution" ratified by a newly elected National Assembly.

The new EPRDF constitution was proclaimed throughout the land, and prescribed parliamentary elections were conducted to establish the Federal Democratic Republic of Ethiopia. Close observers of the scene noted that the blueprint of the Charter had been followed in constructing the Ethiopian coach of state, but many worried about the substance used in the building.

The one-party government coming to, or rather remaining in, power under the new constitution would be part of a lingering transition. But where was the transition going? Had one dyed-in-the-wool communist regime been replaced by another repressive Marxist-Leninist cabal versed in the counterfeit trappings of democratization and capitalism?

Could "crypto-communists" or "nuevo conversos" to the gospel of Adam Smith hoodwink the donor nations and especially the United States into keeping the Front fiscally propped up and blessed at a time when the monied regimes were disparaging other African governments for their democratic deficits and failures as guarantors of human rights? Apparently so.

The EPRDF, adept at everything that's hidden, had demonstrated its resiliency, skill, and tenacity. The party leader, Meles, was a master of *coup d'oeil*, a sixth sense for advantageous tactical situations. Although he occupied a "Seat Perilous," his brand of hard authoritarianism had kept opposition at bay with fine-tuned subtlety. Ethnicity and Marxist-Leninist revisionism had become his essence, his angelic ichor.

The legacy of fear and repression left by the undemocratic TGE did not bode well for Ethiopia under the new constitution. In addition to lacking widespread popular support, the government was in bad need of the missing brain power, the wasted human potential, that remained abroad in the diaspora. Ethiopia, alas, was "wandering between two worlds, one dead, the other powerless to be born."[8]

The final diabolical mask thus was painted on the bottom of the TGE's *kitab*. Then the *debteras* of the EPRDF began work on a new one using many of the same images and patterns. The *kitab* of the FDRE is a work in progress. What will it look like and how long will it be?

NOTES

1. Fikre Tolossa, "Interview with George E. Moose, U.S. Assistant Secretary of State for African Affairs," *Ethiopian Review* 4 (February 1994): 23.

2. See Chester A. Crocker, "Time to Get Serious in Africa," *New York Times*, 28 August 1998, A-23.

3. See, e.g., George E. Moose, Testimony, Hearings Before the Subcommittee on Africa of the House Committee on Foreign Affairs, 103d Congress, 2d Session, 27 July 1994.

4. "Ethiopians Vote on Constituent Assembly," *News from Ethiopia*, Embassy of Ethiopia, Washington, DC, 23 June 1994, 1–2.

5. Marina Ottaway, "From Political Opening to Democratization?" in *Democracy in Africa: the Hard Road Ahead* ed. Marina Ottaway, (Boulder, CO: L. Rienner, 1997), 3.

6. T. S. Eliot, "The Hollow Men," in *The Complete Poems and Plays 1909–1950* (New York: Harcourt, Brace, World, 1971), 58.

7. See Marina Ottaway, "The Ethiopian Transition: Democratization or New Authoritarianism?" in *Proceedings of the 37th Annual Meeting of the African Studies Association*, Toronto, Ontario, 3–6 November 1994.

8. Matthew Arnold, "Stanzas from the Grande Chartreuse," in *The Poetical Works of Matthew Arnold* eds. C. B. Tinker and H. F. Lowry, (Oxford: Oxford University Press, 1950), 299.

Haile Selassie, Emperor of Ethiopia, 1930–1974. Photo courtesy Library of Congress.

Meles Zenawi, President of the Transitional Government of Ethiopia, Prime Minister of the FDRE. Photo courtesy Embassy of Ethiopia.

EPRDF leader Meles Zenawi at the July 1991 "All Party
Conference" in Addis Ababa. Photo courtesy of the author.

Meles Zenawi and Tesfaye Habisso of the EPRDF
at the July 1991 National Conference. Photo
courtesy of the author.

OLF leader Gelassa Dilbo at the July 1991 Conference. Photo courtesy of the author.

Dr. Beyene Petros of the SEPDC at the July 1991 All Party Peace and Reconciliation Conference. Photo courtesy of the author.

Professor Asrat Woldeyes, President of the AAPO, returning from a court appearance in Addis Ababa, June 1993. Photo courtesy of the author.

Part II

THE FEDERAL DEMOCRATIC REPUBLIC OF ETHIOPIA, 1995-PRESENT

CHAPTER 12

Government of the FDRE

With the ratification of the constitution and the establishment of the FDRE, the EPRDF was poised to fully implement its struggle for revolutionary democratic goals. The cast of characters in party and government had changed but little from that of the Transition Period, and direction still came from the hard core leaders of the TPLF and hence, from the Marxist-Leninist League of Tigray. This gave them quite a lot of clout.

The Front continued its political high wire act, balancing between the reality of its ideology and the illusion needed to beguile the monied international community. From the ground, it appeared the party acrobats were more sure of step than previously. Yet, it was obvious that they still worried about tumbling down. They sought a fiscal safety net to catch them should they fall and went about rigging the meshes with strands from internal and foreign sources. Of course, no other party was allowed to perform in the main arena, and those who entered the tent were treated as rubes. The audience was led to applause by the skillful ringmaster who manipulated the crowd with his whip and through his exclusive control of the loudspeaker. In the chapters that follow, we will look at the *mise en scène* of the FDRE's Big Top and see how the Front's act of Revolutionary Democracy has played in Ethiopia and beyond.

DRAMATIS PERSONAE

The newly elected Council of People's Representatives (CPR) and Federal Council (FC) began work on 21 August 1995. The EPRDF and its affiliates held over 90 percent of the seats in the founding congress, so it was no surprise when it elected the Front's General Secretary, Meles Zenawi, as Prime Minister for a five-year term. The Councils also chose Negasso Gidada of the OPDO as the nation's figurehead president. Meles selected his Council of Ministers, composed of EPRDF veterans of the TGE, and was prepared to exercise unrestrained executive power in the parliamentary system sans separation of powers. Presiding over the legislative and executive branches and serving as commander-in-chief of the armed forces, the Prime Minister sat at the apex of the EPRDF/FDRE power structure.[1]

Preoccupation with power motivated the responsible EPRDF leadership at every crucial stage in the development and consolidation of the Front's political hegemony. Persuaded of their own ultimately beneficent purposes as the surrogate of the "oppressed masses," the Front's leaders were prepared to destroy ruthlessly all who stood in their way, to make temporary concessions to the forces which they could not master, and to utilize those willing and unwilling allies who could be induced to join the "struggle" for Revolutionary Democracy.

Armed with a new legitimacy, at least in the eyes of those who wanted to see it, burnished by a "popular mandate," the Front used the reorganization of the government to tighten its hold on political instruments. The judiciary was ethnically cleansed to strengthen the party's monopoly of legal power, and the bureaucracy was purged of those who were not supporters of EPRDF programs. The army was reorganized as a "nonpolitical" entity but remained permeated with party controls. Police and security forces, oppression's enforcers, were used to create among the populace a milieu of pervasive insecurity founded on ever-present fear of the informer and detention houses. Trade unions and other voluntary associations were further subordinated to the party.

Positively, the Front tried to saturate and paralyze the minds of the people with a monolithic stream of agitation and propaganda stressing the superiority of Revolutionary Democracy and the virtues of party leaders. Negatively, it sought to deny citizens access to any alternatives by keeping journalists and political opponents muzzled. The Front also kept people cut off from each other through its killil system of subtle ethnic discriminations.

With the parliament safely packed with EPRDF regulars, the Front's leaders could focus their attention on other sectors of the central government that might yet harbor elements inimical to revolutionary democracy and "the oppressed masses."

THE JUDICIAL SYSTEM

Under the TGE, judges who tried to uphold the rule of law frequently were defeated by local officials who refused to comply with their decisions. The FDRE sought to alleviate this situation, not by firing the local officials, but by restructuring the judiciary and dismissing more than 500 well trained and experienced judges and prosecutors. This action put further pressure on the meager capacities of the judicial system, which had already suffered sweeping political purges after the fall of the Derg. The result was near paralysis of the courts, with most citizens being denied the full protections supposedly provided in the Constitution.[2] One year adjournments became routine in the court system, with supects and defendants routinely spending long months in pretrial detention.

The accused facing trial on political and security charges claim that the government is using the near paralysis of the justice system to neutralize them and their parties, associations, and publications for years at a time without appearing to be directly cracking down on them. Some prisoners held only for the nonviolent exercise of their freedom of expression and association faces long term detention before even coming to trial.

The dismissed judges were replaced by TPLF cadres, who, for the most part, lacked formal training in the law. The government instigated crash courses in a newly created Civil Service College to give the new judges and prosecutors rudimentary knowledge of the legal system.[3] However, as we shall see, knowledge of ethnic origin and party loyalty probably are more significant than jurisprudence in the EPRDF scheme of justice. In discharging the judges trained for the most part at Addis Ababa University's School of Law, the government undermined the efforts of the university, aided by foreign scholars, especially Americans, over a period of more than three decades to build a legal system comprised of rigorously-trained law graduates.

The Front justified its action as an effort to weed out corruption. According to Meles, most of the dismissed judges had been participants in "the brutal injustices of the Derg." The Prime Minister claimed the government was unable to find many qualified judges who are trustworthy—an amazing determination in light of the number of Ethiopians trained in the law.[4] What the judicial *shumshir* (promotion/demotion) did give Ethiopia was the distinction of being the African country with the largest number of untrained judges.

To further assure that judges can be controlled by the party, parliament passed a law denying legal immunity to judges. The law is in violation of an international convention on judicial immunity which Ethiopia had signed. The new law makes it legally permissible to remove judges from their posts and to prosecute those who hand down rulings adverse to the Front. This possibility leaves the judges liable to pressures from the executive branch and undermines the independence of the judiciary.[5]

In addition, the CPR elected three of its members, all representatives of the EPRDF, to the Federal Judicial Administrative Council (FJAC). They joined six judges, also Front members, on the powerful nine person FJAC. The Council is responsible for nominating judges for appointment; for transferring, firing, or suspending judges; for determining their salaries; and for issuing disciplinary and ethical regulations. With such powers entrusted to party regulars, the Front's leaders had little fear that the nation's courts might restrain their activities.[6] Constitutionalism was not to be a cherished value of the FDRE.

DERG TRIALS

The Special Prosecutor's Office (SPO) was established, to international acclaim, in 1992 to create a historical record of the war crimes, genocide, and crimes against humanity committed by officials of the Derg and to bring to justice those criminally responsible for human rights violations. Although the trial of the first group of defendants charged with such crimes during the former regime began in 1994, there was little done in the showcase trials until early 1997. Finally, the SPO concluded its lengthy investigatory process and brought charges of criminal offenses against 5,198 people, of whom 2,246 were already in detention, while 2,952, including the former dictator Mengistu Haile Mariam, were charged in absentia. All defendants who are in custody were scheduled to appear in court in 1998. Many of the defendants were in pre-trial detention for almost six years before they were indicted. In September 1998, thirty-one members of the WPE and military officers were released after having been detained for seven years. The slow pace of the work of the SPO was sharply criticized by senior government officials.[7] Nevertheless, the FDRE boasts that the "Derg trials" are the largest effort by an African country to try its own former oppressive government for its crimes.[8] Critics of the highly publicized "Red Terror on trial," however, see the government's action as a smoke screen to hide its own repressive acts against political prisoners.

THE BUREAUCRACY

A modern authoritarian regime depends on bureaucratic organization to make its control effective. To maintain centralized bureaucracies in the federal system, the EPRDF has used downsizing as an aspect of structural adjustment as an excuse to fire unwanted government officials. The Front also has used *gimgema* (evaluation) and "Peace, Democracy, and Development Conferences" to remove bureaucrats who are not toeing the party line.

Government organizations are required to hold *gimgema* in which they point out each other's weaknesses as well as those of their supervisors. At such meetings, staff evaluations by management are reviewed by the subordinate staff. Appraisals from these meetings serve as the basis for promotions or demotions, increases or decreases in salary, and even dismissals—actions traditionally carried out under law by the Civil Service Commission. Thus, the *gimgemas* effectively have replaced the rules of the Commission and provided EPRDF cadres with a means to penalize those they suspect of being enemies and to reward friends of the Front. Although the party's stress on criticism and self-criticism conjures up libertarian visions of free discussion and the interplay of competing ideas, the *gimgema* in reality is a verbal masquerade used to enforce the Front's authoritarian dictates. In addition to bureaucrats, judicial personnel also have been removed in this way.[9]

A Peace, Democracy, and Development Conference is an assemblage of Front cadres and hand-picked apolitical residents who approve resolutions prepared by EPRDF leaders and place blame on government officials who have failed to conform to party expectations. Such conferences usually are followed by the removal or dismissal of local officials who are replaced by party loyalists. The Front has used this tactic to purge bureaucrats deemed to be "narrow nationalists or agents of foreign powers" in the Oromo, Somali, Afar, and Benishangul-Gumuz Regions and in Dire Dawa.[10]

SECURITY FORCES, POLICE, AND THE ARMY

Terror is the linchpin of the authoritarian FDRE. Elaborately institutionalized by the Front, the system of terror spreads a net over the whole range of society. The state apparatus, especially the security network, the police, the military, the judiciary system, and the administrative structure down to the village level, are used to infuse the populace with fear. Those perceived by the Front to be "enemies" are subjected to nocturnal, unexplained, and thus deliberately terrifying searches, detentions, and arrests. A blanket of secrecy is imposed on these operations, but some of the affronts to human dignity are documented by human rights organizations in a powerful indictment of the FDRE: calculated violence and cold-blooded efficiency are accepted as implicit in the EPRDF's "struggle."

Throughout the country, the EPRDF has established a network of concentration camps,[11] underground prisons, and unmarked detention houses. In these and in the notorious prison system inherited from the Derg, the government has incarcerated, tortured, and sometimes killed prisoners of conscience, political prisoners, and others opposed to the regime.[12] In the chapters that follow, we will look at specific examples of official brutality against individuals and groups.

Responsibility for internal security shifted from the military forces to the police in most regions. The credibility of the new police force, supposedly established under civilian control and made accountable before the law, suffered serious setbacks, however, when the police were involved in some troubling political cases, particularly the May 1997 killing in broad daylight of Assefa Maru, an officer of the Ethiopian Teachers Association and an executive committee member of the Ethiopian Human Rights Council. Also troubling is the fact that police and other officials who interfere with the independence of the judiciary or refuse to obey court orders have not been held accountable before the law by the FDRE.[13]

The government reorganized the army in accordance with the EPRDF strategy document. The old army of the party with a preponderance of Tigrayan soldiers has been reconfigured with recruits from throughout the country. The new national, supposedly apolitical army, still is guided behind the scenes by the EPRDF. In Ethiopia the military has conducted "low level operations" against the OLF, the Somalia-based Al'ittihad, and the Ogaden National Liberation Front. The International Committee of the Red Cross reported that the army used military camps for the detention of OLF activists and supporters.[14] To its credit, the army of the FDRE, along with soldiers of other African nations, has taken part in peace keeping activities in various parts of Africa—reaffirming Ethiopia's commitment to collective security. To strengthen African multinational peacekeeping efforts, the Clinton administration has provided the FDRE with training, four aircraft, and $7.3 million for equipment to "enhance peacekeeping interoperability in a multination context."[15] According to U.S. Ambassador David Shinn, this was "not arming but providing military equipment" for an Africa Crisis Response Initiative. During the Ethio-Eritrean border conflict that began in 1998, the FDRE spent hundreds of millions of dollars on modern armaments.[16]

THE FEDERAL REGIONS

The federal regions, organized along ethnic lines, purportedly enjoyed increased autonomy, with greater local control over fiscal and political issues. In keeping with EPRDF strategy, ethnicity became the foci of regional government and party activity with basic services and social organization based on tribal affiliations. In truth, however, the Front imposed a monolithic pattern on the political life of the regions. In every regional government, a shadow party organization operated as a disciplined phalanx to carry out the will of the EPRDF leadership.

An example of this is evident in the security apparatus of each killil. In theory, security in the regions is in the hands of local militia who act in tandem with military detachments, but ostensibly under local political control. In reality, security committees, consisting of local officials, political cadres of the EPRDF or its affiliates, and army officers, control these "peasant militias." The committee system makes the militia an integral part of the national political structure and places them under the control of the central government through the ruling party apparatus. They provide the interface between local authorities, the militia, the army, and the ruling party, in practice subordinating local security structures to the central authorities.

The federal regions also provided the central government with a subterfuge for refusing to take action on matters petitioned for by citizens. Petitioners, such as farmers from the Amhara Region complaining about new land tenure policies, found themselves in a political no man's land with neither the central nor the regional government responding to their appeals.[17] When circumstances require it, the government can dodge difficult questions by localizing conflicts or take on the ones they want by nationalizing them.

Critics of "decentralizing" power to the killils believe that the federal policy has more to do with divide-and-rule tactics and the allocation of national resources, than justice for the regions. Some liken it to the former Soviet Communist party which retained tight control over its regions through local parties.[18] Apparent devolution, while real power is retained at the center and used repressively, has increased rather than lessened the disharmony of Ethiopia's ethnic groups.

TRANSPARENCY IN THE FDRE

In 1996 the Minister of Information and Culture proclaimed that "unlike past regimes, where the government cloaked its activities in secrecy, the right to know and freedom of the press is [sic] constitutionally recognized in the present day political climate of Ethiopia."[19] Recognition is one thing, uncloaking what the FDRE is doing is something else. Important decisions are made by party leaders behind closed doors. Not a single important political or organizational question is decided by government officials or mass organizations without guiding direction from the party. The Front stands above all, and the leaders do not test their policies in a forum of free speech and fair elections. Instead, they mobilize and enforce consent. At the same time, the elitist notion that only the party can adequately express the true interest of the nation is tempered by pseudo-democratic strains. The traces of faux democracy are widely displayed to present the public view of the nation that the party leaders deem appropriate or necessary to keep the Front in power.

The Front's show is like a five ring circus. The four outer rings provide performing space for the Front's main troupe of supporting and collaborating players: the TPLF in Tigray, the OPDO in Oromiya, the ANDM in Amhara, and the SEPDF in the Southern killil. The center ring features the balancing act of the EPRDF. The ringmaster has the discretion to put the spotlight on any of the rings—or to take it off. The Tigray actors, with their new costumes and expensive accouterments, have drawn most of the audience's attention. Some of the other rings have shabby props and their leads have not received good reviews. Clowns circulate around the periphery of the rings to distract the crowd when the acts falter or when the tight wire walkers in the center ring lose their balance.

Sometimes the spotlight is focused on poor performers to contrast their efforts with the feats of the stars. This occurs when the government publishes in state media detailed reports on officials who are arrested or dismissed for abuse of authority or corruption, such as the former Deputy Prime Minister and Minister of Defense, Tamrat Layne, and his coterie; or when EPRDF members of Parliament are removed from office and indicted for war crimes committed during the Derg regime. Then the ringmaster can brag that his circus is a legitimate show and that his acts are clean. The audience can see it. It's transparent. Using ringmaster logic, Prime Minister Meles believes that his government has been "extremely transparent."[20] But even his friends in the U.S. State Department concede that governmental transparency remains limited. Everyone knows that the Front's circus is planned and controlled in the ringmaster's wagon where only EPRDF artistes are admitted.

A review of the acts of the Front's spectacle will demonstrate the lack of transparency and accountability in government and the use of its instruments to suppress its enemies and sustain its victories.[21]

NOTES

1. "Meles Changes his Title and Retains His Power. TPLF Consolidates Political Grip Over Country," *Ethiopian Register* 2 (September 1995): 17–22.

2. Human Rights Watch. "Ethiopia: Human Rights Developments," New York, NY, 1999; Human Rights Watch, "Human Rights Curtailed in Ethiopia," New York, NY, 9 December 1997. On 16 November 1997, Ethiopia was singled out for having the highest number of dismissals of judges of any country by the Geneva-based Centre for the Independence of Judges and Lawyers.

3. "Graduates Without Experience Appointed Judges," *Ethiopian Register* 5 (April 1998): 13; Editorial, "Clinton and the Ethnic Tyrant," (March 1998): 2–4.

4. "Meles Declares Political Loyalty Key Factor in Appointment of Senior Government Officials," *Ethiopian Register* 4 (July 1997): 20–23.

5. "TPLF/EPRDF Council Appoints Supreme Court Presidents," *Ethiopian Register* 3 (April 1996): 6–7.

6. Ibid; see also, EHRCO, "Cessation of Administration of Justice in Ethiopia," Special Report No. 2/1996, 9 April 1996.

7. "Former Military Officers and WPE Officials Released," *Ethiopian Register* 5 (October 1998): 15; Human Rights Watch, "Human Rights Curtailed in Ethiopia," New York, NY, 9 December 1997; "Senior Derg Official on Trial Passes Away," *Ethiopian Register* 5 (April 1998): 11.

8. "Red Terror on Trial: Additional Benches Speed Up Proceedings," *News from Ethiopia*, Embassy of Ethiopia, Washington, DC, June 1997, 1, 4. Cf. "Derg Officials on Trial," *Ethiopian Register* 3 (July 1996): 17 -19; "Former Military Officers and WPE Officials Released," *Ethiopian Register* 5 (October 1998): 15.

9. "GIMGEMA Marginalizes Public Service Regulations," *Ethiopian Register* 3 (May 1996): 8–9.

10. "Yet More PDDCs & *Gimgemas*: TPLF Trapped in Its Own Ethnic Politics?" *Ethiopian Register* 4 (June 1997): 14–16.

11. Among the most infamous concentration camps are those at Hurso, Didessa, Agarfa, and Bilate.

12. Editorial, "The Persecution of the Oromos," *Ethiopian Register* 4 (October 1997): 3–4.

13. Human Rights Watch, "Human Rights Curtailed in Ethiopia," New York, NY, 9 December 1997.

14. "Ethiopia Country Report on Human Rights Practices for 1997," U.S. Department of State.

15. David F. Gordon, "Africa Today: Worst of Times, Best of Times," *Great Decisions 1998* (New York: Foreign Policy Association, 1998), 60.

16. Quoted in "Meles Declares Political Loyalty Key Factor in Appointment of Senior Government Officials," *Ethiopian Register* 4 (July 1997): 20–23; "From Two-Week War to Weak Peace," *Addis Tribune*, 5 March 1999.

17. "Farmers from Gojjam Flock to Addis Ababa to Lodge Protest," *Ethiopian Register* 4 (April 1997): 6–8; see generally, Stephen Buckley, "Ethiopia

Takes New Ethnic Tack: Deliberately Divisive," *Washington Post*, 18 June 1995, A21.

18. "Ethiopia, Federal Sham," *The Economist*, 16 August 1997, 36; see also, John Young, "Ethnicity and Power in Ethiopia," *Review of African Political Economy* 23 (December 1996): 531–42.

19. "Ministry Opens New Department," *News from Ethiopia*, Embassy of Ethiopia, Washington, DC, September 1996, 5.

20. "Meles Declares Political Loyalty Key Factor in Appointment of Senior Government Officials," *Ethiopian Register* 4 (July 1997): 20–23.

21. See, letter from Kahsay Berhe and Tesfay Atsbeha to the Special Prosecutor, 6 September 1997, published in *Ethiopian Register* 4 (December 1997): 41.

CHAPTER 13

Human Rights in the FDRE

With such countless disgraces, unbearable wounds and pain, under the
merciless gaze of the developed world . . .

—Shamin Azad
"The Most Beautiful Sweet Thing"

Heading the list of the EPRDF's political goals was "materializing the peoples' political and human rights completely." The agenda for this goal is laid
out in the new constitution, which explicitly incorporates among its speci-
fied "fundamental principles," human and democratic rights. Article 10 of
the constitution proclaims:

1. Human rights and freedoms are inviolable and inalienable. They are inherent in
   the dignity of human beings.
2. Human and democratic rights of Ethiopian citizens shall be respected.

Chapter Three of the constitution enumerates some fifteen human rights
that the government cannot infringe, and Article 13 explains that the fundamental rights and liberties included "shall be interpreted in conformity with
the Universal Declaration of Human Rights" and other international human
rights treaties which Ethiopia has accepted or ratified. The Universal Declaration sets forth economic, social, and cultural rights as well as civil and political rights.

Unfortunately, many Ethiopians have learned that listing human rights does not guarantee their protection. The FDRE, with its monopoly of power, has acted ruthlessly against critics of the regime and suppressed the human rights of citizens. The government's army, police, and security forces have had a free hand in crushing any citizens who attempt "to obstruct the exercise of the rights of the masses" (i.e., disagree with the EPRDF or the government). Without an independent judiciary to protect the due process rights of the accused, human rights abuses of individuals or members of organizations expressing opposition to the government are pervasive. Highly respected international human rights organizations such as Amnesty International, Human Rights Watch, and the Ethiopian Human Rights Council, among others, report extrajudicial arrests, torture, disappearances, and murder carried on by the government of Ethiopia. Included in the litany of human rights abuses by the regime are the incarceration of prisoners of conscience, journalists, and leaders and members of opposition political parties and the suppression of peasants, businessmen, religious groups, academics, and members of professional and trade associations.[1] Indeed, the Woyane human rights record contains something to displease about everybody.

In the face of such documented accusations, Prime Minister Meles proclaimed to a 1997 Congress of the TPLF that human rights were now respected in Ethiopia and that peace was firmly established throughout the nation.[2] Meles' position was supported by the U.S. State Department's 1997 "Ethiopia Country Report on Human Rights Practices in Ethiopia."[3] Since the EPRDF came to power in 1991, the annual State Department country report has put the Ethiopian government in the best possible light, conveying the impression that the FDRE is committed to improving human rights and the democratization process. But according to the New York-based Lawyers Committee on Human Rights, the State Department's reports are biased and misleading and create very different impressions of the regime in question, depending on the strength of United States economic and strategic ties.[4] The country report for Ethiopia, with its selective reporting and carefully crafted phrases, has been sharply criticized as being of dubious authenticity in describing the human rights situation.[5] To test the veracity of the assertions of Prime Minister Meles and his American patrons, let us examine some of the actions by the party-in-government against those not actively supporting the programs of the EPRDF.

ARBITRARY ARREST AND TORTURE

The Constitution and the Criminal and Civil Codes prohibit arbitrary arrest and detention, the use of torture, and the mistreatment of prisoners.

Nevertheless, the government has arrested thousands of critics and opponents and has treated many of them in cruel ways. Throughout the nation, but especially in outlying regions, security forces often detain persons without a warrant and frequently do not charge them within forty-eight hours as required by law. The International Movement for Fraternal Union among Races and Peoples has recorded the names of almost 10,000 persons who remain in detention without a day in court.[6] The government blames such lapses on the nation's shortage of judges and prosecutors. Political opposition groups maintain that many of the people detained are held for political reasons. In 1998 the International Committee of the Red Cross estimated that 10,980 Ethiopians were in prison for political or national security reasons.[7] The government denies that it holds persons for political reasons, however.

In remote regions, such as the Somali and Oromo killils, government forces sometimes confront armed dissident groups pressing for self determination on ethnic grounds. Village shakedowns by security personnel followed armed encounters or were used to preempt such engagements. As a result hundreds of civilians have been held under the authority of regional governments that suspected them of supporting armed opposition groups. This particular category of detainees faces the greatest risk of political killings, torture, and harsh and inhumane treatment, mainly at the hands of rural militiamen and other security forces that enforce law and order in remote rural areas. The absence of effective judicial oversight has meant that most of those suffering abuse have had no recourse to legal remedy. Furthermore, their plight frequently goes unreported because the work of most rights monitoring groups is restricted, by the FDRE, to Addis Ababa.[8] A sufficient number of cases have come to light, however, to form what Amnesty International describes as "a pattern of widespread detention, torture, disappearances, and extrajudicial executions of suspected OLF supporters."[9] Similar patterns are documented for members of other opposition political groups throughout the nation.

EXTRAJUDICIAL KILLINGS AND DISAPPEARANCES

Despite government claims to the contrary, the Oromia Support Group has recorded 2,424 extrajudicial killings and 676 disappearances since 1992.[10] The Working Group on Enforced or Involuntary Disappearances of the United Nations Commission on Human Rights lists over one hundred cases of disappearances in Ethiopia during a corresponding period.[11] The U.S. State Department's 1997 Human Rights Report asserts, however, that "there were no confirmed reports, but numerous unsubstantiated reports, of alleged disappearances" in Ethiopia. The same report also states that security forces arrested and held people "incommunicado for several days or weeks."[12] This apparent fallacy may result from the Ethiopian government's requirement "that two years must have elapsed before a court may, upon the provision of sufficient evidence, officially declare a person absent." Apparently many Ethiopians disappear in forced physical absence for periods of less than two years. Their human rights are violated regardless of what amount of time is calculated in constituting an official disappearance, however.

Two incidents of extrajudicial killings by government security forces drew international attention in 1997. Wako Tola, a teacher at the Sandford English Community School in Addis Ababa, was arrested without warrant and detained without indictment for over six weeks at the Central Investigation Office. Visitors found him in good health on 31 March, but the next day Wako died, supposedly of natural causes while in police custody. His body showed signs of bleeding from the nose and mouth. Investigators found no satisfactory explanation for his death. Although he was not indicted, Wako probably was detained on suspicion of being a member of the OLF.[13]

Even more brazen was the murder of Assefa Maru, an executive board member of both the Ethiopian Teachers Association and the Ethiopian Human Rights Council. Eyewitnesses to the event report that while Assefa was walking to his office in Addis Ababa, he was stopped by Federal Policemen and while being interrogated was shot dead by another policeman driving by in a police vehicle. In reporting the incident, government media claimed that the police had shot the leader of a notorious terrorist group at his home while he was trying to escape arrest.[14] Although the government declined to make public the results of an internal investigation into Assefa's death, many Ethiopians could tell the lion by the mark of his claw.

The number of "*ley de fuga*" murders committed by the government is unknown, but anecdotal evidence suggests that an Ethiopian version of the right of police to kill a prisoner trying to escape often is used as a pretext for killing a prisoner purposely set free.

FREEDOM OF EXPRESSION

Article 19 of the Universal Declaration of Human Rights, subscribed to by Ethiopia, declares that "everyone has the right to freedom of opinion and expression; this right includes freedom to hold opinions without interference and to seek, receive, and impart information and ideas through any media and regardless of frontiers." Freedom of expression therefore means that government officials cannot restrict the public debate about public affairs.

In a democracy, free expression is both the foundation and the symbol for the policy-making process. Decision-makers need true and timely information—and the final decision-makers are not prime ministers or prosecutors but the people of the democracy. In such a system, the government cannot control the thoughts, ideas, and facts that enter into the public debate. Furthermore, the public needs an independent press as a necessary restraint on the natural tendency of government to be tyrannical and despotic. In such an arrangement, the press is supposed to serve the governed, not the governors.

The FDRE takes a contrary view. Government-controlled media are used as propaganda tools to promote the Front's programs and to disparage any opposition. Apparently terrified of ideas, rather than challenged and stimulated by them, the EPRDF seeks to keep unapproved and politically incorrect information from the people. One way to do this is by keeping the private press in line and by limiting people's access to foreign journals such as the *Ethiopian Register* and the *Ethiopian Review* that criticize the FDRE and EPRDF.

The FDRE has continued the practice of the TGE of harassing the private press by routine use of detention and imprisonment and the imposition of prohibitive fines and bail amounts on journalists and editors.[15] It has detained more journalists in the past four years than any other African government. Amnesty International reports that over 200 journalists of the Ethiopian private press have been detained under the 1992 Press Law.[16] Some journalists were imprisoned for as long as three years; one was killed; two disappeared, and twenty-six were exiled, among whom are the chairman, vice chairman, and general secretary of the Ethiopian Free Press Journalists Association.[17] In October 1998 a joint explorative mission of the International Press Institute and the International Federation of Journalists found that sixteen journalists were in prison and thirty-one had pending criminal cases. Most were detained for writing or publishing articles which police claimed were defamatory or "incitement of conflict between people." In fact the journalists were imprisoned because the articles were critical of the government.

Such harassment by the government has doubtlessly been an important factor in the declining number of newspapers published since the EPRDF came to power. By 1998 only twenty weekly newspapers still appeared regularly,[18] and distribution of private newspapers outside of Addis Ababa was prohibited. The government was selective in its disabling of the media. Most newspapers and magazines that dealt with substantive issues were forced out of business. Those allowed to continue as evidence of a "free press," for the most part, are those concerned with trivial or superficial issues.

The government carries on a campaign of harsh criticism against the remainders of the independent press. FDRE officials and the government media castigate most of the private publications as being unprofessional and printing inaccurate and untrue articles. None of the magazines or newspapers condemned of irresponsible reporting is in English. They are all in Amharic or Oromigna—making it difficult for foreign observers to judge them. Reputable Ethiopian critics, however, question how such publications as *Tobia*, *Ruh*, *Muday*, *Tseday*, *Alef*, and *Africa Qend* can be characterized as irresponsible in light of the depth of analysis and level of abstraction of their articles.[19]

The most ruthless action against press freedoms was the arbitrary arrest of the general manager and three editors of the highly respected weekly newspaper, *Tobia*, by government agents and the torching of its offices. A suspicious fire gutted part of the editorial offices of the publishing company where the paper is published. The nearby fire brigade incredulously arrived forty-five minutes after the first call for help was received. Publication of *Tobia* was halted for three months while editors in Ethiopia and abroad appealed for donations to help the newspaper get the equipment needed to resume services.[20]

The FDRE denies access by private journalists to government press conferences, despite the fact that the Press Law requires the government to be accessible to those seeking information. Government officials frequently ignore this provision and deny access to information even to government journalists. Thus, officials in the land with "thirteen months of sunshine," eclipse the "sunshine" legislation guaranteeing the availability of information about governmental activities to the press as well as to the general public. Such harassment and persecution of the free press has resulted in the condemnation of the FDRE by the International Federation of Journalists and by associations of journalists in the United States, Europe, and Africa.[21]

In May 1998 the New York-based Committee to Protect Journalists (CPJ) cited Prime Minister Meles as one of ten leaders of different countries which it labeled as enemies of the press. The CPJ found that Meles, "lauded by U.S. Policy makers as one of the new generations of African leaders for his ostensive contributions to the democratization of Africa, is in fact an autocrat who attempts to suppress all press criticisms of his regime." Thus, on World Press Freedom Day and the fiftieth anniversary of Article 19 of the Universal Declaration of Human Rights which enshrines freedom of speech and the press, the Prime Minister of Ethiopia was listed among the world's most notorious enemies of the press, along with General Sani

Abacha of Nigeria, Burma's Senior General Than Shwe, Cuba's Fidel Castro, Indonesia's President Suharto, and China's President Jiang Zemin.[22]

In an interview, Prime Minister Meles defended the policy of denying the private press access to government press conferences. He analogized the practice to that of limiting admittance to White House press conferences. In similar fashion, Meles said, "liars and name-callers" will not be given access in Ethiopia. "They can scribble as they like, but when they violate the law, we will take them to court and make them get their punishment." The Prime Minster maintains that journalists are arrested because they write stories that foment ethnic hatred or compromise national security. When asked why the private press was allowed to exist at all, Meles replied:

We did not want their existence, but we have two alternatives. One is to prevent them from writing. Even if we do so, they will still go on saying whatever they want about our present situation. The second option is to let them do what they want. This is a newly gotten freedom, but they have no audience for their reports, for the people do not pay attention to them.[23]

The Prime Minister's statements reveal the Front's distorted view of the press. In democratic countries a press free of government control is a vital part of the political system based on the will of the people. As part of its "watchdog" function, the press needs the freedom to report abuses of power by public officials. The people must be able to receive news critical of the government and exchange information and opinions about public affairs without interference by government officials. The press must prevent officials from covering with the veil of secrecy their common routine activities, for the liberties of the people never will be secure when the transactions of their rulers can be concealed from them.[24] The private press of Ethiopia that risks punishment under a Free Press Law when it publishes criticism of government can hardly be expected to inform the public effectively.[25]

ETHNIC JUSTICE

A corollary of the "rights of the masses" is a system of justice based not on universal principles but rather on ethnic or party considerations. The roots of this system probably have their origin in the TPLF, a liberation front based on ethnicity and ideology. During the dictatorship of Mengistu Haile Mariam, the TPLF was ensnarled in bitter combat with both the Derg and the Ethiopian People's Revolutionary Party (EPRP) that also was opposed to Mengistu's dictatorship. Surrounded by enemies while fighting on their home turf in Tigray Province, the TPLF developed a paranoid distrust of anyone who was neither a Tigriña speaker nor a true believer in the party's cause. Under such circumstances, issues of justice were based on ethnic or family considerations.[26] Abstract theories of what is just or unjust did not apply. What was important was the ethnicity of the offender or victim. For the TPLF cadre, any act that could be construed as contrary to the interests of a Tigrayan was held to be *prima facie* unjust. Conversely, any criminal offense that a Tigrayan might commit against a non-Tigrayan was not an injustice so long as the perpetrator was a member of the TPLF or a Tigriña speaker.[27]

When the TPLF expanded into the EPRDF, this perverted sense of justice was transferred to a larger front and eventually to the ruling party. Under the FDRE's ethnic federalism, such EPRDF front parties as the Oromo People's Democratic Organization (OPDO) or Ethiopian Somali Democratic League (ESDL) may practice ethnic or clan justice in their respective bailiwicks in administrative regions. In a larger sense, however, justice now depends upon loyalty to the government or to the ruling EPRDF in whatever guise. An act perpetrated on a member or sympathizer of the EPRDF by an "outsider" or non-EPRDF supporter is automatically unjust and punishable. On the other hand, the party-affiliated can determine who are "the ruling classes" or "oppressors" and hammer away at them with impunity. EPRDF leaders in the provinces are especially notorious for extralegal "justice" against whomever they consider enemies. Under such circumstances, the protection of human rights by the FDRE is a fiction.[28]

THE ROLE OF THE INTERNATIONAL COMMUNITY

Officials of the FDRE frequently make statements that equate the expression of concern for human rights by representatives of the international community with interference in the internal affairs of the country. Such was the case in April 1998, when at the conclusion of a closed meeting of East African leaders, Prime Minister Meles directly told President Clinton that he should not try to tell him how to rule.[29]

The donor nations generally have acquiesced in the FDRE's abuses of human rights in exchange for Ethiopia's help in promoting economic progress, stability in the Horn, and diplomatic and military containment of perceived threats from terrorists and Islamic fundamentalists in neighboring Sudan. According to Human Rights Watch, this has led to firm commitments of aid, and less resolve as to the conditioning of that aid on human rights improvements.[30] In doing so, the donors legitimate the persecutors.

Although the European Parliament has passed resolutions criticizing the government for human rights abuses, Ethiopia receives more aid from the

European Union (EU) than any other country in the world.[31] After South Africa, Ethiopia is the second largest recipient of U.S. aid in sub-Saharan Africa, and according to Susan Rice, U.S. Assistant Secretary of State for Africa, the FDRE is to be applauded for its progress in human rights and democratization.[32] In light of its human rights record, however, the Ethiopian government enjoys disproportionate moral and financial support from the EU and the United States. There is little pressure on the Woyane to go beyond mere formalities of a democratic system.

UNKEPT PROMISES

Despite the government's adoption of international norms of human rights, the FDRE, by committing abuses and atrocities, still claims a "right to be monstrous" to its own citizens. Some apologists for the regime try to justify it with theories that rights should be sacrificed in favor of order, economic development, or repression. Human rights are not universal, some argue, but represent Western values being projected into their non-Western society. The Secretary General of the United Nations, Kofi Annan, a Ghanaian, refutes arguments against universality, noting that it is not people who reject universality of human rights but some government leaders.[33] Annan's sentiments are echoed by Vaclav Havel who contends that:

Human rights are universal and indivisible. Human freedom is not separate from these: if it's denied to anyone anywhere, it is therefore denied, indirectly, to all. This is why we can't remain silent in the countenance of evil or violence; silence merely encourages evil and violence.[34]

The record of *les esprits méchant* of the EPRDF/FDRE has made a mockery of the constitutional mandate of respect for inviolable and inalienable human rights and freedoms. The lack of freedom of action in the judiciary, the legislative bodies, and the press leaves power over civil liberties concentrated in the hands of the ruling party. "The degree to which the security forces behave in the defense of liberty, the degree of arbitrariness in the use of power by the ruling group and the relationship of the various organs from the center to the localities"—all contribute to the sullied record of the FDRE in this area.[35] With the government's concept of justice based on ethnic or party considerations, only certain Ethiopians enjoy protection of human rights. The rest of the people are beyond the pale of such safeguards. The violation of basic decency—of the rules that make human life possible and tolerable—is an undeniable affront to all Ethiopians.[36] By fomenting ethnic violence and perpetuating a political culture based on persecution of opponents, the government has abandoned its responsibility to protect its people.

When the EPRDF's "moderate" methods to coerce uniformity of sentiment fail, the government must resort to an ever-increasing severity. Strife within the country becomes more bitter as the FDRE's pressure toward conformity becomes greater. As a result, the government foments the cruelty and pain and hatred raging beneath the everyday surface of things. Palliations usually include comparisons of the more subtle oppression of the present regime to the threat and use of brute force under the Derg. Nevertheless, reports of international human rights organizations and even the U.S. Department of State's Bureau of Human Rights unequivocally attest to the FDRE's role in violent, uncivilized treatment of critics.[37] Viewed through the prism of moral choices, it seems inexplicable to commend one evil tyranny over another.

The few human rights violations conceded by the Ethiopian government are blamed on local officials and the lack of a democratic culture and history of respect for human rights. According to the country report of the U.S. Department of State, the federal government cannot protect constitutional rights at the regional level where local authorities were unwilling or unable to do so.[38] Nevertheless, there is clear evidence that the central government has been involved in human rights abuses. Central planning was obvious in the shooting of three unarmed Oromo in Addis Ababa in October 1997 and the subsequent imprisonment of sixty-five others, including elders, businessmen, journalists, and human rights activists who were labelled as terrorists. The government claimed these killings and arrests were carried out because the offenders belonged to an OLF cell that was responsible for bombings in Addis Ababa and Dire Dawa earlier in the year or were members of OLF "support groups."[39]

The 1997 bombings have become the FDRE's weapon of choice in persecuting political opponents. The government earlier had claimed that the bombings were the work of Al'ittihad, a Somali-based opposition group that had actually claimed responsibility for the explosions. Subsequently, in the trial of Dr. Taye Wolde Semayat, president of the Ethiopian Teachers Association, the government claimed that he was leading an Amhara terrorist cell of the "Ethiopian National Patriots Front" that was responsible for the bombings.

The Oromia Support Group in Great Britain has received first hand reports directly from victims, their close relatives and eye-witnesses that reveal a clear pattern of human rights abuses throughout Ethiopia. Some of these accounts show how suspected supporters of opposition political groups are pursued and tracked down over many miles before being detained, disappeared, or killed. The role of "local officials" in these violations and in the street killings in Addis Ababa appears to be minimal.[40] Similar incidences consistent with a centrally planned policy are reported in cases of Ethiopians seeking political asylum in the United States[41]

Lessons from history tell of the ultimate futility of such attempts to compel coherence. From the Roman drive to stamp out Christianity as a challenge to its pagan unity down to the terror of the Derg as a means to Ethiopian unity, dictatorial rulers have failed in their efforts to prescribe what will be orthodox in politics, nationalism, or other matters of opinion. The EPRDF should heed the warning of a sage American jurist: "Those who begin coercive elimination of dissent soon find themselves exterminating dissenters. Compulsory unification of opinion achieves only the unanimity of the graveyard."[42]

Until democratic principles, norms, values, and procedures are constantly applied in Ethiopia, human rights will not be protected. The record of the FDRE demonstrates that these standards are not being met and that human rights suffer accordingly.

NOTES

1. See, e.g., Getachew Haile, "Violation of Human Rights of Ethiopians by the Tigray People's Liberation Front," *Unraveling Human Rights Abuses in Ethiopia: Ways and Means of Alleviating the Problem*, Proceedings of a Human Rights Week Observance and Electronic Mail Conference, 3–8 March 1997 (Medford, MA: ISCEPC, 1997), 38–43.

2. "TPLF/EPRDF Congresses Wound Up Without Addressing Crucial Political Issues," *Ethiopian Register* 5 (February 1998): 13–14.

3. Bureau of Democracy, Human Rights, and Labor, "Ethiopia Country Report on Human Rights Practices for 1997," U.S. Department of State, Washington, DC, 30 January 1998.

4. "Critique: Review of the U.S. Department of State's Country Reports on Human Rights Practices," Lawyers Committee for Human Rights, New York, 1995, 1996, and 1997.

5. See, e.g., "Oromia Support Group, Human Rights Abuses in Ethiopia, Press Release, January/February 1998," No. 21, 17–20.

6. "U.F.E.R.'s Report to the UN," *Ethiopian Register* 4 (June 1997): 18, 20.

7. International Committee of the Red Cross, *Annual Report*, 1 June 1998.

8. Human Rights Watch, "Human Rights Curtailed in Ethiopia," New York, NY, 9 December 1997.

9. Urgent Action, 18/98, Amnesty International, London, 21 January 1998.

10. See the running tally of "Human Rights Abuses by the Ethiopian Government Since 1992" updated bimonthly by the Oromia Support Group and published in its newsletter, *Sagalee Haaraa*.

11. U.N. Economic and Social Council, Commission on Human Rights, Report of the Working Group on Enforced or Involuntary Disappearances, Ed/CN.4/1998/43, 12 January 1998.

12. Bureau of Democracy, Human Rights, and Labor, "Ethiopia Country Report on Human Rights Practices for 1997," U.S. Department of State, Washington, DC, 30 January 1998.

13. Oromia Support Group, "Urgent Action, May 8th 1997, Death in Custody of Wako Tola."

14. Oromia Support Group, "Urgent Action, June 1997, The Shooting of Assefa Maru." By its actions, the EPRDF has qualified for inclusion in the next edition of *Le Livre Noir du Communisme* (*The Black Book of Communism*). First published in France in 1997, the Black Book is an encyclopedia of Communist atrocities around the world, from 1917 to the present, all scrupulously recorded and presented, with a tally of a hundred million deaths. Future editions may well include the thousands of extrajudicial murders committed by the EPRDF, influenced as the Front is by its authoritarian communist roots.

15. See, e.g., "More Journalists Jailed, but Fewer Are Killed," *New York Times*, 15 March 1996; Azeb Ze Mariam, "The 'Invaded Spaces' of the Ethiopian Mind: The Press Law," *Ethiopian Register* 3 (May 1996): 22–27; Danna Varsnick, "Freedom of the Press in Ethiopia: The Plight of Independent Journalists," *Ethiopian Register* 4 (January 1997): 26–29; Human Rights Watch, "Human Rights Curtailed in Ethiopia," New York, NY, 9 December 1997.

16. Amnesty International Report 1997: Ethiopia, Amnesty International, London.

17. Editorial, "Clinton and the Ethnic Tyrant," *Ethiopian Register* 5 (March 1998): 2–4; International Press Institute (Vienna) and International Federation of Journalists (Brussles), "Review of Situation of Detained Journalists," Toronto, 21 October 1998.

18. "Ethiopia Country Report on Human Rights Practices for 1997," U.S. Department of State.

19. Shumet Sishagne, "The Travesty in Ethiopia," *Ethiopian Register* 4 (September 1997): 25–26.

20. "Police Detain *Tobia*'s Editors while Suspicious Fire Guts Office," *Ethiopian Register* 5 (February 1998): 6–7; "*Tobya*'s Publication Resumes," (June 1998): 16–17; "*Tobia*'s Editors Released after 6–7 Months Detention without Charges," (September 1998): 12–13.

21. See, e.g., International Federation of Journalists and International Press Institute, "Review of Situation of Detained Journalists," Toronto, 21 October 1998.

22. Committee to Protect Journalists, "Attacks on the Press in 1997: Ethiopia," New York, 1998; "Prime Minister Meles Cited As Enemy of The Press," *Addis Tribune*, Week of 08/05/98; see also, Editorial, "World Press Freedom Day and Ethiopian Journalists," *Addis Tribune*, Week of 08/05/98.

23. "Meles Declares Political Loyalty Key Factor in Appointment of Senior Government Officials," *Ethiopian Register* 4 (July 1997): 20–23.

24. The sentiment is that of the American revolutionary democrat Patrick Henry.

25. Bill F. Chamberlin, "Speech and Press," in *The Oxford Companion to the Supreme Court* ed. Kermit Hall, (New York: Oxford University Press, 1992), 808–816.

26. "Customary law" is defined in ethnic terms, but in "civil law, the community is a nation." Mahmood Mamdani, *Citizen and Subject: Contemporary Africa and the Legacy of Late Colonialism* (Princeton, NJ: Princeton University Press, 1996), 109–137. For the history of the EPRP and its battles with the TPLF, see Kiflu Tadesse, *The Generation Part II, Ethiopia Transformation and Conflict* (Lanham, MD: University Press of America, 1998).

27. Assefa Negash, *The Pillage of Ethiopia by Eritreans and their Tigrean Surrogates* (Los Angeles: Adey Publishing, 1996), 86–92.

28. See, e.g., "A Dangerous Semblance of Justice," *Ethiopian Register* 5 (September 1998): 15. The existing system of ethnic justice made one Addis Ababan shemagele long for the earlier *leba shay* method of detecting criminals. In the early twentieth century, *leba shay* was a whimsical traditional mode for finding criminals. A young boy was drugged and set loose in the neighborhood. The house closest to where the youngster finally collapsed would be declared the abode of the guilty. "Under *leba shay*, there was at least an element of chance that you would not be punished," said the shemagele. "With the Woyane, it's a sure thing." Interview with anonymous shemagele, Addis Ababa, 5 July 1992. For a description of *leba shay*, see, Bahru Zewde, *A History of Modern Ethiopia 1855–1974* (Athens: Ohio University Press, 1991), 121, 123.

29. *The Economist*, 4 April 1998.

30. Human Rights Watch, "Human Rights Curtailed in Ethiopia," New York, NY, 9 December 1997.

31. Minutes of European Parliament, Resolution on Human Rights in Ethiopia, 16(f) B4–0785/97, 18 September 1997; "British Development Assistance in Partnership with Ethiopia, Summary Fact Sheet: 1997, Department for International Development, London, May 1997.

32. Susan Rice, Presentation to African Studies Association, Cleveland, Ohio, 15 November 1997.

33. Felice D. Gaer, "Human Rights: What Role in U.S. Foreign Policy?" *Great Decisions* (New York: Foreign Policy Association, 1998), 31–40; see also, Mary Robinson, "Toward *Never* Again," *Yale Law Report* 42 (Fall 1995): 2–6.

34. Vaclav Havel, "True Democracy Demands Moral Conviction," in *On Prejudice: A Global Perspective* ed. Daniela Gioseff, (New York: Doubleday, 1993), 606–608.

35. Mammo Muchie, "The Surgical Operation of Ethiopia without Anesthetics: Andreas Eshete's Defense of Ethnic Federalism," *Ethiopian Register* 5 (April 1998): 18–22.

36. See William A. Galston, *Liberal Purposes* (New York: Cambridge University Press, 1991), 38–39.

37. See, e.g., Human Rights Watch, "Ethiopia: Human Rights Developments," New York, NY, 1999; Human Rights Watch, "Human Rights Curtailed in Ethiopia," New York, NY, 9 December 1997; Amnesty International Report 1997: Ethiopia; Freedom House, "Freedom in the World," New York, NY, 1997; Reuters, "Subject: World Jurists Say Ethiopia Suppressing Dissent," Geneva, 1 May 1995; "Ethiopia Country Report on Human Rights Practices for 1997," U.S. Department of State.

38. Bureau of Democracy, Human Rights, and Labor, "Ethiopia Country Report on Human Rights Practices for 1998," U.S. Department of State, Washington, DC, 26 February 1999.

39. Trevor Trueman, "Human Rights Violations in Ethiopia," Virtual Seminar on Indigenous and Minorities' Rights, University of St. Andrews, Scotland, 1–20 June 1998, 1, 8.

40. Ibid.

41. From the author's experience as an expert witness in political asylum cases in 1995–1999.

42. Justice Robert Jackson's opinion of the U.S. Supreme Court in *West Virginia State Board of Education v. Barnette*, 319 US 624 (1943). Jackson also said, "The most odious of all oppressions are those which mask as justice."

CHAPTER 14

Freedom of Association in the FDRE

While individuals suffer in most cases of human rights abuse in Ethiopia, the real target of outrage is the group. Freedom of association, one of the bedrocks of human rights, has been abrogated by the EPRDF as part of its monopoly of power. Central to that party's suppression of political opposition has been control of the country's socioeconomic substructure of social organizations. A significant number of human rights cases in Ethiopia have dealt with the rights of individuals acting as members of organized religious, political, and economic associations, acting in their behalf or in their name, and utilizing organizational resources and power.

A THEORY OF FREEDOM OF ASSOCIATION

One of the dominant facts of twentieth century living, regardless of the stage of a society's economic development, is a preponderance of voluntary associations.[1] In such an organization-dominated society there are only a few times when the individual, speaking for himself, and acting for himself, is able to wrench his destiny into his own hands. More often, it is the organization which controls the destiny of the individual, acting as a member of the organization, by furnishing him the stability and security deemed so desirable today.[2] The growth of the importance of large organizations is a reflection of the increased complexity of modern society, in which organized groups of business, labor, and agricultural interests have emerged as significant political forces while the scope of governmental power has steadily increased.[3] Under such circumstances, a right to freedom of association emerges as one of the most important in a democratic society.

Early in the twentieth century, a distinguished group of English scholars, led by Frederic W. Maitland, Neville Figgis, and Harold J. Laski, presented a powerful argument against the tendency, which they saw as growing and dangerous, of the modern state to deny to the other associations a proper share in guiding and expressing the social life of men and women. In its more extreme form this school of pluralism, which received its name from the assertion that the state must surrender its claims to people's exclusive primary allegiance, has not been accepted. Yet, its significance has grown with the rise of its diametrical opposite—totalitarianism.

Essential to totalitarian thought is that men and women have no right to associate for purposes that do not fit the plans of the state; that it is the right and the duty of the state to make all associations mere agents for carrying out state purposes and to destroy those which it cannot control. By contrast, in a democracy organizations of civil society strengthen the political role of the people beyond the ballot box and provide a voice for the disparate interests unrepresented by political parties.

The Charter of Rights of the United Nations, the Constitution of the FDRE, and the constitutions of several nations speak specifically of freedom of association.[4] The modern concept of the right of association, like the right of property, is actually a group of rights. The right to assemble and petition and the right to communicate are essential to the broader rights of association. Rights to admit members, to discipline and even to expel them, to choose officers and to specify their powers, and to acquire, hold, and expend funds—in short, to provide for the internal government of the group—are rights that also are important to effective association.[5]

The concept of the rights of association is concerned with the rights which each of the diverse types of associations may claim and the regulations which justly may be imposed upon them. Diverse problems arising from the activities of a multitude of associations so different in their forms and purposes constitute the unified conception of a law of association.

The relationship between the state and voluntary associations in a particular nation-state defines freedom of association for that nation. In Ethiopia, the *de jure* basis of this relationship is spelled out in Article 31 of the Constitution: "Every person has the right to freedom of association for any cause or purpose. Associations which undertake acts that lawlessly subvert the rule of law and constitutional rule are prohibited."

Article 31 would appear to guarantee a broad concept of the right of association, actually encompassing a group of rights. Not only are rights of individuals to associate protected under this concept, but also the rights of groups are defended against arbitrary governmental regulation. A review of what Article 31 really means for associations will provide a standard by which to judge the status of freedom of association in Ethiopia.

MASS ORGANIZATIONS: LEVERS OF THE PARTY

The Albanian dictator, Enver Hoxha, regarded by many as the role model of TPLF/EPRDF leaders, viewed mass organizations as "levers of the (communist) party for its ties with the masses."[6] Associations in the Hoxha regime carried out political, executive, and organizational work in such a way as to enable party directives to be correctly understood and implemented by the population at large. Thus, the Albanian communists relied on mass organizations to achieve political socialization. Associations were controlled by party cadre who used public funds for their maintenance. The EPRDF has followed the Hoxha archetype in its actions against a host of voluntary associations.

OPPOSITION POLITICAL PARTIES

In a democracy, a political party is a team of men and women seeking to control the governing apparatus by gaining office in a duly constituted free and fair election. A party is supposed to serve as a linkage institution connecting voter preferences with actual government policies.[7] In the EPRDF scheme of governance, neither of these democratic ideas about parties is respected. The Front, after winning the initial elections, has created a situation that will ensure its hegemony and make it possible "to win without interruption."[8] The EPRDF uses the complete arsenal of state powers to make "revolutionary democracy" the governing ideology of society. The linkage goes the wrong way: it runs from government policies to the people, instead of vice versa. At the same time, the EPRDF works to discredit the views of "the enemy," opposition political parties.

As a result, any non-Front political parties demonstrating strength are effectively debilitated—especially outside of Addis Ababa, where 95 percent of the population lives. In the capital they are only allowed to have offices for the benefit of the international community.

Many opposition parties have been forced to shut regional offices. For example, in Northern Wollo, EPRDF officials forced AAPO members to denounce their party as a *neftegna* or "Amhara colonizer" organization. Those refusing to do so were threatened with imprisonment and the loss of their agricultural land. Following the kidnapping and three month detention of the head of the woreda AAPO branch by Front cadres, the other local AAPO Committee members, in fear of being arrested, fled the woreda, putting an end to local party operations. In Dire Dawa, shortly after the FDRE was established, a local AAPO official, who had repeatedly reported to his party that Front cadres had warned him to stop his work for the AAPO, was beaten and assassinated by government officials—prelude to the shutting down of the local AAPO office.[9]

Likewise, regional offices of the OLF have been forced out of business. Thousands of reports received by the Oromia Support Group unequivocally show that suspicion of membership in the OLF or even being closely related to such a suspect is enough to result in detention or worse punishment.[10]

Far too many Ethiopians have learned that open, peaceful opposition to the Woyane regime is a risky undertaking. It is an act of *lese majestie* to question the wisdom of entrusting the fate of the nation to the EPRDF. Members of legal political parties and organizations, time and again, have found themselves threatened and beaten or incarcerated for taking part in politics and expressing their beliefs.[11]

When the promises of democracy and protection of human rights by the FDRE turned out to be spurious, members of opposition parties had to take their political beliefs and activities underground or face possible persecution by the government. With political action in the open proscribed, secret operations of legal organizations also were penalized.

A typical case is that of a married couple who were active members of the AAPO in a provincial town and participated in open and secret meetings, contributed money to the organization, attempted to recruit new members, and wrote and distributed papers and pamphlets to raise public awareness of human rights abuses, the lack of democratic processes, and the suffering endured by Amharas and others under the ethnic policies of the EPRDF.[12] For this "crime," they were arrested at their home by soldiers and taken to the jail of the local peace and stability committee office. There, the husband was tortured and the wife was raped by government officials. The next day they were released after being warned by EPRDF soldiers to end their AAPO activities. The husband continued his work for the AAPO and later was imprisoned for a year for daring to take part in what are supposed to be democratic processes. When he was released and barely escaped an assassination attempt against him, he and his wife decided it was time to leave Ethiopia if they could.

Another case involved a woman accused of being "anti- government" because of her activities in behalf of the AAPO in the provinces. She was apprehended in the middle of the night by uniformed security officers who broke into her room, arrested her, and searched her possessions without a warrant, handcuffed her, beat her, and literally threw her into a filthy jail cell where she was imprisoned for nine months. During her incarceration, she was interrogated and threatened with torture and long-term imprisonment unless she cooperated with government officials by identifying people affiliated with the AAPO or the organization's financial contributors. When she refused to become an *agent provocateur* for the government, she was brutally raped on three different occasions by government security officers. After bond was posted for her by a friend, the accused was released after being warned by EPRDF officials that if she did not cooperate with them by providing information they requested about the AAPO, she would again be imprisoned. Thereafter, she and her family were harried by government officials and supporters of the EPRDF. She was required to register every other day at the kebele office. Her house was searched several times, and during one such search, the AAPO member had a weapon pointed at her by a hostile security official. Fearing for her life, she eventually was able to leave the country.

Since March 1996, members of the AAPO have been especially targeted as victims of the government's persecution. At that time, in conjunction with a government effort to disarm the civilian population, forces of the FDRE arbitrarily arrested second and third tier supporters of the AAPO. The reason no first tier officers were arrested was because they were all previously arrested, in hiding, or in exile abroad. For AAPO members in Ethiopia, the current round of persecution by the Government is counted as the "seventh wave" since the EPRDF came to power in 1991. There were four waves of persecution before the arrest of Dr. Asrat and three subsequently.

Many opposition politicians have fled abroad, and others have been in prison for much of Meles' rule. Six central committee members and sixteen other top leaders of the AAPO are in detention.[13] Government accusations that the AAPO or the SEPDC are terrorist groups waging war against the state are made without producing much evidence that these parties use or advocate violence.[14]

Leaders of opposition parties say the government often denies them permits to hold rallies.[15] For instance, in January 1997, the AAPO complied with the necessary formalities to stage a "Release Asrat Candle Vigil" in Meskel Square. Leaders of the AAPO were instructed to collect the permit from the killil office on the following Monday. On that day, however, a government official informed the AAPO by telephone that the vigil could not be held. When pressed for reasons why permission was denied, officials offered a potpourri of excuses: the square was needed for another function; the vigil would create traffic congestion; the size of the group was too large for authorities to assign sufficient security personnel; the square lies in an important route of high level officials.[16] The planned for and publicized meeting had to be cancelled, and freedom of association was scuppered by government's careful misdirection.

Many hotels and *kebeles* have been unwilling to rent their halls to the AAPO for fear of retaliatory action by Amhara National Democratic Movement (ANDM) officials. At the AAPO's sixth anniversary celebration in Bahir Dar in 1998, ANDM cadre waged a propaganda campaign to keep people from attending the meetings of the AAPO "warmongers." Kebele residents, workers, and students were warned that there might be violence in the meeting. Policemen and armed soldiers kept watch on the hall while ANDM cadres tried to register residents who were entering. Nevertheless, the hall was packed and the meeting was conducted without any disruption.[17]

Exorbitant fees preclude the opposition from using government-owned media, and the nation's only private media outlet is a radio station owned by the ruling party. Opposition leaders also complain that their phones are tapped.[18]

When the Southern Ethiopia People's Democratic Coalition (SEPDC) tried to take part in Woreda Council elections in the Southern Ethiopia killil in December 1997, the EPRDF put up obstacles to prevent its candidates from registering for the elections. The Front deliberately misinformed SEPDC candidates about registration deadlines and bogus requirements concerning proof of residency in the kebeles and letters of support from EPRDF officials in zonal and woreda administrations. Honest kebele officials who registered and issued identity cards to SEPDC candidates were summarily fired. As a result of the officially condoned "dirty tricks," none of the SEPDC candidates were elected.[19] Hampered in similar ways by the Front, virtually all campaigns by the opposition are unavailing.

Dr. Beyene Petros, leader of the SEPDC and a former official of the TGE, argues the regime allows just enough freedom to keep major donors quiet. "A functioning multi-party system is nonexistent," he said.[20]

To avoid the charge that Ethiopia does not have multiparty elections, the National Election Board (NEB) points out that some sixty parties are legally registered; fifty-six are regional while the rest operate at the federal level.[21] What the NEB fails to mention is that 95 percent of all parties are affiliated with the ruling party.[22] This vainglorious numbers game has been played by the EPRDF since the 1992 elections to detract attention from the compelled absence of the opposition political parties capable of mounting serious challenges to the EPRDF. Behind the multi-party mask lies a solid one-party system. Opposition groups are allowed to exist but the ruling EPRDF never loses an election.

The cards are stacked against any who might challenge the hegemony of the EPRDF. The electoral system favors the ruling party, but even more important is the rewards system. People are rewarded for their vote by not having their supply of food, especially sugar and salt, or fertilizer cut off by kebele officials. Workers in pro-Front trade unions get the best pay and conditions; student party members are first in line for scholarships. All this binds people into a blurred entity consisting of the central government, the region, and the ruling party.

According to Prime Minister Meles, the government has "no policy of intimidating the opposition." Meles states that from personal experience, he is aware of "what happens when peaceful, legal dissent is muzzled," and he concludes that "if for no other reason than maintaining stability, we must allow dissent." The Prime Minister avers that the opposition is "marginalized" because they offer no alternatives to the EPRDF's five-year development program. "A mature opposition is not just rejectionist but also one that puts forward its own alternatives," he said.[23]

Instead of criticizing the FDRE from abroad, the opposition should go into the field to win the hearts and minds of the peasants as the TPLF/EPRDF had done while fighting the Derg. According to the Prime Minister, "Any political group which has a popular agenda cannot be marginalized by repression of whatever magnitude." Meles contends that the opposition, operating under conditions far better than those in which the TPLF had labored during the civil war, would achieve success only if they built institutions "rooted in the countryside." The government, he indicates, could not prevent the opposition from accomplishing such an objective.[24]

But the government, through constant harassment and interference, has prevented the opposition from accomplishing much at all. The reality is that government use of violence and terror precludes, from the start, any other group from presenting an agenda by *peaceful* means. By the time of the 1995 elections, all non-EPRDF political organizations had been rendered practically impotent though some continued to exist in a precarious limbo of quasi-legality. But EPRDF toleration was based solely on expediency and the good behavior of representatives of those parties daring to dissent from the Front's programs. A handful of opposition parties, notably the AAPO and CAFPD, preserve a precarious presence in Addis Ababa—their activities in the contryside effectively curtailed.

The Prime Minister has warned opposition groups that since they are "anti-democratic both in terms of their objectives and their approaches, it is futile to expect them to make a positive contribution to the democratic process in the country." The government press claims that the attempt of narrow nationalists (the OLF and others) to secede by force has been crushed. Likewise, national chauvinists (the AAPO and others) have been defeated in their attempt to impose their hegemony by acting "under the mask of human rights protection, mass organizations and trade unions."[25] Nevertheless, according to the Prime Minister, the forces of revolutionary democracy must remain alert to challenges to the constitutional order by these chauvinist forces.

In the politics of the FDRE, authority derives from above rather than from below. The oppressed masses are given periodic opportunities to register their approval of Front leadership; there is no effective way in which they may register their disapproval since no meaningful alternatives are allowed to be presented to them. The EPRDF leadership is rich in sanctions to enforce its centralized control, and prudently, few opposition party members have shown an inclination toward martyrdom.

All of the evidence gives credence to the findings of EHRCO that the EPRDF controls all major aspects of political and public life:

The opposition groups with a vested interest in Ethiopian affairs have been marginalized from the political scene. The activities of some of these groups have been restricted to Addis Ababa, where they have what remains of their offices. Those that set up branch offices outside Addis Ababa in 1992 and 1993 have been driven out of the provinces, and they cannot operate even in Addis Ababa without the permission of the EPRDF."[26]

LESSONS FOR THE TEACHERS

Long established professional and trade associations have been targets for takeovers or enervating hostilities by the ruling party. The Ethiopian Teachers Association (ETA), a multiethnic, transconfessional institution founded in 1949, represented more than 120,000 teachers and promoted the professional interest of members and the development of education in Ethiopia. The EPRDF targeted the ETA for dismantling and reorganization on ethnic lines.

When the TGE went about restructuring Ethiopian education on the basis of killils with teachers' assignments correspondingly following ethnic or linguistic paths rather than those of high quality instruction, the ETA protested. The government attempted to mute this criticism by putting the association out of business. On 23 October 1994, the Ministry of Interior issued a certificate of legalization to a newly-spawned EPRDF teachers' union claiming that the old ETA had been disbanded because "it was part of the now defunct Derg government." The government then froze the ETA bank account and, backed by a court order, expropriated more than U.S. $1 million of the association's funds.[27] When the ETA challenged these actions, the government retaliated. Defiant teachers who did not follow the EPRDF line were denied salary increments and pension rights or were suspended or dismissed from their jobs. Dissident married couples were posted to newly carved ethnic homelands and sometimes separated because of their ethnic backgrounds. Many were transferred to different schools or to remote areas in violation of Ministry of Education regulations. Financial contributors to the ETA were labelled as "anti-government" and discharged. In sum, over 2,000 teachers were dismissed for political reasons. As a further indignity, the EPRDF deducted a percentage of salaries of all teachers for support of the puppet teachers' union created by the government.

Government security forces ransacked the association's Addis Ababa offices and placed them under the control of EPRDF loyalists. All of the 133 ETA branch offices were closed by repressive measures of the government and the offices and properties were expropriated by the Front. Officers of the association became special targets of vexation. Armed security officers broke into and illegally searched the home of ETA president Dr. Taye Wolde Semayat. On 30 March 1996, upon his return from a business trip to Europe, Dr. Taye was arrested at the Addis Ababa airport and has been imprisoned since that time. He was not indicted until 5 August when he was charged with forming an illegal organization with the aim of violently overthrowing the government and planning and executing acts of terrorism. Throughout his imprisonment on unproven charges, Dr. Taye has been vilified by the government controlled media and he was placed in a death-row cell know as the "darkness cell" and kept in chains twenty-four hours a day for fifty-seven consecutive days—in violation of Ethiopian law.[28] In mid-1999 Dr. Taye was sentenced to fifteen years imprisonment.

Other ETA leaders have been imprisoned and some killed—the murder of Assefa Maru, ETA's vice president, by police in broad daylight being the most infamous example.[29] The secretary general of the organization fled to the United States. On 17 September 1998, EPRDF security forces surrounded the Addis Ababa headquarters of the ETA and demanded that the remaining officers hand over everything belonging to the organization to the government's new "ETA." By the end of 1998, the ETA was hardly surviving as a badly damaged association.

The FDRE chose unwisely in making examples of Dr. Taye and Dr. Asrat of the AAPO, both of whom were well-known outside of Ethiopia. Dr. Taye received his Ph.D. in political science from the University of Missouri and before he was elected president of the ETA, he collaborated in research studies with American political scientists. Dr. Asrat was internationally renowned as Ethiopia's leading surgeon. Both men were faculty members of AAU and were among the forty-two academics summarily fired by the TGE in 1993.

The government faces a heavy burden of proof in convincing foreigners that know these men that they would be capable of carrying out the crimes with which they have been charged. Even more grievous, is the government's gormless assumption that Asrat and Taye would be so inept as to get caught in the fabricated circumstances cited as "evidence" against them. Testimony of witnesses in court about the tortuous methods used by security agents in coercing confessions and statements from them about the alleged activities of Taye and Asrat also undermines the government's case.[30] In making *cause célèbres* of two of the country's noted intellectuals, the FDRE has further eroded its *bona fides* in the international community.

Pressure from the international community (especially the British), professional associations and human rights organizations, and a relentless campaign by Ethiopians within and outside Ethiopia finally resulted in the release of Professor Asrat from his hospital prison cell on 27 December 1998. Government media stated that the FDRE had suspended Asrat's trial on the basis of medical evidence that his life would be endangered unless he received medical treatment abroad. Suspension implied that charges against Dr. Asrat had not been dropped and could be reactivated in the future. Meanwhile, Professor Asrat went to Houston, Texas, where he received much needed medical care. He died in Philadelphia on 14 May 1999.

ACTIONS AGAINST TRADE UNIONS

The Confederation of Ethiopian Trade Unions (CETU), the nation's largest and oldest union, was likewise the target for takeover by the ruling party. After several years of trying, the combined forces of the government and party cadres succeeded in gaining full control of the CETU on 24 April 1997. Using clandestine techniques, the EPRDF gained majority control of executive and audit committees of eight federations that decided to reorganize CETU and administer its property regardless of the results of a case pending before the courts.[31] After a series of management-sponsored meetings with members of trade unions of various industrial federations, an assembly of carefully selected pro-EPRDF members voted to replace the existing constitution of the CETU with a revised version. The new constitution reduced the power of the union's General Congress and gave it to the Council, which is composed of the executive committees of the various member federations. This enabled pro-EPRDF federations leaders to control the CETU thus avoiding the need of getting the approval of workers' representatives for the decisions the Council takes in the name of the Confederation. New pro-EPRDF officers were elected, and they passed a resolution calling for charges to be brought against the former leadership of CETU "for the various offenses they have committed against the Confederation." Former CETU president Dawi Ibrahim and other union officers, fearing for their lives, fled into exile abroad.[32]

The removal of the independent trade union leaders and the control of CETU's leadership by the TPLF/EPRDF cadres was part of a plan published in Amharic in a secret document, *Plan of Activities to be Implemented through Addis Ababa Organizational Unit from among the Political Works to be Carried out by the Trade Unions*.[33] The document gave details for a scheme to change the balance in the party's favor by increasing the EPRDF-front's control from six to seven federations through the removal of "diehard opponents from the Plant Unions and the Federation Councils" such as the Chemical and Energy Federation as well as Tourism, Hotel and General Services Federation. Although the EPRDF unit acknowledged its lack of firm support at the level of Plant Unions, it claimed that its victory in the control of the seven Federation Councils would enable it to get an upper hand in the CETU Council which was to be newly organized.

The secret document also described how party organs at various levels coordinate their activities to remove or neutralize all opposition to EPRDF control and facilitate the formation of a new CETU controlled by the party. The EPRDF's takeover of the CETU was another casebook demonstration of the "box within a box" technique used so successfully by the Front. Although the EPRDF/FDRE's actions against the CETU sparked protests from international labor groups, the objections came too late. The lid of the box was shut. When queried about the EPRDF's actions against CETU and theETA, Prime Minister Meles replied that "the government has nothing to do with the internal problems of the confederation of free-trade unions or the ETA."[34] He did not mention the role of party cadre in his answer.

The method of control used by the EPRDF was illustrated by events at a general meeting of members of the Industrial Federation of Banking and Insurance Trade Unions (IFBITU) called to elect its leaders. The gathering was disrupted by Front labor cadres who seized the podium and refused to let an election be conducted. Despite protests from rank and file membership, the cadres refused to give up the podium and allow the election to proceed. When the Federation members began to walk out of the hall in protest, about fifty EPRDF sympathizers remained behind to conduct a sham election and usurp the leadership of the Federation using their own preselected candidates. Realizing the aim of the cadres, members returned to the hall to prevent this. The ensuing melee ended in a stalemate when the staff of the meeting hall turned off the lights and drove everyone out—one of the few times that the bullying technique of the Front's CETU henchmen did not succeed.[35] Nevertheless, the IFBITU has been quietly shut down: the original federation was declared illegal and a new one recognized by the government.[36]

RAISING THE RENTS AND IRE OF BUSINESSMEN

Businessmen of Addis Ababa felt victimized by EPRDF policies when in 1997 rents in government owned shops were raised dramatically, some as high as 1,000 percent. Those who suffered from rent increases closed their shops and held a massive protest rally at Meskel Square on 17 May 1997. Two days later, the merchants, traders, and businessmen went on strike to get the attention of authorities and to urge a solution to their crises. On a mid-day radio broadcast, regional authorities warned strikers that business premises would be sealed by the government unless the businessmen opened them by 3:00 p.m. Immediately after the deadline, premises still not open were sealed. Eighty-four businessmen thought to have coordinated the strike were detained and 1,100 shops sealed.[37] Businessmen could get their premise unsealed by admitting they had committed an offence by striking and by appealing for a pardon. The coordinators of the strike would not be pardoned and were punished by having their trade licenses revoked, their shops taken away from them, and formal charges brought against them. None of these penalties are provided for by law.[38] The licenses of ninety-one businesses eventually were canceled as punishment for those who had protested.[39]

Coercing confessions from citizens and requiring them to appeal for a pardon whenever they exercise their rights of free speech, petition, and association are gross violations of human rights. Strikers at the Commercial Bank of Ethiopia and Addis Ababa University student protesters also have had to admit guilt and to beg the government for a pardon in order to get reinstated in employment or to attend classes.

The major business associations, the chambers of commerce, also have been reorganized by the FDRE. Since the beginning of the Transition Period, the Ethiopian Chamber of Commerce had been critical of some of government's economic policies and practices. In 1997, to squelch such organized criticism of the Front's policies by the private sector, the Ministry of Trade and Industry overhauled existing chambers of commerce and set up ethnic-based organizations in their place. The new chambers of commerce and industry were established at the woreda, killil, and federal levels in order to be compatible with the "free market economy and the federal administrative structure." Under the new arrangement, members of the business community have to be organized into associations based on the economic or trade sector of their particular business. State enterprises as well as private business organizations may be members. Representation at the various chambers is indirect through membership in a business association. By "ethnicizing" the new chambers, providing for the indirect representation of individual businesses, and allowing public enterprises to be members, the EPRDF should be able to exercise more control over the "vacillators" and petty bourgeoisie.[40]

PLOWING UNDER THE PEASANTS

Peasants, who constitute 80 percent of the population, live and work on land owned by the state according to the constitution of the FDRE. Rural people are EPRDF tenants who risk losing their lands if they criticize or anger the ruling party. Under an "agrarian reform" program of the Region 3 (Amhara province) administration, hundreds of farmers from Gojjam were dispossessed of their land which was handed over to supporters of the ruling party. Farmers appealing the rulings were rebuffed by officials at the woreda, zone, and killil levels. Angry peasants then went to Addis Ababa to protest being driven off their land at gun point by EPRDF military. The central government offered the farmers no relief on the grounds that under the FDRE's system of federalism, decisions regarding land distribution should be made at the regional level. The protesting farmers were told to return to their homes or face being charged with organizing and participating in an illegal organization.[41]

Under the Region 3 program, peasants who had been landowners during the reigns of Haile Selassie or the Derg cannot own more than one hectare (less than 2½ acres) of land each, while "poor farmers," who were "peasants oppressed by the former regimes" are entitled to three hectares. Any peasant who works for the present regime, however, can obtain as much land as a poor farmer. The effect of this reform is to dispossess farmers with land not exceeding ten hectares in order to benefit poor peasants whom the EPRDF is trying to attract as allies.[42]

THE PARTY IN THE ACADEMY

At Addis Ababa University, as we have seen, academicians who were not submissive to the dictates of the government were summarily dismissed from their positions.[43] Government controls of higher education were further augmented by new policies at Addis Ababa University and other institutions. Beginning in June 1996 elected deans and directors of faculties and research institutes of the university were replaced by new appointees, contrary to long established tradition.[44] Collegial governance of the university has been replaced by governmental management. In addition, AAU is being "restructured" to prepare its students for what the government calls "self-employment and proficiency in skills that will enable them to participate in the economic development of the country."[45]

To facilitate "monitoring" of faculty at Alemaya University, a security office of the TPLF was set up on campus. Dissident faculty and students could be called there for frequent interrogations and sometimes beatings. Several of the faculty were arrested on campus and taken to the nearby, infamous Hurso detention camp where they were incarcerated and tortured. Department heads and administrators who still did not knuckle under to TPLF pressures and who stood up for academic freedom were demoted or fired. All remained under close surveillance from security forces. Such actions lowered the morale of faculty and students and badly damaged the intellectual integrity of the university.[46]

As part of a government-initiated structural adjustment program, Alemaya University lost three of its faculties: the Faculty of Agricultural Engineering was moved to the Tigray Region, the Faculty of Agricultural Economics to the Amhara Region, and the Faculty of Forestry was merged with the Wondo Gennet Forestry and Wildlife College.[47] The propriety of this weakening of the comprehensive agricultural curriculum of Alemaya University has been questioned by the higher education community.

While keeping AAU and AUA at bay, the government in 1998 established four new "universities" in the regions governed by the quartet of component parties of the EPRDF. Tigray University came into being by the redesignation of Mekele Business College as a university college. In the southern home of the SEPDF, Awassa University incorporated the Awassa Agricultural College, Dilla Teachers' College, and Wondo-Guenet Forestry College. In OPDO territory, Oromiya University was built from the foundation of the Health Science Institute at Jimma. In Bahir Dar, in the bailiwick of the ANDM, the Polytechnic Institute combined with a teacher's college to form Amhara University.[48] It remains to be seen what quality of education will come from the further stretching of Ethiopia's limited higher education resources.

The FDRE also downgraded Kotebe Teachers College, a junior college in Addis Ababa, to a teacher training institute[49] and converted the Harar Teacher Training Institute into a military training center.[50]

Student councils under the control of Front cadres have been set up in every junior and senior secondary school.[51] In the nation's schools, as well as in the universities and other settings, freedom of assembly is controlled by a myriad of nontransparent, unpublished rules, and regulations.

NEUTERING NONGOVERNMENTAL ORGANIZATIONS

Under the EPRDF strategy, NGOs exist to serve their members' interest and to provide organized support for Revolutionary Democracy. Government-organized NGOs or "GONGOS" serve the party's purposes while masquerading as actors in a pluralist society. Bona fide NGOs that have not demonstrated their support of EPRDF programs in development, relief, and monitoring work have been subjected to pressures to conform. Their development workers have been special targets of party cadre to be "won over to the side of the Front."

In a 1997 interview, Prime Minister Meles revealed that his government was promulgating new laws to gradually force the international NGOs to close down their offices.[52] All NGOs were ordered to register with the Ministry of Justice, and conflicting policy and administrative regulations have left NGOs in a state of confusion and uncertainty. The government's granting of work permits for NGO personnel is notoriously slow. Newly founded organizations have found it difficult to register, and some already existing organizations have been "deregistered."[53]

The government has created further restrictions on existing NGOs by promulgating an "NGO Code of Conduct." Although the FDRE views NGOs as "an important part of the freedom of association enshrined in the Constitution," such freedom, according to a government spokesman, should not "be used to advance illegal enterprises." The government defines "illegal enterprises" to suit party purposes, and the Code of Conduct is thus needed "to ensure the integrity of the NGO sector."[54]

The most open attacks by the FDRE have been against human rights organizations, which Meles has accused of trying to dictate to his government what it should do to protect human rights. The Ethiopian Human Rights Council (EHRCO), which correctly could be called "the great injustice collector" for its straightforward reporting of human rights violations, applied for, but was not granted registration as an NGO for eight years. The government froze the organization's bank account containing locally-raised and foreign-donated funds and threatened EHRCO with prosecution by the Ministry of Justice. The FDRE contends that EHRCO is a "political organization," i.e., a group obstructing the hegemony of revolutionary democracy. Similar charges used by the government to harass ethnic human rights groups, including the Human Rights League (Oromo), the Oromo Ex-Prisoners for Human Rights, and the Ogaden Human Rights Committee, have forced most of them to operate clandestinely.[55]

The EPRDF knows full well that NGOs are crucial in the process of effective monitoring and enforcing of human rights norms. The international community relies on the reports and studies of NGOs when allegations of human rights violations by a particular state are examined. Those reports are distributed to the media, national authorities, and international bodies. To prevent NGOs from using the information that they have gathered in Ethiopia to lobby national and international bodies in the defense of human rights, the FDRE attempts to discredit the organizations. In addition, members of EHRCO's Legal Committee, Assefa Maru and Tesfaye Taddese, have been murdered in strange circumstances, and another member, Mengistu Wassihun, fled into exile after threats against his life were made by TPLF security forces.[56]

To deflect international criticism of the regime's human rights abuses, the House of Peoples' Representatives held a widely publicized "Human Rights Conference" in May 1998. Representatives from sixty-eight countries were invited to participate in the meeting that was to "set the stage for the establishment of a Human Rights Commission and Ombudsman in Ethiopia."[57] Notably excluded from the invitation list were Amnesty International, Human Rights Watch, EHRCO, the Human Rights League, and other Ethiopian NGOs critical of the government, as well as individual activists and scholars who have voiced opposition to EPRDF policies. The Front's products of the conference, a new "Human Rights Commission and Ombudsman," will receive an implied blessing from the foreign participants and be used to further disparage the existing NGOs monitoring the human rights situation. It remains to be seen if the commission will be more than a propaganda vehicle of the government.

POLITICIZING THE PATRIARCH

The Ethiopian Orthodox Church (EOC) also has been drawn into the EPRDF's political struggles. When the Front came to power, a nominating committee of religious leaders chose a new "Patriarch" or head of the church. One of the archbishops on the nominating committee thought the election had been "manipulated from the outset."[58] Abune Pawlos, the new Patriarch, was a Tigrayan who had spent a number of years in the United States and held a Doctor of Divinity degree from Princeton. His tenure has been stormy, marred by accusations that he is a tool of the EPRDF and that the EOC is being reorganized along ethnic lines. Under Pawlos' administration, priests have been assigned to their appropriate ethnic killils, and critics of the Abune have been disciplined—some prevented from entering church grounds.[59]

The Abune frequently is a target of public disdain while he performs his priestly duties. As a result, he is closely guarded by TPLF militia. The most disturbing event of Pawlos' patriarchy occurred on 9 January 1997, when a monk, Bahtawi Fekade Sellassie, attempted to present a petition to the Abune and was shot dead on the steps of Estifanos Church in Addis Ababa. The shots that killed the monk were fired from an area where clergy were seated around the Patriarch. The government media announced that the monk was carrying a sword and attempted to assassinate Abune Pawlos before being killed by "an individual"—an account disputed by those present.[60] This and other acts of violence in and around churches have alienated the Patriarch from his spiritual flock and have contributed to the EPRDF goal of exploiting internal contradictions within the EOC leadership to weaken any opposition to the Front.[61]

FREEDOM OF ASSEMBLY

The right to assemble is part-and-parcel of the right of association and is a fundamental human right. Under Ethiopian law, organizers of political meetings and demonstrations are required only to notify appropriate government authorities prior to convening an event. Nevertheless, peaceful demonstrations have been denied by government fiat. The usual practice is for the FDRE to restrict freedom of association through a *de facto* permit system under which it can delay in acknowledging notifications and declare events which go ahead anyway as illegal and subject to dispersal and arrest of participants.[62]

An example of this occurred in Addis Ababa on 27 May 1997 when representatives of three large opposition groups, CAFPDE, SEPDC, and AAPO, requested permission from the government to hold a demonstration at Meskel Square to mark the anniversary of the fall of the Derg and to protest the policies of the EPRDF. Government officials at first denied permission, but later, two days before the scheduled demonstration, gave it their approval. Rally organizers were unable to use government-controlled radio or television to publicize their gathering and did not have time to print and distribute fliers about the rally. Under these pressures, the organizing committee decided to postpone the protest until 1 June by which time fliers could be printed and dispersed. Government officials, however, put a further obstruction, a "Catch 22," in the way of citizens trying to express their political views by denying "permits" for distributing fliers to residents of

Addis Ababa. Rally organizers had a date and place for a demonstration and thousands of fliers announcing it but no way of effectively advertising the event. Officially damned if they did and damned if they didn't, the rally organizing committee postponed the demonstration indefinitely and instead issued a joint statement—a lame excuse for participation in so-called democratic processes.[63]

Two months earlier, AAU students had run afoul of the obnubilating government policy. Then, about 500 AAU students took to the streets in support of Amhara farmers protesting against their being dispossessed of their farmland. Police detained 200 of the marchers and claimed that the demonstration was illegal because the students did not get the necessary permission. Students had submitted written notification to the Addis Ababa Administration, along with a petition signed by 425 students. In order to be released, the students had to admit being wrong and write a letter requesting the government pardon them for knowingly participating in an illegal demonstration. They also were required to promise to be subjected to "legal action" by the government if they again took part in such a demonstration.[64] Such requests for pardon with threats of unspecified punishments hanging over their heads implies the forfeiture of the students' constitutional right of peaceful assembly.

FREEDOM OF ASSOCIATION DENIED

In many nations the participation of citizens in political parties and voluntary associations has been a training ground for democracy. Self-government works best when sovereignty is dispersed and citizenship formed across multiple sites of civic engagement.[65] As de Tocqueville noted, "Practicing self-government in small spheres impels citizens to larger spheres of political activity."[66] That is exactly the reason the EPRDF/FDRE seeks to deny freedom of association and meaningful participation in political organizations to its citizens.

Thus, despite the guarantees of Article 31 of the constitution, the government has shamefully enjoined the basic right of Ethiopians to join with others in the pursuit of certain non-EPRDF/FDRE aims, be they private, public, political, social, or economic. The rights of the group in the state as well as the right of individuals to associate have not been protected. Freedom of association, like other human rights, is fettered.[67]

NOTES

1. Herbert A. Simon, *Administrative Behavior* (New York: Macmillan, 1957), 101–102.

2. Chester I. Bernard, *The Functions of the Executive* (Cambridge: Harvard University Press, 1956), 3.

3. David. E. Lilienthal, *Big Business: A New Era* (New York: Harper, 1953), 131–136.

4. See for example the *Basic Law* of the Federal Republic of Germany (Grundgesetz), Article 9, Point 1; Article 20; *Constitution of Japan*, Article 21.

5. See generally, Robert A. Horn, *Groups and the Constitution* (Stanford: Stanford University Press, 1956); Glenn Abernathy, *The Right of Assembly and Association* (Columbia: University of South Carolina Press 1961), 171–252; Charles E. Rice, *Freedom of Association* (New York: New York University Press, 1962); David Feldman, *The Constitutional Right of Association* (Chicago: University of Chicago Press, 1963).

6. Raymond Zickel and Walter R. Iwaskiw, eds., *Albania: A Country Study* (Washington, DC: Library of Congress, 1994), 179–180. In a November 1989 interview with *The Independent*, Meles said approvingly, "the nearest any country comes to being socialist as far as we are concerned is Albania." Quoted in Ben Parker, *Ethiopia, Breaking New Ground* (Oxford: Oxfam UK, 1995), 21.

7. Kay Lawson, ed., *Political Parties and Linkage: A Comparative Perspective* (New Haven: Yale University Press, 1980), 3.

8. TPLF/EPRDF, "TPLF/EPRDF's Strategies for Establishing its Hegemony & Perpetuating its Rule," English translation of TPLF/EPRDF document originally published in June 1993, *Ethiopian Register* 3 (June 1996): 20–29.

9. "AAPO Official Assassinated in Dire Dawa," *Ethiopian Register* 3 (January 1996): 8.

10. Oromia Support Group, "Human Rights Abuses in Ethiopia, Press Release-January/February 1998," 20. For an account of atrocities against Oromo seen by a British nurse, see Sue Pollock, "Ethiopia—Human Tragedy in the Making," Oromia Support Group, March 1996; "Breaking the Guilty Silence," *The Scotsman*, 13 April 1996, 10–14; Kirsty Scott, "Human Tragedy in the Making," *The Herald* (Glasgow), 10 February 1996.

11. See, e.g., the reports documented in *Sagalee Haaraa*, the Newsletter of the Oromia Support Group, published in Great Britain, and in *Moresh*, published in Minnesota by the Ethiopian Amhara Organization.

12. The cases cited in this chapter are taken from actual political asylum cases. Names of claimants are withheld to protect their anonymity.

13. Stephen Buckley, "Ethiopia: A Rights Violator? Foes Say Foreign Aid Props Up System of Widespread Abuses," *Washington Post*, 13 April 1998, A17; Human Rights Watch," Ethiopia: Human Rights Development," New York, NY, 1999.

14. "Ethiopia, Federal Sham," *The Economist*, 16 August 1997.

15. Neka Tibeb, "Interview," *Moresh* 3 (Oct/Nov 1995).

16. "AAPO Denied Permission for Holding the Third Candle Vigil in Meskel Square," *Andinet* 3 (1 February 1997).

17. "AAPO Celebrates 6th Anniversary in Bahir Dar," *Ethiopian Register* 5 (March 1998): 11.

18. Human Rights Watch, "Human Rights Curtailed in Ethiopia," New York, NY, 9 December 1997.

19. "SEPDC Participates in Woreda Election," *Ethiopian Register* 5 (February 1998): 9.

20. Buckley, op. cit.

21. *News from Ethiopia*, Embassy of Ethiopia, Washington, DC, September 1996.

22. Buckley, op. cit.

23. "Meles Declares Political Loyalty Key Factor in Appointment of Senior Government Officials," *Ethiopian Register* 4 (July 1997): 20–23.

24. Meles' statements are from a meeting with American Ethiopianists in Washington, DC, on 20 October 1995; see, Theodore M. Vestal, "Yes, Prime Minister, But . . . : An Open Letter to Prime Minister Meles Zenawi," *Ethiopian Register* 2 (December 1995): 30–32.

25. "TPLF Warns Local Opposition, *Ethiopian Register* 4 (July 1997): 16–17.

26. EHRCO, "Violence Does Not Solve Problems," Special Report No. 13, Addis Ababa (2 May 1997).

27. Assefa Negash, "Brief Survey of Educational Development, ETA's Current Struggle and Human Rights Violations in Ethiopia," *Unraveling Human Rights Abuses in Ethiopia: Ways and Means of Alleviating the Problem*, Proceedings of a Human Rights Week Observance and Electronic Mail Conference, 3–8 March 1997 (Medford, MA: ISCEPC, 1997), 44–56.

28. Ibid.; see also, Letter, ETA Executive Committee to Meles, 4 June 1996; EHRCO, "Report on the Detention of Dr. Taye Woldesemayat," Special Report No. 3/1996, Addis Ababa (27 June 1996); "The Framing Up of ETA's Dr. Taye Wolde Semayat," *Ethiopian Register* 3 (September 1996): 30–35; "'You Risk Your Life Unless You Testify Against Dr. Taye W/Semayat et al'—Torturers," *Ethiopian Register* 5 (March 1998): 13–16; "TPLF Judge Orders Police to Keep Dr. Taye W/Semayat in Chains Indefinitely," *Ethiopian Register* 5 (September 1998): 5–6; "Chains Removed from Dr. Taye Wolde Semayat's Hands," *Ethiopian Register* 5 (November 1998): 9.

29. EHRCO, Special Report No. 14, 13 May 1997; "The TPLF Destroys the Independent ETA," *Ethiopian Register* 5 (October 1998): 8.

30. See, e.g., "Court Hears More Gruesome Tales of Torture," *Ethiopian Register* 5 (May 1998): 10–19; "Court Hears More Testimonies on the Torture of Professor Asrat's Co-defendant," *Ethiopian Register* 5 (June 1998): 6–9; Lisanua Fitihaye, "Professor Asrat Woldeyes—Victim of TPLF's Political Conspiracy," *Ethiopian Register* 5 (July 1998): 20–29; "At the TPLF Court of Justice," *Ethiopian Register* 5 (September 1998): 14–15; "Professor Asrat's Court Hearing Sus-

pended," *Ethiopian Register* 6 (February 1999): 5–6; "London Gives Professor Asrat a Hero's Welcome," *Ethiopian Register* 6 (February 1999): 6–7.

31. "Concerted Move to Replace CETU by Surrogate Confederation," *Ethiopian Register* 4 (February 1997): 13–14.

32. "TPLF's Anti-Free Trade Union Campaign Culminates in Control of CETU," *Ethiopian Register* 4 (June 1997): 13–14.

33. Ibid.

34. "U.F.E.R.'s Report to the UN," *Ethiopian Register* 4 (June 1997): 18, 20.

35. "Federation of Bank and Insurance Trade Unions Prevented from Holding Elections," *Ethiopian Register* 5 (April 1998): 8.

36. Lara Santoro, "Cracks in Ethiopia's Calm Facade," *Christian Science Monitor*, 23 April 1998. Residues of the old federation remain until courts rule in pending cases.

37. EHRCO, Special Report No. 18, 15 September 1997.

38. EHRCO, "Illegal Measures Against Businessmen," Special Report No. 16, Addis Ababa (3 June 1997); "Violation of the Right to Work," Special Report No. 18, Addis Ababa (15 September 1997).

39. "Bureau Illegally Cancels Trade Licenses," *Ethiopian Register* 4 (October 1997): 12–13.

40. "Ethnic-Based Chambers of Commerce to Replace Existing Ones," *Ethiopian Register* 4 (October 1997): 7–8.

41. Saba Seyoum, "Ethiopian Peasants Revolt Against Land Reforms," Agence France Presse (14 March 1997); "Gojjam Farmers Appeal to Federal Government," Africa News Service (14 March 1997); "Amhara Farmers Must Toe the Line," Indian Ocean Newsletter (29 March 1997).

42. "Farmers from Gojjam Flock to Addis Ababa to Lodge Protest," *Ethiopian Register* 4 (April 1997): 6–8; see also Mammo Muchie, "The Ethnic Enclosure of the Ethiopian Peasantry," *Ethiopian Register* 6 (February 1999): 18–23.

43. See Chapter 6, Supra.

44. "AAU's Elected Faculty Deans and Directors Replaced by Appointees," *Ethiopian Register* 3 (June 1996): 15.

45. *News from Ethiopia*, Embassy of Ethiopia, Washington, DC, March 1998.

46. Testimony from political asylum cases. Names of claimants are withheld to protect their anonymity.

47. "Alemaya University to Lose Three of its Faculties," *Ethiopian Register* 3 (January 1996): 9.

48. *News from Ethiopia*, Embassy of Ethiopia, Washington, DC, May 1998.

49. "Kotebe Teachers College Downgraded to a Teacher Training Institute," *Ethiopian Register* 4 (October 1997): 9– 10.

50. "Harar Teacher Training Institute Converted into Military Training Center," *Ethiopian Register* 5 (January 1998): 16.

51. "Government to Organize Student Councils," *Ethiopian Register* 4 (April 1997): 13–14.

52. "NGOs Banned from Employing Public Servants without Clearance," *Ethiopian Register* 5 (February 1998): 15.

53. Human Rights Watch, op. cit.

54. *News from Ethiopia*, Embassy of Ethiopia, Washington, DC, March 1998.

55. Human Rights Watch, op. cit. See also Kjetil Tronvoll, "Contextualising Human Rights and Democratisation Support: External Aid to the NGO Sector in Ethiopia," Norwegian Institute of Human Rights, December 1997. In 1999 the block on EHRCO's bank account was removed by court order.

56. "Another Member of EHRCO Assassinated," *Ethiopian Register* 5 (July 1998): 12–13.

57. *News from Ethiopia*, Embassy of Ethiopia, Washington, DC, May 1998.

58. "Interview with His Grace Abune Yosef, Archbishop of Dire Dawa and Western Harerge," *Ethiopian Register* 5 (January 1998): 32–35.

59. Koki Abesolome, "The Tormented Soul of a Cloned Patriarch," *Ethiopian Register* 5 (January 1998): 18–23.

60. "Petitioning Monk Shot Dead on Commemoration Day of St. Estifanos," *Ethiopian Register* 4 (February 1997): 15–16.

61. "Tigrawi Clergymen Call for Abba Pawlos' Removal," *Ethiopian Register* 5 (June 1998): 17.

62. Human Rights Watch, op. cit.

63. Ethiopian Email Distribution Network, 6 June 1997.

64. "University Students Demonstrate Against Discriminatory Land Redistribution," *Ethiopian Register* 4 (May1997): 7, 9–11.

65. Michael Sandel, *Democracy's Discontent* (Cambridge: Belknap Press, 1996), 347.

66. Alexis de Tocqueville, *Democracy in America* (New York: Mentor Books, 1956), vol. 1, 68.

67. See also, Theodore M. Vestal, "Freedom of Association in the Federal Democratic Republic of Ethiopia," Boston University, African Studies Center, Working Paper No. 210, 1998.

CHAPTER 15

The Mischief of Ethnic Factions
in the FDRE

There are two main factors contributing to Ethiopia's dismal record in the protection of human rights. One can be traced to the strategy of the EPRDF with its concomitant restraints on individuals and groups perceived as opposed to the hegemony of the ruling party. The other, mistrust and hatred among ethnic groups, grows out of the EPRDF's theory of governance.

The EPRDF's ethnic federalism emphasizing rights of "nations, nationalities, and peoples" is diametrically opposed to the ideology of nationalism and a "Greater Ethiopia." In the FDRE, ethnic groups are identified, territorially fixed and "killilized," and are handed over to ethnic parties. Unions and professional associations also are forced to organize on an ethnic basis. This is in contrast to democratic countries where the free play of class, gender, ethnic, and other interests all are subordinated to the respect of the universal and inclusive attributes of citizenship.

When rights are primarily seen from the perspective of ethnic groups or class, they are shorn of their universality and inclusiveness and distorted into becoming privileges enjoyed only by those who bestow upon themselves the identity of the true ethnic. The primacy of individual rights makes possible the respect of collective rights of all sorts. But the primacy of group rights does not at all entail the respect of individual rights.[1]

THE "SCHWEINHUND WITHIN" AND SYNDROME E

Ethnic hatreds spawned by this scheme are the source of abuses of human rights documented in the tragic cases of many Ethiopians seeking political asylum in the United States. In such cases, ethnicity often played a role in the claimants being arbitrarily arrested, incarcerated without charge or trial, and tortured by security forces of the government.[2]

In most instances, the perpetrators of these indecencies verbally abused the claimants because of their ethnicity even while torturing them. In carrying out hate crimes against ethnic and political "others," EPRDF zealots, with the endorsement of state power behind them, perpetrate unspeakable moral outrages against fellow Ethiopians. With power corrupting, and absolute power, which is what security personnel enjoy, corrupting absolutely, the EPRDF cadre and their collaborators have unleashed the great beast, the capacity for outraged, uncontrolled, bitter, and bloody violence that lurks beneath all the norms of legal and institutional behavior in normal society.[3] The scabrous security patrols of the EPRDF, with their resilient capacity for cruelty, are ruled by a malevolent spirit, what the Germans call "der innere Schweinhund," or the evil spirit within.

In oppressive actions against their countrymen, EPRDF security forces exhibit the symptoms of "Syndrome E," a blood-lust characterized by killing without emotion, identified by Dr. Itzak Fried of the UCLA Brain Institute.[4] According to Fried, Syndrome E is a kind of "cognitive fracture" that often proves contagious. It provides a sense of elation around violence and transforms nonviolent people into killing automatons who attack women and children without remorse or pity. Syndrome E is characterized by repetitive violence, obsessive ideas, group reinforcement, and a psychological "compartmentalization" that allows sufferers to detach themselves emotionally from their deeds. All of these characteristics are present in most of the human rights abuses of torture and worst punishments meted out by casually brutal EPRDF security forces.

Furthermore, according to medical clinicians with extensive experience in the treatment of torture-related trauma, it is difficult for torture victims to heal, to surmount their experiences if the torturers are regarded by the society or world at large as exercising legitimate political authority.[5] Unfortunately, in Ethiopia, the torturers can continue their work with impunity. Thoughtful analysts worry about how many years it will take to heal this divisive pathology spread throughout a diseased body politic.

In Ethiopia the world is witnessing ethnicity gone awry. The division of Ethiopia into ethnic administrative regions was mandated by the government. The people did not have an opportunity to approve the idea at the grass roots level. Until they do, ethnic federalism must be viewed as an artificial system imposed from above.

Instead of ethnicity referring to cultural-linguistic communal groups, built around ties of real or putative kinship, taking pride in the in-group, common consciousness, and identity of the group—as is the case in most multi-ethnic societies—under the FDRE, cultural prejudice and social discrimination against "others" have been encouraged and perverted into denying others basic human and economic rights. The government purposefully has tried to gull the people into believing the cause of their pitiable condition is ethnicity. This ethnicity run wild exaggerates differences, intensifies resentments and antagonisms, and sharply divides races and nationalities. Mutual suspicion and hostility are bound to emerge in a society bent on defining itself in terms of such jostling and competing groups.[6]

In ethnic killils, officials ruthlessly use political dominance, economic exploitation, and psychological oppression to drive out members of other ethnic groups who may have lived in the regions for decades—or to make life miserable for those who remain. Under the color of law, conflict and violence have been whipped up in response to imaginary threats from ethnic outsiders. As a result of this "informal repression," the covert use of private sector surrogates by the government to attack opponents or critics, the cult of ethnicity has produced bitter constraints on the peace, harmony, and integration of the nation's society.[7] The endgame of such identity politics is self-pity and self-ghettoization, and ultimately, political instability. As Arthur Schlesinger, Jr., has noted: "The meanness generated when one group is set against another, the 'built-in we-they syndrome' has caused more dominating, fearing, hating, killing than any other single cause since time began."[8]

THE ALCHEMY OF ETHNIC DISTRUST

The EPRDF's recipe for the alchemy that changes prejudice into human rights abuse, torture, and murder can be observed in the party's record of fostering inter-ethnic hatred since it came to power in 1991. There are four basic ingredients.

First, history. A historic grievance is kept festering by the retelling of events, real or imagined, that puts another ethnic group in a bad light. Perhaps this ploy is more significant where the oral tradition is still vital in communications. EPRDF cadres and their servitors skillfully stir up the most sensitive memories of lingering antagonisms long after the people who were offended are gone. Ethnic resentment of conquerors or rulers of decades or centuries ago is remembered as if events happened yesterday. The memory is honed by bitterness over perceived government favoritism toward one group or the other in the past or currently. Such resentment breeds resentment, hatred fuels hatred, and the resulting animosities generate flights from neighborliness and largeheartedness necessary for a commonwealth.

For example, the government has returned houses nationalized by the Derg to previous owners in Tigray, but not elsewhere. Property rights are withdrawn from some and bestowed on others purely on the basis of ethnicity. Those discriminated against feel they are victims of economic terrorism, and new ethnic grievances are brewed.[9]

The second ingredient is contempt. One group perceives the other as dirty, slothful, deceitful. The besmirched return contempt for contempt: the accusers are arrogant, devious, aggressive, and mean-spirited. This animus is fueled by members of both groups characterizing those of the other in terms dripping with bigoted contempt. When Ethiopians, with a natural bent for talk, go on a *chikachik* binge of verbal verbosity aimed at the "other," the brine of hostile criticism is further agitated.

Contempt also is exacerbated by what the author Solomon Deressa calls the inability of Ethiopians to hear one another coupled with "the demonic pride" Ethiopians take in their contempt for the "other." According to Solomon, if an Ethiopian says to a member of another ethnic group, "Your father burned my house down and my only child died in the fire," his or her knee-jerk response is likely to be, "How dare you? Since when do the likes of you have the right to mention the likes of my father?"[10] This belligerence, even in the face of basic human pain, is bound to have direct impact on intensifying old animosities, and the EPRDF well knows how to aggravate this weakness.

The third ingredient of the hateful brew is poison. To move any ethnic group, say, Tigrayans, from disliking another, say, Amharas, to fighting them requires another ingredient—a toxin. If the leader of a political party identified with a particular ethnic group, such as the All Amhara Peoples Organization (AAPO), can be convicted of plotting to overthrow the government, regardless of how trumped up the charges or how spurious the trial, the toxin of inter-ethnic hatred will be swallowed by the gullible. The horrors inflicted on those protesting the incarceration of Dr. Asrat Wold-eyes in the Central High Court in Addis Ababa in September 1994 is a classic example of officially condoned poisoning that spread throughout the country to the point that the AAPO and its surviving members are but a shell, a remnant of what was a strong and growing political party. Party regulars have been tormented, imprisoned, tortured, and murdered[11]—and the cause of their persecution ultimately can be traced to their ethnicity. Similar poisons have been plentifully stirred into the mixture by the astute actions of EPRDF cadres.

Such toxins are a component of Front propaganda. For instance, the EPRDF journal, *The People's Custodian*, asserts that "only by eliminating the Oromo educated elite and capitalist class will the Oromo people be freed from narrow nationalism. Only the class division can account for the explanation of narrow nationalism." In contrast, "Revolutionary Democracy affirms and struggles for the political supremacy of the proletariat, the peasant, the lower intellectual classes and the oppressed urban dwellers . . . against their common class enemies." The journal concludes that the Front "must be in a position to eradicate all narrow nationalists" as part of the "struggle for peace, democracy, and development."[12] The journal's diatribe was prelude to an intensified government campaign of abusing and even killing Oromo and plundering their property in 1997–1998.[13]

The fourth component of the mixture of calumny is domination. Ever since the EPRDF set itself up as the dominant power in the Transitional Government, there has been domination by one ethnic group over others. This is the case whether carried out by the Woyane in the central government or by its surrogates in the regions. The regional governments controlled by EPRDF ethnic front parties were set up to provide domination by one group at the expense of all others in the killil, a cynical and resentful closing off of others. Such domination generates the pernicious corrosion of resentment that prods concern and foreboding. The dominant group requires that *you* recognize that *we* have nothing in common with one another. The result has been governmental licensing of oppression and the denial of human rights to the "others."

Thus, in Ethiopia, the recipe for the culture of mistrust that changes prejudice into murder can be observed—history, contempt, poison, and domination by one group[14]—all contributing to the revulsion coefficient of the nation.

IS BENEVOLENT ETHNICITY POSSIBLE?

With the genie of ethnic distrust out of the bottle and with a number of Ethiopians actuated by a common passion adverse to the rights of other citizens or to the aggregate interests of the community, what can be done to control their effects? What answer is there to the contention that ethnic pride, the identity of groups, and exclusiveness of its members is "born in the bone?" Is the dye too deep in the Ethiopian wool? Can virtue be found in the current exposure of ethnic animosities?

The Ethiopians' answers to these questions will shape the future of the nation. The present regime has exposed every possible negative feeling of oppression and human suffering inflicted by one group upon another in the past. All the cards are on the table. What is the next play? Does the nation continue its ethnic dance macabre with its resultant spirit of gloom? Or can lessons learned produce a society where the Ethiopian's "Schweinhund within" is replaced by "ein gutter Geist, ein bessres Ich," a good spirit, a better person? Are Ethiopians big enough as a people to extinguish their banked ancestral rages?

There can be a benevolent side to ethnic belonging, a positive appreciation of one's own social roots in a community and cultural group without necessarily disparaging other groups. Ethnicity can provide material as well as emotional support networks for individuals in society. Identifying with an ethnic group fosters a sense of belonging as part of an intermediate level of social relationships between the individual and society.[15]

There also can be a democratic side of ethnicity: the rights of members of each ethnic group to be secure in their lives and property, as well as secure from arbitrary arrest and punishment, and for them to enjoy equal opportunity in real terms in trade, business, employment, schooling, and the enjoyment of social amenities. In a democracy the equal rights of all ethnic groups are recognized and ethnicity is a tool in the fight against privilege and nepotism.[16]

Benevolent ethnicity can be attenuated by the development of a public culture of a democratic society committed to seeking forms of social cooperation which can be pursued on a basis of mutual respect between free and equal persons. This cooperation does not imply the coordination of social activity by the government, but simply involves the acceptance of certain common procedures to regulate political conduct. It must also contain "fair terms specifying the basic rights and duties of citizens within society, so that the benefits produced by everyone's efforts are distributed fairly between generations over time."[17] Such a common adherence to ideals of democracy and human rights is precisely what has held the American people together in the absence of a common ethnic origin.[18]

Democracy in Ethiopia will require institutions and laws, but it also will depend on what might be called democratic dispositions. These include a preparedness to work with others different from oneself toward shared goals; a combination of strong convictions with a readiness to compromise in the recognition that one cannot always get everything one wants; and "a sense of individuality and a commitment to civic goods that are not the possession of one person or of one small group alone."[19]

Ethiopia, then, must liberate itself from the stifling past and enter into a new era with an interweaving of separate ethnic strands into a new national design. To secure the public good and private rights against the danger of ethnic factions, and at the same time to create a truly democratic government, is the great object to which freedom-loving Ethiopians should direct their thoughts and their individual actions.

NOTES

1. Editorial Office, Montreal, "Dialogue and Good Faith," *Ethiopian Register* 5 (April 1998): 33, 35.

2. Theodore M. Vestal, "Documented Sacrifice: The Experience of Young Ethiopians Now Seeking Political Asylum Abroad," *Ethiopian Register* 4 (August 1997): 30–33.

3. Harold L. Nieburg, *Political Violence: The Behavioral Process* (New York: St. Martin's Press, 1969), 103–104.

4. Joby Warrick, "Psychology: Syndrome Suspected in Genocidal Acts," *Washington Post*, 29 Dec 97, A2.

5. Jack Saul, "Forgotten in the Hoopla: Tibet's Young Torture Victims," *New York Times*, 1 November 1997, A29.

6. Arthur M. Schlesinger, Jr., *The Disuniting of America* (New York: W. W. Norton, 1992), 112.

7. See, International Centre Against Censorship, *Deadly Marionettes: State-Sponsored Violence in Africa*, Article 19, London, October 1997, iii, 1. The term "informal repression" was coined in South Africa in the late 1980s and refers to the practice of dictatorial governments using "private sector" surrogates to stimulate ethnic violence between communities which had previously lived together in harmony.

8. Schlesinger, 110.

9. Editorial, "The TPLF's Housing Policy & Practices," *Ethiopian Register* 4 (February 1997): 3–5.

10. Solomon Deressa, "The Poem and Its Matrix," in *Silence Is Not Golden: A Critical Anthology of Ethiopian Literature*, eds. Taddesse Adera and Ali Jimale Ahmed, (Lawrenceville, NJ: Red Sea Press, 1994), 177.

11. For reports of harassment of AAPO, see *Moresh* 2, 3, 4 especially Apr/May, July/Aug, Aug/Sep, Dec 1994; Aug, Oct/Nov 1995; Neka Tibeb, "Speech," *Andinet*, 1 February 1997, 3.

12. *Hizbaawi Adera* (*The People's Custodian*), December 1996–February 1997, quoted in *Sagalee Haaraa*, Newsletter of the Oromia Support Group, January/February 1998, 6.

13. "Urgent Action, AFR 25/04/98, International Secretariat, Amnesty International, London, 16 February 1998.

14. Credit for the recipe for turning prejudice into murder belongs to A. M. Rosenthal in describing what happened in India during communal rioting following destruction of a mosque in Ayodhya in 7 December 1992; see, "The Alchemists of Murder," *New York Times*, 2 March 1993, A21; cf., Gordon W. Allport, *The Nature of Prejudice* (Boston: Beacon Press, 1954), 14–15: five degrees of negative action in a fateful progression: 1) antilocution; 2) avoidance; 3) discrimination; 4) physical attack; 5) extermination.

15. Okwudiba Nnoli, "Ethnicity," in *The Oxford Companion to Politics of the World* ed. Joel Krieger, (New York: Oxford University Press, 1993), 280–284.

16. Ibid; see also, Alemante G. Selassie, "Ethnic Identity and Constitutional Design for Africa," *Stanford Journal of International Law* 29 (Fall 1992): 1–56.

17. John Rawls, "Justice as Fairness: Political Not Metaphysical," *Philosophy and Public Affairs* 14 (1985): 223–51.

18. Schlesinger, 118.

19. Jean Bethke Elshtain, *Democracy on Trial* (New York: Basic Books, 1995), 2.

CHAPTER 16

The Economy of "Revolutionary Democracy"

Since coming to power in 1991, the EPRDF has been committed to a market economy for the country. Most of the legislation in force during the Derg regime restricting a market economy and private business has been abolished. Although a substantial number of public enterprises are still owned and run by the government, many of these eventually will be privatized. State ownership was to be limited to certain strategic sectors including civil aviation, the railway, energy, mining, the chemical industry, telecommunications, insurance, and banking.[1] Changes in the global economy, however, forced the EPRDF leaders to modify their plans and privatize parts of some of these sectors.

In 1994 the EPRDF announced a Five Year Development Program with the goals of improving the infrastructure and the climate for investments with assistance from the International Monetary Fund (IMF) and World Bank. The program focused specifically on projects in health, education, agriculture, roads, and mining.[2]

As part of the strategy for attaining the Front's economic goals, the EPRDF *nuevo conversos* of capitalism secretly established a substantial number of large "private" companies in the names of party cadres. The firms, operating in Ethiopia and abroad, have a total capital of hundreds of millions of dollars.[3] How did the Front, an armed movement with a narrow social base in a devastated area of a poor country, accumulate such capital in a relatively short time?

CAPITALIZING PRIVATIZATION

The massive capitalization for such ambitious undertakings began with donations and contributions by exiled members and supporters of the TPLF, but more importantly, it gained impetus from illicit sources. Former TPLF officials have testified to shady fiscal dealings by the party to provide income for the organization. In the 1980s such nefarious schemes as the sale of relief food donated by aid agencies via Sudan for the people of Tigray helped fill the party coffers. The Relief Society of Tigray (REST) was used as the fulcrum for bilking well-meaning NGO representatives who bought and distributed the same grain over and over again in areas controlled by the TPLF. In addition to relief assistance, donor agencies gave the TPLF medicine, agricultural tools, heavy machinery, road construction equipment, transport vehicles, and spare parts—all supposedly for the rehabilitation of Tigrayan refugees in the Sudan or farmers in drought-affected areas. Instead, those donations were sold to Sudanese buyers to finance the TPLF's war activities and to invest in income-producing businesses, such as printing, vehicle repair, and commercial farming in the Sudan. During the civil war, TPLF fighters raided and looted Derg-held towns, robbed banks, pillaged hospitals, and ambushed Red Cross and other relief agency convoys carrying food and medical supplies. The plunder from these forays was supplemented by war booty abandoned by the Derg in its final months. Millions of dollars in tax revenues also were paid by people living in the areas controlled by the Front. In sum, the TPLF had accumulated wealth as well as military power before the final overthrow of the Mengistu regime.[4]

Since the TPLF expanded into the EPRDF and assumed power and control of public finances in 1991, millions of dollars have been transferred from the government treasury to the party. In one instance, former Prime Minister Tamrat Layne was involved in a scheme in which the EPRDF sold medicine to the Ministry of Health and then took money from the budgets of public hospitals to "reimburse" the Front for medicines the party had distributed in various regions during the civil war.[5]

Further, the government's fiscal policies have favored state enterprises and companies allied with the Front. Tax breaks are extended to party-approved businesses, and using its power to control the banks of the country, the Front has extended credit at very low rates or given direct start-up capital to its affiliated companies.[6]

At war's end, the EPRDF took over a number of economic institutions and government-owned companies that the party has used for its own ends. Cash generated by these enterprises has been used as start-up money for party firms. Public property, such as construction equipment, machinery, and vehicles, that fell into EPRDF hands was sold to foreign buyers or converted into fixed assets for companies set up by the Front.[7]

The EPRDF's vast network of "free" enterprises has been established in the names of individuals, who coincidentally are party members. In virtually every sector of the economy, *nuevo conversos*, former revolutionary politicians, have transmorgified into shareholders and managers of million dollar "private" businesses. In the process these "crony capitalists," high ranking members of the Front, such as Sebhet Nega and Siyie Abraha, among others, have become millionaires while providing the party with income. To staff these businesses, the party again has turned to its own. EPRDF cadres and members, many lacking in requisite formal education and experience, have been hired as well-paid administrators and foremen.[8]

In addition to the "private," EPRDF-controlled sector, the other major player in the Ethiopian economy is its largest foreign investor, the Ethio-Saudi al-Amoudi family.[9] Led by Sheik Mohamed al-Amoudi, the family owns the holding company, Midroc, the Sheraton Addis, and some twenty other companies in major sectors of the economy.[10] It is rumored that private and governmental capital from Kuwait and Saudi Arabia help finance the family's investments in Ethiopia. Although the nature of the connection between the al-Amoudi clan and the EPRDF is not publicly known, the Front so far has not hindered the growth of the family's businesses. Midroc, in turn, was a sponsor of the "Addis Forum" held at the Addis Sheraton in March 1998 to encourage trade and investment in Africa and Ethiopia.[11] It apparently was Sheik Mohamed who alerted the EPRDF that Deputy Prime Minister Tamrat Layne was misappropriating public funds. The Sheik presented evidence in the case *in camera* to the Federal High Court in February 1998.[12]

THE ROLE OF NGOs

As part of the party organization activity, Front cadres collect "voluntary contributions" from farmers, civil servants, factory workers, and the business community—most of whom fear economic reprisals against them should they be niggardly in "donating." The funds so contributed for both political organizations and the ethnic-based "development" associations affiliated with them are at the disposal of the parent party. In theory, the development associations are NGOs that mobilize local resources for the development of small-scale infrastructure and social services for their ethnic constituencies. In reality, no one, other than the political organizations that control the associations, knows how the money is spent, and the parent groups make good use of this arrangement to gain additional revenues. The

Front's NGOs also put pressure on non-EPRDF economic actors which might pose a threat to the hegemony of the party.[13]

"Non-profit" relief organizations set up by EPRDF member parties, such as REST, are exempt from paying taxes on revenues and import taxes, and through agreements with international donor agencies receive aid in foreign currencies. The lack of transparency in their operations makes it possible for party-sanctioned NGOs, while posing as benevolent ethnic self-help groups, to directly serve the political and economic interests of the EPRDF.[14]

A classic example of this strategy was the TPLF's establishment in 1995 of *Tikal Igri Mitkal Tigray* ("Rehabilitation of Tigray"), a profit-making NGO with over a million dollars in paid-up capital. This entity came into being through the "donation" of shares of party-controlled companies to the "Endowment Fund For the Rehabilitation of Tigray" (EFFORT). Such donations are exempt from sales taxes and thus provide the Front with a fiscally painless reallocation of capital of some of its companies. EFFORT then made its resources available to *Tikal Igri Mitkal Tigray*, the center of large-scale investment in Tigray Region.[15]

While Front-affiliated NGOs are used to bolster support of the party and to control the economy, NGOs of political organizations not affiliated with the EPRDF either have been banned or severely restricted. When the AAPO attempted to form a famine relief organization in 1994, the government denied its request on the ground that aid agencies "must be free from political affiliation."[16] Holding the AAPO to such a test while looking the other way at political affiliations of REST and the rest of the EPRDF-endorsed aid associations is typical of government partisanship of the politically correct.

Well-established and reputable relief groups, such as the Gurage People's Self-Help Organization, the Oromo Relief Organization, the Gonder Development Association, and the Wollo Development Association have been the targets of debilitating harassment by the EPRDF. Rival ethnic aid associations affiliated with the Front, however, are encouraged by the government to operate in the areas vacated by those non-EPRDF groups.[17]

The Political Party Registration Proclamation provides another example of a two-track system used to deny other organizations the benefits accruing to the Front. Under the law, "a political party which has attained legal personality may not directly or indirectly engage in commercial and industrial activity."[18] Before and after the proclamation was issued in 1993, individuals, "revolutionary democratic forces," and NGOs had set up income-generating business companies in behalf of the EPRDF. The acts of the Front to the contrary not withstanding, the proclamation makes it illegal for any non-Front political organization to get funds from such sources.[19]

Through the establishment of million dollar companies, smaller businesses, and profit-making NGOs, the EPRDF is carrying out its strategic objective of dominating the economy. The power of party-owned companies especially is felt in such sectors as construction, industrial production (including textiles, cement, marble, and pharmaceutical drugs), agricultural production (with special focus on livestock and cash crops), transport (both public and freight), consultancy, publishing, advertising, import-export, wholesale trade and distribution, and transit services. Many of the private companies that are not associated with the party have been marginalized, and even some state enterprises are not able to successfully compete with Front concerns.[20] As a result, Ethiopia is now a free-market kleptocracy run directly or indirectly by the Woyane.

One of Ethiopia's most admired businesses has not done well under EPRDF management, however. In 1997 Ethiopian Airlines acknowledged a decline in income which had been dramatically exceeded by expenditures. The low morale of employees was purportedly reflected in the deterioration of work efficiency and poor quality of service provided customers.[21]

JOINT VENTURES

Beginning in 1997 the Woyane expanded the scope of its economic activities by setting up joint ventures with non-Front individual businessmen and companies and organizations (with EPRDF companies maintaining majority ownership). The Front also became more active in the financial sector and created the nation's largest "private" bank, *Wegagen*, with working capital of Birr 60,000 million.[22] The increase in the number of banks, the expansion of the banking system, and the introduction of regulatory changes could reduce the costs of banking, encourage savings, attract investment funds, and stimulate economic growth—all a part of the liberalization of the financial system, a course of action advanced by the IMF and the World Bank. Critics of the EPRDF maintain that the Front has contorted objectives of financial liberalization and other structural adjustment programs to 1) prove its compliance with the recommendations of international lending institutions and Western donor countries to obtain further loans, 2) as a Western-sanctioned economic weapon to attack non-Tigrayans, and 3) as an instrument to enrich its supporters, cadres, and leaders.[23]

In January 1998 the EPRDF leadership announced three significant changes in the Front's development strategy "to benefit the rural people."[24] The telecommunications sector, the production of hydroelectric power, and the defense industry were opened to foreign investors.[25] Party leaders were willing to allow private investments in the construction of infrastructures of these sectors, but they stressed that distribution activities linked with these infrastructures would remain in the state's hands.

THE AGRICULTURAL SECTOR

In its fight against poverty, an overarching goal of the FDRE is to increase agricultural production. With 80 percent of the population in farming, agriculture accounts for over half of Ethiopia's Gross Domestic Product and 85 percent of export earnings. Prime Minister Meles avers that "no government can impose its will on peasants" and believes that the nation's agriculture will improve under a governmental policy of "hands off the peasants."[26] The peasantry are free to make their own decisions about what crops to plant and when and where to sell them.[27]

Apparently agricultural production did improve, for in early 1997 Meles announced that Ethiopia had achieved self-sufficiency in grain production. Furthermore, the country had produced more than 500,000 tons of surplus grain for export, including 1,246 metric tons of maize sent as relief aid to some 40,000 drought victims in northern Kenya.[28] The optimistic report of the nation's improved agricultural output was diminished, however, when in December 1997 the Disaster Prevention and Preparedness Commission appealed to foreign donors for food aid amounting to over half a million metric tons to feed over 4 million food deficient Ethiopians.[29] The unpredictable rains of the highlands again raised problems in the agricultural sector that tarnished the government's claim that agricultural output had increased by 50 percent over the previous two years. The maize that was shipped to Kenya traveled through the Borana and Bale zones of the Oromo killil, parts of Ethiopia where hundreds of thousands of people were suffering from food shortages.[30]

Agricultural production, of course, is tied closely to land tenure, and the various regional administrations have leeway under the constitution to implement land policies in different ways according to traditional local practice. Peasants are guaranteed access to land, their only social security, but they cannot sell it. The land that is left after reallocation to peasants will be available to be leased by commercial farmers.[31] Experiments under the new regime may bring improvements, but skeptics worry that the lack of land alienation through sale or mortgage may stymie agricultural production.

PARTIALITY FOR TIGRAY

Because of the dominant role played by the TPLF in the EPRDF, it is not surprising that the Tigray Region has received the lion's share of economic

benefits from Front activities. Tigray has become the center for new factories manufacturing, among other things, pharmaceutical products, cement,
and other building materials. The infrastructure of the region is being improved by the construction of irrigation dams, roads linking different wore-
das, airports in the main towns, schools, special vocational training centers,
colleges, clinics and hospitals, and water supply systems. Electricity and
telephone services are available in many of the towns. The massive Tiss
Abay Hydro-Electric Power Project, now under construction on the Blue
Nile, primarily will benefit Tigray when completed.[32] The outpouring of
economic benevolence on Tigray at the expense of other parts of the nation
is described by Assefa Negash as "the pillage of Ethiopia."[33]

The marked imbalance between the reconstruction activities in Tigray
and in the other regions was justified by Prime Minister Meles as a function
of the constitutional division of power between the Federal Government
and the Regional States. Since each regional state is responsible for the
overall development of its domain, according to Meles, the dynamic economic growth in Tigray is attributable to the successful efforts of the Tigray
Regional State.[34] The Prime Minister failed to note that the Central Government has provided Tigray with more development resources than have been
available to other regions and that Tigray was receiving 85 percent of all international aid to Ethiopia.[35]

THE FACADE OF "FREE ENTERPRISE"

For public consumption, the EPRDF extolls the virtues of economic liberalization, a free market, and the privatization of state-owned enterprises.
Behind the scenes, however, most of the Ethiopian economy is under state
ownership or control. Rural land belongs to the state and not to the farmers
and is parceled out by the Front to secure political support of the peasants.
Key sectors of the economy, including banking, manufacturing, foreign
trade, mining, and transportation are either dominated by EPRDF-owned
companies or controlled by the state.[36] Enterprises that have been privatized
have been "sold" at low prices to the party faithful, frequently Tigrayans
and Eritreans, in what has been termed unfair bidding competitions.[37] Privatization deals have been criticized for their lack of transparency: prices,
buyers, terms or method of privatization or the destination of the proceeds
have not been made public. Included in the nationalized businesses and assets sold are buildings, factories, and houses confiscated by the Derg and
never returned to their former owners. The government has announced
plans for additional privatization of 115 state companies, with an estimated
value of 40 billion birr, during the next few years.[38]

The Front, with its *nuevo conversos* and crony capitalists, comfortably occupies "the commanding heights of the economy." The EPRDF has devised an encyclopedic stock of anticompetitive weapons, and they have adroitly found ways to restrain trade, rig markets, and suppress competition. According to international financial institutions, the EPRDF controls or owns more than 80 percent of the Ethiopian economy.[39]

NOTES

1. See "Economic Goals" in TPLF/EPRDF, "TPLF/EPRDF's Strategies for Establishing its Hegemony & Perpetuating its Rule," English translation of TPLF/EPRDF document originally published in June 1993, *Ethiopian Register* 3 (June 1996): 20– 29; see also, Sisay Asefa and Ahmed Hussen, "Perspectives on Economic Development in Ethiopia," in *Ethiopia in Broader Perspective*, eds. Katsuyoshi Fukui, Eisei Kurimoto, and Masayoshi Shigeta, Vol. III, (Kyoto: Shokado, 1997), 671–681; Daniel Teferra, "State and Economic Development: The Case of Ethiopia," in *Proceedings of the 41st Annual Meeting of the African Studies Association*, Chicago, IL, 29 October–1 November 1998.

2. See Tamrat Layne, Prime Minister, "Ethiopia's Transitional Period Economic Policy Draft," in Amharic, Nehassie 1983 (August 1991); TGE, *Economic Policy of Ethiopia During the Transitional Period*, Addis Ababa, November 1991; *Ethiopia: Policy Framework Paper 1992/93–1994/95*, September 1992; *Ethiopia: Policy Framework Paper 1993/94–1995/96*, 15 July 1993, unpublished Policy Framework Papers (PFP) prepared by the TGE in collaboration with the IMF and World Bank.

3. Awualom Aynekulu, "The Emerging Monopolies of the TPLF," *Ethiopian Register* 3 (July 1996): 20–32.

4. Ibid. Unlike the EPLF, the TPLF has few generous contributors abroad; critics of the TPLF maintain that the Woyane buys support in Europe and North America by paying its supporters.

5. Ibid.

6. Ibid.

7. Ibid.

8. Editorial, "TPLF Inc.: From Rags to Riches," *Ethiopian Register* 3 (July 1996): 3; for an extensive profile of "the EPRDF business empire," including companies linked to the EPRDF, TPLF, ANDM, OPDO, and SEPDF, see Assefa Negash, "Ethiopian Non-Governmental Business, A Preliminary Survey, Part I: Companies Controlled by or Associated with EPRDF-Member Organizations," Amsterdam, September 1996.

9. Assefa Negash, "Ethiopian Non-Governmental Business, A Preliminary Survey," Amsterdam, September 1996, 7–9.

10. "Sheraton Addis Inaugurated," *Ethiopian Register* 5 (April 1998): 9–10.

11. "Addis Ababa Hosts International Business Forum," *Ethiopian Register* 5 (April 1998): 12–13.

12. Oromia Support Group, Newsletter, *Sagalee Haaraa* (March-May 1998), 2.

13. "The Emerging Monopolies of the TPLF," 23–24.

14. Ibid.

15. Awualom Aynekulu, "The Emerging Monopolies of the TPLF, Part II" *Ethiopian Register* 3 (August 1996): 14–22.

16. "The Emerging Monopolies of the TPLF," 24.

17. Ibid., 24–25.

18. Proclamation No. 46/1993.

19. "The Emerging Monopolies of the TPLF," 25.

20. "TPLF's Business Influence in the Financial Industry on the Rise," *Ethiopian Register* 4 (June 1997): 10–13; "The Emerging Monopolies of the TPLF, Part II," 18–21.

21. "Ethiopian Airlines Acknowledges for First Time Decline of its Income," *Ethiopian Register* 4 (September 1997): 6; "Ethiopian Airlines Marks Golden Jubilee Under Crisis," *Ethiopian Register* 3 (June 1996): 5.

22. "TPLF's Business Influence in the Financial Industry on the Rise," *Ethiopian Register* 4 (June 1997): 10.

23. Editorial, "The Perils of Ethnic Banking," *Ethiopian Register* 4 (August 1997): 3–6.

24. "Meles Off-Loads Some," *The Indian Ocean Newsletter*, 17 January 1998, reprinted in *Ethiopian Review* 8 (January-March 1998): 12.

25. "Highlights of Meles Zenawi's Press Statements," *Ethiopian Register* 5 (February 1998): 11–13, 14; "TPLF/EPRDF Congresses Wound Up without Addressing Crucial Political Issues," *Ethiopian Register* 5 (February 1998): 13–14.

26. Theodore M. Vestal, "Meles' Meeting with American Ethiopianists," *Ethiopian Register* 3 (February 1996): 20.

27. Stephen Buckley, "Africa's Agricultural Rebirth—Production Soars in Ethiopia, Others Recast Farm Policies," *Washington Post*, 25 May 1998, A18.

28. "Meles Announces Ethiopia is Self-Sufficient in Food Supply," *News from Ethiopia*, Embassy of Ethiopia, Washington, DC, February 1997.

29. "US Provides 25 Million in Food Aid," *News from Ethiopia*, Embassy of Ethiopia, Washington, DC, January 1998; "Over 4 Million Ethiopians Face Risk of Starvation," *Addis Tribune*, 5 December 1997, 1.

30. "Drought and Famine in Eastern and Southern Ethiopia," *Ethiopian Register* 4 (April 1997): 10, 13. Famine and food supply in Ethiopia are accessed generally in John Prendergast, *Peace, Development, and People of the Horn of Africa* (Washington, DC: Bread for the World, 1992).

31. "Meles' Meeting with American Ethiopianists," 20.

32. Awualom, 22.

33. Assefa Negash, *The Pillage of Ethiopia by Eritreans and their Tigrean Surrogates* (Los Angeles: Adey Publishing, 1996), 31–40.

34. Awualom, 22. In 1997 CAFPDE published figures showing investment share distribution in various regions of the country both in absolute and relative amounts. Tigray had by far the largest investment: over 2 billion Ethiopian birr accounting for 45 percent of the total. Addis Ababa came in a poor second with 886 million Ethiopian birr or 18.8 percent. CAFPDE, *Alternative* 1 (1997): 7.

35. Anonymous source in the U.S. Embassy in Addis Ababa, 2 July 1998.

36. "TPLF Inc.: From Rags to Riches," 3.

37. Ejigou Demissie, " 'Privatization' of Public Enterprises in Ethiopia: TPLF Style," *Ethiopian Register* 3 (April 1996): 23–27; *Addis Tribune*, 25 December 1998.

38. "Public Enterprises Worth 40 Billion Birr Ear-Marked for Privatization," *Ethiopian Register* 5 (April 1998): 14; by the end of 1998, The Ethiopian Privatization Agency had sold 176 nationalized enterprises totalling 2.5 billion Birr. *Addis Tribune*, 25 December 1998.

39. "TPLF Inc.: From Rags to Riches," 3.

CHAPTER 17

The Political Theory of the EPRDF

The leaders of the TPLF and EPRDF doubtlessly share a sense of historical mission, a belief in their own destiny as agents chosen to carry forward a program of profound social reconstruction of first Tigray, and then of Ethiopia. They view their "struggle" as not only changing who was in power but changing the system, an overthrow of the "exploiting classes" and a victory for the "exploited classes." The leaders are an intelligent group who have honed their political skills over time, learned from the mistakes of their predecessor governments of Ethiopia, and have adopted the best models furnished by the experience of former Marxist-Leninist regimes throughout the world. The Front's brand of post–Cold War socialism is a most comprehensive political doctrine. "Revolutionary Democracy" and the means of achieving it are spelled out in a large volume of documentation in which the Front's theoreticians give reasons that underlie their philosophical doctrines. Unfortunately, the party's documents, for the most part, are secret.

Thus, many parts of the EPRDF's political theory are closed to public investigation. Its content must be surmised from: (1) the content of a few of its secret documents that have come into the hands of the free press which has published them; (2) the public addresses or remarks of party leaders, especially Meles Zenawi; and (3) the writing of party members who describe activities of the party-in-government or defend them against critics. From these sources, what political theory of the Front emerges?

THE THEORY OF THE PARTY

The EPRDF's leaders agree that politics, not economics, is the fundamental agent of historical change. In the same way that Lenin led his party to power by endorsing the bitter resentment of the Russian underclass,[1] the EPRDF has sought to govern by playing upon animosities between Ethiopia's different ethnic groups.

The TPLF, originally dedicated to Tigrayan separatism, broadened its purpose when circumstances permitted and took on the mantle of liberator of the nation. But the Front was "left without any logical way of envisioning its collective future other than as a collection of liberated ethnic entities."[2] This necessitated the creation of ethnic "homelands" where none had existed before, the rewriting of Ethiopian history, and the derogation of nationalism. The Front also activated and neutralized "nations and nationalities" through its one-party rule and ingratiated itself to donor nations as a champion of democratization, social equality, and the self-determination of "peoples."[3]

Implicit in the writings of EPRDF leaders is a "victim mentality." The exploited masses that must be protected by the Front were victims of oppressors that include the monarchy, the Derg, the *neftegna* system, imperialism, or the Western-dominated worldwide course of modernization. It was the political incursion and economic exploitation by these oppressors that undermined the peoples' place in society and humiliated the ethnic "nations." The EPRDF contends that this victim status will not end until, through struggle, the goals of Revolutionary Democracy are realized. Such a perception makes it difficult for party leaders to compromise with those in the political opposition they view as "the elite" or "oppressors."

Leaders of the EPRDF, following in the steps of their hero Lenin, also believe that politics is the continuation of war by other means. The Prime Minister frequently uses battlefield analogies to describe political situations.[4] Party rhetoric emphasizes the struggle to realize the goals of Revolutionary Democracy, and political opposition is referred to as the enemy. In the EPRDF political wars, the Front has nearly all the arms and the opposition must be sworn to nonviolence. Because the state has a monopoly of force, the Woyane contend it ought to have a monopoly of loyalty as well. Anyone who looks like a potential opponent faces the possibility of being imprisoned or brutalized into silence.

The significant role played by the TPLF/EPRDF in defeating the armies of the Derg is rightfully memorialized as the chief point on the party's escutcheon, but the civil war is long over. Although it might be argued that sinister designs on the escutcheon's field, embodied as authoritarian governance, were necessary during the transition period, that four-year rite of passage has ended. Instead of using rhetoric and actions befitting a parliamentary democracy, EPRDF officials continue to use those appropriate for war making.

To attain political and economic goals, the EPRDF serves as an omniscient vanguard party made up of professional revolutionaries. The party's goal is the realization of Revolutionary Democracy built upon a new pragmatic economic system dictated by changing world conditions. The Front's leaders recognize the advantages of flexibility and have encouraged temporary deviations from the party's earlier goals. In the EPRDF Five Year Development Program, the leaders admit that toleration of capitalist activity is in a sense a retreat, but they never deny that they have lost interest in constructing socialism.

Revolutionary Democracy, like its predecessor doctrine, dialectical materialism, is an ideology of absolute truth understood correctly only by Meles and his comrades. A small elite of professional revolutionaries, subject to an authoritarian command structure and strict party discipline, anticipate the country's needs and best interests and lead the masses through the oxymoronic theory of "democratic centralism." Under this form of party governance, discussion of a topic ceases once a decision has been taken and orders from the center are binding. In EPRDF practice, centralist tendencies have always overwhelmed the democratic and participatory ones.

The Party's strength comes from selected, dedicated, indoctrinated, and rigidly disciplined cadre and members. Through placements in positions of power the Front works a leverage over society that will make up in power of coercion what it lacks in power of persuasion. In the bureaucracy, EPRDF cadre used prerogatives of ideological knowledge to brand political opponents as "enemies of the people" and remove them from office. Similar tactics are used to stifle dissenting opinions in the general public by condemning as dissidents those who think differently. Obeisance to party dogma is mandatory.

Nevertheless, the elite party seeks to mobilize the masses and draw them into participation in public life. For this purpose, it develops two means—organization and propaganda. To organize the masses, the Front creates a vast network of auxiliary organizations and associations extending into every field of endeavor. Cadre infiltrate all groups, and Front orthodoxies are strictly enforced through censorship and pressures to conform.

Propaganda activities are divided into long-range indoctrination and short-term arousal or agitation. The state's propaganda machine glorifies the Front as the active incarnation of class and ethnic consciousness whose strength is fed by the trust of the spontaneously oppressed masses and their "feeling that the party is the objectification of their will" (obscure though this notion may be to the masses).[5] The EPRDF's theory manifests a deep distrust of the masses, however, by excluding its members from a substantive influence over the decisions which affect them. Public opinion is irrelevant. Meaningful political debate takes place behind closed doors. The Woyane do not test their policies in a forum of free elections; instead, they mobilize and enforce consent. The population's political role is to turn out regularly and vote in favor of the party-selected candidates, including loyal and exceptionally diligent members for whom this is a reward.

Since the Front came to power in 1991, there have been three major developments relating to the EPRDF: (1) all other parties, not members of the Front, were suppressed; (2) the function of the Front changed from carrying out the revolution to that of governing the country; and (3) within the party itself, a small elite group from the TPLF Politburo exercised centralized control of the EPRDF by placing its most powerful members in key positions on the EPRDF Standing Committee, which set and executed policy.[6]

THE THEORY OF GOVERNANCE

In the TGE and FDRE certain principles remained more or less constant in the EPRDF pattern of governance. Chief among them were the extension of democratic centralism over the entire system of government; the priority of economic growth; the primacy of ethnic groups in a cultural revolution emphasizing nations, nationalities, and peoples rather than citizenship in a greater Ethiopia; and the willingness to apply terror, the threat of indiscriminate and unlimited violence against anyone suspected of dissenting from the party's will.

In government the party enforces its dictates on the populace with iron discipline. The individual is ground down by the all-encompassing power of the state. Revolutionary democracy frees individuals only for life in a thinly disguised one-party dictatorship that suppresses individual freedom in expectation of a future society to be liberated from poverty and backwardness.

The EPRDF set up a system based on a succession of party-dominated organizations in the countryside, villages, factories, and cities. This pyramid of associations in each constituent region culminates in the Council of Peoples' Representatives at the apex of the federal government. But while it appeared that the council exercised sovereign power, this body was actually governed by the EPRDF. The party and the state were one.

For the administration of the country, the relevant organization is the purported autonomous ethnic region, but again, central control over the killils is exercised by the Front. The party-in-government became a significant employer, the owner of substantial property, a large bureaucracy, and an institution from which millions of members and their families acquired a certain social status. In relations with the outside world, the Front has pursued the national interests of the state through fostering fruitful relations with governments of the capitalist countries and even with foreign investors of capital who are willing to play under the rules of the EPRDF's investment game.

By espousing the processes of democracy and the protection of human rights and by adopting a form of free-market capitalism, the Front now has the proper "hardware" for acceptance in the post–Cold War world of cyberspace. Unfortunately, it has little of the necessary "software"—the institutions of governance, constitutionalism, a watch-dog press, or independent courts, civil service, parliament, and police and security forces.[7]

In short, the EPRDF/FDRE, with its few pragmatic differences, is a palimpsest of the traditional communist party states of the twentieth century. The old Marxist-Leninist parchment has been reused with some of the earlier theoretical writing erased. Traditional communist states were defined in terms of four related characteristics. All based themselves on an official ideology, Marxism-Leninism, which was derived from the theories of Marx, Engels, and Lenin, and which provided the vocabulary of politics in the states as well as the basis on which the rulers claimed to exercise authority. Second, the states were ruled by a single communist party within which power was highly centralized. The third distinguishing feature was the party's control at all levels of a wide range of institutions, including the press, the trade unions, and the courts. Finally, the economy was largely or entirely in public ownership, in line with the Marxist doctrine that private ownership of productive resources involved the exploitation of workers by those who employed them.[8]

The EPRDF model of post–Cold War Marxism deviates from the traditional form in creating its own ideology of Revolutionary Democracy, a variation on a theme by Lenin; by not calling itself or its surrogates a communist party but ruling through a rigidly centralized power command; by directing society's institutions but also encouraging the formation of nominally autonomous associations that are dominated by the party; and by controlling the economy with a facade of private ownership in which "party capitalists" or "Revolutionary Democratic forces" invest as one individual in those economic sectors in which the state has no direct influence.[9] This is revisionism tinged with rue for the old line Marxists.

The leaders of the EPRDF are post–Cold War masters of illusion. They have answers for any question that might be raised about their political or economic activities—so long as one does not probe deeply the response.

For example: Question: Does the FDRE have democratic elections? Answer: Yes, and our elections have been declared "free and fair" by international observers who have watched the masses line up at designated polling places and put ballots in boxes.

Q: Do you have multi-party elections? A: Indeed we do, and we have sixty—count them—sixty political parties registered with the National Election Commission.

Q: Are human rights protected? A: Yes. Our constitution guarantees human and social rights, and the government is setting up a Human Rights Commission and Ombudsman to make sure their protections are enforced.

Q: Do you have a free press? A: Our legislature passed a proclamation establishing freedom of the press and the existence of private newspapers and magazines affirms its vitality.

Q: Are you liberalizing the economy? A: The government has opened the economy to foreign investment, especially in joint-ventures, and many state enterprises are being privatized.

All these replies appear logical and politically correct in EPRDF terms. But they are partial truths—accepted all too facilely by diplomats from donor nations. A more careful analysis merits a response of "Yes, but . . . " because the statements are misleading. In answering such questions, the Woyane adopts the FDRE attitude toward the available material. The action of such an attitude is rather like that of a sieve. Only what is relevant to the attitude gets through. The rest is thrown away. The real relevance and truth of what gets through the mesh then depends on the relevance and truth of the attitude. Leaders of the EPRDF have proved adept at using language to conceal rather than to reveal.[10] It has been convenient for them to find shelter behind a calculated lack of political definition. The Front's leaders personify the new form of authoritarianism, the "subtler tyrannies" of the post–Cold War world.[11]

NOTES

1. See, e.g., Alfred G. Meyer, "Leninism," in *The Oxford Companion to Politics of the World* ed. Joel Krieger, (New York: Oxford University Press, 1993), 356–358.

2. Donald N. Levine, "Paul Henze & the EPRDF," *Ethiopian Review* 5 (November 1995): 31–35.

3. Tesfaye Demmellash, "Reckoning with the Woyane Critique of Ethiopia: the Imperative of Counter-Criticism," *Ethiopian Register* 3 (September 1996): 16–20.

4. See, Theodore M. Vestal, "Yes, Prime Minister, But . . . : An Open Letter to Prime Minister Meles Zenawi," *Ethiopian Register* 2 (December 1995): 30–32.

5. The EPRDF's use of propaganda is similar to that of Lenin; see, Robert A. Dahl, *Preface to Democratic Theory* (Chicago: University of Chicago Press, 1956), 234.

6. "Colin Legum's Propaganda for the TPLF," *Ethiopian Register* 3 (May 1996): 10.

7. See Thomas L. Friedman, "Oops! Wrong War," *New York Times*, 7 April 1997.

8. See, e.g., Stephen White, "Communist Party States," in *The Oxford Companion to Politics of the World* ed. Joel Krieger, (New York: Oxford University Press, 1993), 167–169; see generally, Merle Fainsod, *How Russia is Ruled* (Cambridge, Mass: Harvard University Press, 1959).

9. See Worku Aberra, "Ethnicism: The Ideology of a *Worari* State," *Ethiopian Register* 4 (June 1997): 22.

10. See George Orwell, "Politics and the English Language," in *The Collected Essays, Journalism and Letters of George Orwell* eds. Sonia Orwell and Ian Angus, (London: Secker & Warburg, 1968), 127–140. Is the EPRDF's use of language a modern version of "wax and gold"?

11. See Robert D. Kaplan, "Was Democracy Just a Moment?" *Atlantic* 280 (December 1997): 55–80.

CHAPTER 18

Next Steps Towards Democracy

Since the FDRE came into being, the crypto-communists of the EPRDF have adroitly consolidated their hold on Ethiopia. Building from their base in Tigray, the Woyane have put into place many of the organizational structures and operations to accomplish the goals of "Revolutionary Democracy" envisioned in the Front's strategy document.

A SELF-EVALUATION OF THE EPRDF

Speaking before the Third Congress of the EPRDF in late 1997, Prime Minister Meles gave a progress report on the party's efforts in expanding its social base since the party's second congress five years earlier. The most extensive work had been done in the rural areas of the killils where the EPRDF was operating. According to Meles, the Front's organizational structure had improved in terms of the number and quality of its members. Areas controlled by the TPLF were the party's bulwark, but there were significant gains in areas where the ANDM and SEPDF were operating. Continued fighting in Oromiya and the resistance of the OLF appear to have challenged the Front to maintain "the quality of members of the OPDO." The party's main task will be to strengthen members of the EPRDF and to extend current rural organizational work into the towns. The Prime Minister reported that the EPRDF's outlook and views had been inculcated satisfactorily at the rural level although there were differences from place to place.

The Front found its political and organizational work in urban areas more difficult—especially in Addis Ababa and the towns of Oromiya. Intellectuals in towns had not been drawn into the organization, Meles contended, because the party had focused its efforts on rural areas where the EPRDF has had more experience and because some member organizations were "relatively young" and "did not have as much experience as others." The Prime Minister did report some success in towns in the Amhara and Tigray killils.[1]

The Front's achievements in organization were diminished by the continuing widespread discontent with many of the regime's policies. Although suppressed, the opposition remains a latent force resisting the EPRDF's hegemony. In rhetoric reminiscent of the Front's strategy document, Meles ruled out any reconciliation with opposition forces by declaring that the EPRDF will strengthen its struggle against those forces "who are trying to bring about changes in the constitutional system by opposing the constitution, by directly or indirectly violating the constitution and by applying pressure on the government through use of force or diplomatic means."[2] He did not elaborate on the meaning of "opposing or violating the constitution."

The Prime Minister had reason to be concerned about pressures on the government from diplomatic means or the use of force. The FDRE continued to face armed opposition from the OLF in the Oromo region and the Ogaden National Liberation Front in the Somali region. Anti-government violence by other groups, including the Ethiopian Unity Forces and the Ethiopian Patriotic United Front, also was reported, although their strength was not clear. In late 1997 government forces attacked the bases in Somalia of Al'ittihad, an Islamist organization which claimed responsibility for bombings in Ethiopia.[3] In general, the EPRDF seemed firmly entrenched and Prime Minister Meles secure in his leadership in early 1998.

WAR WITH ERITREA

In the spring of that year, however, a forceful surprise came from Meles' long time ally, the EPLF. Before Eritrea's independence, Meles and Issayas had agreed on an ambitious model of economic integration that would benefit both economies. Eritrea would develop its industries and use its ports to become an import and export zone, while Ethiopia would be the supplier of raw materials, agricultural goods such as teff and coffee, and foreign exchange. Both countries announced that all movement of people and goods would be entirely unfettered, and Ethiopia would have free access to Eritrea's ports. The birr, Ethiopia's currency, would be used in both nations.

Eritreans in large numbers flocked into neighboring Tigray and through-out Ethiopia where they bought goods with local currency and exported them in dollars.[4] Many Ethiopians, but especially the *nuevo conversos* of the EPRDF, resented this privileged access to Ethiopia's resources, prod-ucts and markets enjoyed by Eritrean businesses. In late 1997, when Eritrea introduced its own currency, the nafka, as part of a secret arrangement that Meles and Issayas had made to use the nakfa and the birr as legal tender in both countries, the *nuevo conversos* revolted. A strong faction within the TPLF forced Meles to renege on his deal and to require the use of hard cur-rency (U.S. dollars) in bilateral trade between Ethiopia and Eritrea.[5]

In Eritrea prices rose and commerce started slowing down. In reaction to what Eritreans saw as a Tigrayan-sponsored sabotage of the nafka, all im-port and export duties on Ethiopian-bound goods were raised. In turn, Ethiopia announced that instead of continuing to utilize Eritrean ports, it would use Djibouti as its main port—further depriving Eritrea of significant government revenues. This mutual economic strangulation led to the out-break of full-scale hostilities between the two states—disguised as a border dispute.[6]

On 12 May 1998 Eritrean forces occupied the rocky Badme triangle on the Tigrayan border. Both sides massed troops and heavy weapons at strate-gic sites along their common border. Within a month they locked in fierce battle and Eritrea and Ethiopia unleashed warplanes on bombing raids against each other.[7] Hundreds of soldiers were killed, up to 300,000 civil-ians were displaced, and economic activity on both sides of the border was disrupted. The conflict-related migration of tens of thousands of civilians from each side raised allegations of widespread human rights abuse, "ethnic cleansing," and "recurrent humanitarian problems."[8]

In late June, the two sides agreed to a cease-fire. Efforts by the United States and African nations to mediate a peace accord were of no avail, how-ever, and tensions along the border remained high Both Ethiopia and Eritrea continued a bitter propaganda war and spent hundreds of millions of dollars to buy planes, tanks, and artillery, mostly from Russia and Ukraine, as well as from China and France. U.S. officials estimated that 450,000 soldiers were massed along the border. In February and March 1999 hostilities flared again along fronts in Badme and Tsorona. As many as 15,000 battle-field casualties were reported in a bloody version of modern trench warfare. A nasty war of attrition continued, caused in part by what one observer called the two nations' "knack for stubbornness."

What started as a small war engineered by Eritrea largely for economic reasons provided Meles with an opportunity to shore up his ebbing home base support in Tigray. The Prime Minister had much to gain if he could successfully repulse outside aggression, recapture Ethiopian territory invaded by Eritrea, and demonstrate to the Ethiopian people and especially to the *nuevo conversos* that he was getting rid of EPLF dictation which had been the source of discord within the TPLF. To accomplish this, Meles took on the mantle of an Ethiopian nationalist, strange clothing indeed for the ethnic federalist. Further, the EPRDF leaders used the war as a means to call the whole nation to act in accordance with the will and terms of the Front. Of the opposition political parties, only the OLF openly sided with Eritrea during the fighting. While the internecine warfare raged between the old comrades at arms, concerned observers worried how either of the poor nations could afford a prolonged conflict.

DIPLOMATIC PRESSURES ON THE FDRE

Diplomatic pressures on the government of Ethiopia were building too. For the first time, Ethiopians in the diaspora succeeded in organizing major united political opposition groups, and their lobbying of host countries caused some to question the propriety of unconditioned development aid to Ethiopia.

In a report to Parliament, Meles articulated his response to those who would use the threat of reducing aid to pressure his government to improve its record in human rights or democratization. The Prime Minister stated that no one could force his government "to do what we do not believe in as a matter of principle. . . . It is futile to assume that if we do not believe in something as a matter of principle, a donor will force us to do so. It is not in our tradition to bow down to pressure."[9]

A NEW TURN IN RELATIONS WITH THE
UNITED STATES

"Is it possible that any villainy should be so dear?"
—*Much Ado About Nothing*, 3.3 109–110

"Well, a Horn for my money, when all's done."
—*Much Ado About Nothing*, 2.3 59–60

Meles' resolve apparently was tested when he attended a meeting of six East African leaders with President Clinton in Entebbe, Uganda in March 1998. The purpose of Clinton's tour of Africa was to promote a new American policy toward the continent with an emphasis on trade and investment.

In Entebbe, Meles, along with leaders of Kenya, Tanzania, Uganda, Rwanda, Congo, and the Organization of African Unity, signed an agreement to work toward building more democratic governments in their countries. The communique issued by the leaders contained vague pledges about protecting human rights and expanding trade. It also contained loopholes and caveats that would allow one-party rule like that of the EPRDF to continue. All that Meles really agreed to was to "pursue a dialogue on democratization" that "recognizes there is no fixed model for democratic institutions" and "explore alternative approaches to the democratic management of cultural diversity."[10]

In the talks Clinton indicated that he might support more debt relief for East African countries and promised to restore direct American aid to Africa to about $813 million a year. But in return Clinton made it clear that the United States expected economic and political changes that would insure human rights, expand their democracies, and create a stable environment for investors. Apparently, it was in response to such American expectations that Meles, along with Kenya's Daniel Arap Moi, bluntly told Clinton that "he should not try to tell them how to rule."[11]

Meles' hubris was surprising in light of the praise that had been bestowed upon him by Clinton. The President had spoken highly of Meles as one of a new generation of African leaders, who were more independent, more assertive, unfettered by the blinders of Cold War ideology, and pragmatically committed to economic and political reform.[12] Perhaps Clinton, himself, had been blunt in telling Meles to get his democratization act in order. Or perhaps Meles was playing to his gallery by standing up to the "imperialists."

The disagreement may reflect the Americans not only hailing "the new face of Africa"[13] but at the same time turning a new face towards Africa. In the post-cold war world, Muslim fundamentalism has been the center piece of Western foreign policy objectives toward Africa. That was the case in Ethiopia, where, immediately after the fall of the Derg, the United States seemed content to back the EPRDF as the best bet to maintain stability in the Horn and to serve as a counter to Islamic fundamentalism in the Sudan. Some American officials argued that the United States should not push Meles to strengthen the democratization process, either because authoritarianism is what Ethiopia needs, or because, as the U.S. Department of State maintains, the EPRDF has already put Ethiopia on the path toward democracy. But increasingly, American officials recognize that a stable world order is essential to the security of the United States and that this requires recognition of the causes of human insecurity, among them the lack of inclusiveness in democratic processes and abuse of human rights that lead to conflict.[14]

Stability and prosperity in Ethiopia and an optimal environment for western investment depend on the establishment of a more liberal and inclusive state in which a diversity of interests can bargain, share, and alternate power with each another. While it is in American interest to work closely with Ethiopia to deal with the Sudan, the viability of such a policy is at risk so long as Meles presides over a divided and unstable polity.

The U.S. strategy appears to be based on supporting and continuing cooperation with the Meles government while maintaining pressure on the EPRDF to improve the democratization process in order to sustain the country's limited progress. As we have seen, the theory, strategy, and practice of the EPRDF limit the possibility that meaningful reforms will be made, however. The most trenchant possibility for moving the Front to strengthen the rule of law and transparency and accountability of government, to respect human rights, and to ensure electoral competition, is through tying U.S. developmental aid to such improvement.

The Clinton administration has pointed out that democratization and the rule of law are good for business and economic investment. As the President put it: "Freedom is a powerful engine of progress."[15] Business leaders as well as human rights organizations have argued that "economic development—particularly the alleviation of poverty—is best served when people are free to band together and speak out about threats to their well-being." In addition, a foreign policy that places a high priority on human rights encourages resolution of disputes through dialogue and institution-building.[16]

Critics of a human rights foreign policy worry that it will undermine U.S. relations with a strategic "frontline state" bordering the Sudan. The choice between the promotion of human rights and democracy on the one hand, and a concern for regional stability on the other, however, is a false dichotomy. The United States can pursue both. The vigorous promotion of democracy will not damage the bilateral relationship with Ethiopia or compromise other foreign policy goals.[17] It is in Ethiopia's strategic interest to join the United States in containing the Sudan, and Meles may grumble but he will not jump ship simply because the United States continues to urge further democratization in his nation.

Until the president's African tour, the Clinton administration had swept aside the criticism that while the United States is genuinely committed to Africa's economic development, Washington had been glossing over abusive human rights practices of its allies such as Ethiopia, Rwanda, and Uganda. The United States defended its continued involvement with repressive regimes as "constructive engagement," ironically the same term used to justify contact with South Africa under apartheid in the 1980s.[18]

Constructive engagement with a new emphasis on human rights and democracy might make U.S. policy more compelling, and it would be morally right. Indeed, the most visible U.S. policy approach to human rights has been stopping egregious violations, particularly assaults on the physical integrity of individuals such as arbitrary arrests, torture, and political killings.[19] In such cases, the United States leads by example and uses its considerable diplomatic resources to create a coherent way of controlling human rights abuses. Washington's policy of constructive engagement should be backed by a clear and unequivocal authoritative statement as to what it expects of the relationship. The statement should declare that the United States expects Ethiopia to become a more open and freer country. The important factor is to stop ignoring repression and abuses in Ethiopia. Such a policy might well be emulated by other donor nations that have expressed concern about Ethiopia's deficits of democracy and human rights abuses.

In his remarks during a tour of the People's Republic of China in June 1998, President Clinton, perhaps unknowingly, set an agenda for a human rights approach towards Ethiopia and other nominally allied nations ruled by autocrats. He declared personal freedom the mandate of the twenty-first century. "We are convinced that certain rights are universal," the President said. "I believe that everywhere, people aspire to be treated with dignity, to give voice to their opinions, to choose their own leaders, to associate with whom they wish, to worship how, when, and where they want."[20]

Many of Clinton's statements made to the Peking University audience about human rights and democracy apply directly to Ethiopia and its relations with the United States. For example, at Peking, the President said, "We believe, and our experience demonstrates, that freedom strengthens stability." To paraphrase the President's comment on China, Ethiopia's "greatest source of strength resides in the minds and hearts of its citizens. It is profoundly in your interest—and the world's—that those minds be free to reach the fullness of their potential."[21] Can the Clinton administration be held to extend such lofty goals to its policy toward Ethiopia?

So long as the United States claims leadership of the free world, it should evince a keen interest in democracy in foreign nations. To walk away from those who believe in America and the ideas it represents to those who demean democracy and crush human rights is, of course, betrayal of United States history and promise. This is especially the case in Ethiopia, where generations were taught by dedicated American teachers or worked in U.S.-led businesses; and where many Ethiopians, when forced to leave their homeland, demonstrated their affinity for the United States by going there to live in far larger numbers than any other place. Ethiopians literally have voted for the American way with their feet. For such trusting friends, must the United States continue to look the other way when Ethiopia's rulers make a mockery of democratic processes and commit gross indecencies against their people? Why must the United States give the tyrannical zealots of the EPRDF so much honor, respectability, and absolution—all simply for playing a role in averting instability in the Horn and for holding the line against terrorist alliances and Islamic fundamentalism? The Cold War is over and the Kissinger-inspired idea that Americans should support authoritarian rulers because they could assure stability is a thing of the past. The United States does not have to condone savagery, much less assist it.[22] Why can't the United States, in its foreign policy towards Ethiopia, live up to its own concepts and principles and show moral fortitude? If the Clinton administration would match its actions in Ethiopia with the President's rhetoric in China, it could.

THE UNITED OPPOSITION

Meanwhile, some Ethiopians in the diaspora, who with good reason are less than sanguine about the help of the United States in bringing democracy to Ethiopia, have acted. They believe that they are compelled to deal with their own problems rather than relying on external forces. Three organizations, the International Ethiopian Action Committee for Unity and Democracy (IEAC), the Ethiopian National Congress (ENC), and the Coalition of Ethiopian Opposition Political Organizations (CEOPO), especially have made notable strides in uniting political opposition activities.

The IEAC

The IEAC, a non-partisan Ethiopian patriotic movement, came into being in April 1997. It is dedicated to the promotion of Ethiopia's "national interest" for unity, democracy, development, respect for human rights and the rule of law. The IEAC, composed of a group of 100 activists, most of them residents in the United States, has successfully organized demonstrations in eleven countries protesting the dictatorial policies of the EPRDF. Truth squads or *yeiwnet budin* of the Action Committee have challenged EPRDF spokesmen and their American apologists in public meetings in North America and London, and the IEAC has been an effective counter to EPRDF propaganda activities overseas.[23] For the Action Committee, truth is tyranny's ultimate vulnerability. The Woyane may be a particularly hard case, but, in the end, they will not be immune to the veracity of the IEAC.

The IEAC's political actions would be pointless unless they were grounded in sound theory.[24] The ancients have said that snow covers Mount Ras Deshan, not because it is so high but because it is so deep. What is extremely high is deep. So too must the high aspirations of the Action Committee show profound depth in its theories. Thus, it is important for the IEAC to develop a meaningful declaration of principles. For a start, there should be agreement that: 1) government should exist to provide economic security for the people and to put an end to the suffering caused by poverty, disease, and famine; 2) a united and democratic Ethiopia should be governed by representatives of the people chosen in fair multiparty elections; 3) the government should function under prospective, publicly articulated rules that protect the citizen's human rights and do not institutionalize the dominance of one ethnic group over another; 4) the government of the EPRDF has not performed these tasks according to the will of the Ethiopian people; and 5) therefore a united opposition should persevere in a sustained act of public relations to keep the image of a deserving, suffering, nondemocratic Ethiopia so well illumined that public opinion in the donor nations, representing respect for the values of democracy and human rights, will be brought to bear on changing the conditions of governance in the FDRE.[25]

The Action Committee is making headway in articulating such a declaration of principles acceptable to Ethiopians of good will as well as propounding the opposition's vision of a post-EPRDF Ethiopia. Members of the IEAC, frustrated in missing the chance to found a new democratic government and civic society in 1991, want to be prepared when the next opportunity arises.

The ENC

The much larger, popularly-based ENC was established in Atlanta in October 1997 and serves as a forum to bring Ethiopians together in a united front in the struggle for national survival against the EPRDF regime. Members are committed to a united and democratic Ethiopia that is governed by the rule of law and that does not institutionalize the dominance of one ethnic group over any other. The ENC in pledged to creating a meaningful connection between politics in the diaspora and the reality of events in Ethiopia. The organization marshalls human and other resources for this task but does not vie for political power or engage in partisan politics as a member of the opposition.[26] The ENC is composed of a "Congress" that represents all Ethiopians who support Ethiopian unity and a "Senate" composed of groups opposed to the ethnic policies of the FDRE. The wish of the ENC is "that they may all be one," *ut unum sint* as Ethiopians.

The Second Congress of the ENC held in May 1998 passed resolutions: 1) condemning TPLF and EPLF policies that have promoted individual prosperity and party interests of the Woyane while dividing and ruling the nation on the basis of ethnicity and conflict instigation; 2) objecting to the deaths and displacement of Ethiopians due to the war between the TPLF and EPLF; 3) demanding the release of all political prisoners and the proper medical care for Professor Asrat; 4) noting the duplicity in the government's establishing of a human rights commission while denying recognition to human rights organizations set up by ordinary citizens; 5) requesting Western governments, especially the United States, international financial and economic institutions, and other donors to stop the unreserved financial support they give to the tyrannical regime; 6) appealing to opposition parties "to make a common stand and to give the appropriate response to the requests that the Ethiopian public is making" in regard to the fighting between the TPLF and EPLF; 7) pleading to religious leaders, both inside and outside Ethiopia, to excommunicate those causing bloodshed in the fighting in northern Ethiopia; and, 8) calling on Ethiopians in the diaspora to join with the ENC in bringing together all the political parties and national and regional groups in opposition to the repressive twin regimes of the TPLF and EPLF.[27]

The ENC builds upon earlier efforts by Ethiopians to bring together associations, groups, and individuals in a uniting umbrella opposition organization. In 1991 the Coalition of Ethiopian Democratic Forces (COEDF) was formed from a number of fronts active when the Derg fell. COEDF in turn was one of forty-two opposition groups that in 1993 organized the Council of Alternative Forces for Peace and Democracy in Ethiopia (CAFPDE) which has its headquarters in Addis Ababa under the close surveillance of the EPRDF. CAFPDE was followed by the Ethiopian Unity Coordinating Committee (EUCC) organized in 1994 to unify opposition political parties "devoted to unity-in-diversity of the Ethiopian people and state." In 1996 EUCC led almost all of the opposition political groups in signing an agreement creating the Alliance for Democracy and National Unity in Ethiopia (ADNUE) and in creating a Shengo of Ethiopian civic organizations from throughout the United States and Canada.[28] All of these predecessor organizations, in their unique ways, contribute to the idea of unity, and their experience informs the work of the ENC.[29]

Most of the significant opposition groups have responded to the ENC's invitation to join the umbrella organization. Among those represented at a September 1998 meeting in Bethesda, Maryland to plan the organization of the "Senate" were the pan-Ethiopian COEDF, the Ethiopian Democratic Unity Patriotic United Front, SEPDC, the Afar Revolutionary Democratic

Unity Front (ARDUF), the Tigray Alliance for National Democracy (TAND), the Gambella National Democratic Alliance (GNDA), and Moa Anbessa, a party advocating a constitutional monarchy. This "group of seven" passed a Joint Declaration of Principles of Ethiopian Opposition Organizations" that articulated the goal of unity, democracy, and justice for the Ethiopian people and opposed "the policies of the EPRDF, which deny respect for democratic rights and practice favoritism among citizens" under the divisive structure of ethnic federalism.[30]

To promote harmony between member groups, the ENC has offered such organizations flexibility to follow different approaches to express their aspirations. Habte Giorgis Churnet, one of the architects of the ENC, foresees the development of "conservative" and "liberal" political parties as well as ethnic-based parties as discordant elements are blended in the processes of the Senate.[31]

The ENC offers a compelling image of Ethiopia's future. They have created a popular coalition organized in such a way that different ethnic, linguistic, and religious groups can work together. Thus, the ENC reflects and serves the diverse purposes of all groups and interests within it. The creation of the ENC was made possible by the major opposition forces being willing to compromise and to agree upon an institutional structure that provides a reasonable guarantee that their interests will not be affected in a highly adverse manner in the course of democratic competition. Agreements about institutions were achieved, even though the opposition groups involved had conflicting interests and visions, because institutions shape the opportunities of realizing specific interests and the groups involved understand that institutions have this effect.[32] In doing this, the Congress has modified the signature industry of the nation: obstreperousness. The factories that formerly produced nothing but arguments and negativity among the opposition now are turning out substantive positive products. As the Bethesda "Senate" meeting proclaimed: "We have more in common than we have previously appreciated."[33]

With the basic agreement reached, opposition groups started talking about issues that bind rather than fracture. The parties involved evinced a new spirit of leadership and a new culture learned in the ways of democracy. This was a major accomplishment for the leaders of opposition groups, who must hold their followers' loyalty but not reproduce their uncompromising attitudes in negotiating with others. The leaders agreed that the procedures of democracy allow for divergent outcomes and that they locate commonalities on the way to difference.[34] In doing this, participants have shown a generosity of spirit to open themselves to such frank and serious discussions.

The opposition parties have demonstrated a commitment to "working for a state of affairs where most agree on fundamentals where their lives impinge on one another, and are prepared to exercise forbearance and adopt democratic means of resolving disputes where they do not agree."[35] This has required them to listen to what others have to say and to be willing to accept reasonable accommodations or alterations in their own views. As a result, the deliberations of the ENC have increased the rigor, coherence, and clarity of its programs.

The spirit of compromise among opposition groups is a necessary but not sufficient condition for the ENC. Equally important is the removal of divisive issues from the coalition's agenda.[36] Instead of trying to resolve a century's residue of hatred and grudges, can the opposition impose upon itself a strategic self-censorship, a cleverly formulated gag rule to shift attention away from areas of discord and toward areas of concord? Can they use what John Rawls calls "the method of avoidance" to leave selected topics undiscussed for what they consider their own advantage?[37] By tying their tongues about the sensitive questions that divide them, the opposition can secure forms of cooperation and unity otherwise beyond their reach.

Sometimes important objectives can only be achieved so long as they are left unspoken. This is common practice in liberal democratic states where members of political parties, in order to present a united front, refrain from publicizing their internal conflicts, or where legislators refuse to officially discuss questions which, if placed under the control of electoral majorities, would be detrimental to the common good.

The Coalition of Ethiopian Opposition Political Organizations

Also in September 1998 eight political opposition groups (COEDF, ARDUF, SEPDC, TAND (all of whom also are members of the "Senate" of the ENC), CAFPDE, MEDHIN, the Tigray-Tigrayan Ethiopians for Social Democracy (TTESD), and the Oromo National Congress (ONC)) met in Paris to form CEOPO. At the meeting designated Paris II to differentiate it from the Paris I conference held in 1993, Dr. Beyene Petros of CAFPDE and SEPDC was elected chairman of the new group that is committed to creating a democratic environment in Ethiopia whereby a government may be established by the free vote of citizens. CEOPO was organized in anticipation of member groups' participating in parliamentary elections in the year 2000. Although CEOPO soft-pedaled the government's policy of killilization, its goals were similar to those of the ENC: a commitment to democracy, the rule of law, and respect for human rights; recognition of the multiethnic nature of the Ethiopian population and the importance of defending Ethiopia's sovereignty and unity; acceptance of a federal system based on democratic equality rather than on ethnic separation; and the necessity of a multiparty system.[38] On 31 January 1999 the CEOPO held a rally in Addis Ababa to condemn Eritrean aggression against Ethiopia and to urge the EPRDF government to positively respond to the oppositions' call for national dialogue.

The similarities in the goals of CEOPO and the ENC are encouraging signs that the two major coalitions might merge. Such a truly united front, with diversity and inclusiveness in membership and with clearly stated objectives, would be in position to carry on a national dialogue with the EPRDF to ensure a transition to a genuine multi-party democracy. The Eritrean border dispute with its concomitant conflict between Meles and Issayas provides the opportunity for such a national dialogue. But a meaningful dialogue will come only from an opposition organization of such collective strength and dedication to shared principles that the EPRDF can ignore it only at its own peril.

One of the most divisive issues a united opposition must face is the question of secession or the "national question," in the rhetoric of the Woyane. This issue especially is pertinent to the country's largest ethnic group, the Oromo. Although many Oromo support the idea of one nation, the OLF, with its goal of an independent Oromia, has so far remained aloof from union with other opposition groups.[39] Critics of the OLF's go-it-alone attitude believe that it plays into the EPRDF's divide and rule strategy. Without doubt, the presence of an association of Oromo, the Oromo National Congress, has enhanced greatly the work of the united opposition.

Modern Ethiopian history is replete with examples of admired achievements when Oromo and other ethnic groups have cooperated in common cause: the victory over the Italians at Adwa; the nationalist resistance to Mussolini's fascism; the struggle against feudalism; and the patriotic resistance to the Derg. A new synthesis of political action by Oromo with other freedom-loving Ethiopians would provide a sharp challenge to the EPRDF regime.[40]

By joining other opposition groups in a united front, the Oromo have demonstrated that they share a reasonable political conception of justice or a core morality with other Ethiopians. This core morality, based on basic tenets of the Judeo-Christian-Islamic traditions, is differently elaborated in the cultures of the various ethnic groups.[41] But the core commonalties are the basis on which public discussion of fundamental political questions can proceed and be reasonably decided, not of course in all cases, but in most cases of constitutional essentials and matters of basic justice.[42] From that base, Ethiopians could develop social cooperation "guided by publicly recognized rules and procedures that those cooperating accept and regard as properly regulating their conduct."[43] This would be a major change from the socially coordinated activity of the past in which orders were issued by the Emperor, the Derg, the EPRDF, or some central authority.

By agreeing to cooperate and to accept certain liberal principles of justice as a way of operating, Ethiopians could fashion a workable alternative to the endless and destructive civil strife that has plagued them during the past quarter century. Central to such an alternative are the promotion of tolerance and understanding among ethnic groups and religions and a deep respect for everything that would constitute "otherness," a respect acquired from understanding the positive values in other cultures.[44] In the same way that Ethiopians can inherit the pain and guilt of earlier generations, so too can they inherit understanding, civility, and grace in dealing with others. The participation of Oromo is a significant factor in such an effort.

The opposition can utilize its scarce resources more effectively if Oromo, Somali, and other groups dodge the irksome issues of unity or secession—at least for the time being. If they possess the talent and will, opposition leaders can then negotiate a settlement—a system of power sharing and mutual accommodation in the interest of all major factions. By cultivating the arts of omission, opposition leaders may liberate the deliberative sense of the community, the opinions the majority holds when it discusses matters in a consecutive, disciplined, fact-minded and thoughtful way.[45] By postponing the discussion of its most divisive issues, the opposition might increase its capacity to solve the underlying problems when they can no longer be repressed—after a democratic government is established in Ethiopia.

It is the establishment of such a government that should be the overriding mission of the opposition. How to bring about such a change is the most salient and troublesome question facing those concerned with bringing democracy to Ethiopia. At the very time donor governments are signaling an interest in partnership and the need for more mature relations based on mutual self-interest with Ethiopia, it is evident that a major part of the citizenry no longer consents to and indeed rejects the current political order.[46] The Christian Science Monitor cites experts who suggest that Meles' "government has the backing of only 5 percent of the population."[47] In these circumstances, political prudence alone, as well as a commitment to the principle of democracy and active promotion of democratization, demands that the donor nations not commend a regime whose legitimacy is in dispute but rather that they strive to establish conditions that allow better reasoning about the proper reconstruction of the political order. A united ENC and CEOPO, a national democratic coalition accepted as a legitimate voice of opposition, could bring pressure to bear on the donor nations to seek such peaceful change.

If it were the best of all possible worlds, this could be done by bringing together the government of Ethiopia and the opposition in structured discussions to create the climate for the restoration of conditions in which all parties can reason fairly and honestly about the proper reconstruction of the constitutional order so that the daunting tasks facing the government of Ethiopia can be pursued with the support of and according to the will of the Ethiopian people. But is a negotiated transition to democracy a possibility?

The stereotypical EPRDF member is seen as an obdurate, hard core Marxist-Leninist who would not budge a centimeter on maintaining sole governing power in the narrowly based, highly repressive regime. Is it possible, however, that within the government of the FDRE, there are forces that would enter into peaceful negotiation if that were seen as the most promising framework for the realization of their interests? Cracks in the facade of TPLF/EPRDF unyielding unity appeared in the responses of some members to secret economic deals between Meles and Issayas and to the fighting that erupted between Ethiopia and Eritrea. Increasing numbers of Tigrayans question the TPLF's divisive politics and collaboration with the EPLF. They fully realize that Meles and Issayas have not brought peace to their countries nor have they won legitimacy in large sections of the population.[48]

Would some of the current rulers opt for democratic compromise if faced with the alternative of an open, possibly violent, conflict and of a democratic solution which requires compromise but provides security? Are there moderate members of the government sufficiently concerned about their private economic interests as to see virtue in negotiation? If such principals are absent or cannot act, then establishing a democratic government in Ethiopia may be possible only if the dictatorship is defeated by force.[49] A peaceful route to change would be preferable, and a united ENC/CEOPO, a truly national democratic coalition composed of the united opposition can pave the way.

ENDING THE CONSPIRACY OF SILENCE AND BRINGING ABOUT CHANGE

Open the bonds of wickedness, dissolve the groups that pervert justice, let the oppressed go free, and annul all evil decrees. . . . Then your light will burst forth like the dawn.

—Isaiah

Until 1998 the story of Ethiopia under EPRDF rule remained generally unreported or overlooked by most of the world, unlike the stories of Tibet, Burma, and South Africa where Nobel Peace Prize winners have vividly dramatized the plight of their people. Instead, Ethiopia suffered from a conspiracy of silence. Representatives of donor nations, playing to their own strategic interests, are among the conspirators, as are some journalists and academicians.

Ethiopians of the diaspora are vociferous critics of the regime, but their jeremiads are ignored or downplayed as part of the conspiracy. All too often, as they rage against the dying of the light that was Ethiopia, they are talking to sympathizers, and the difficulty of making themselves heard is intensified by many Westerners' indifference to or ignorance of events in Africa. Within Ethiopia, those who have maintained their powers of integrity and their capacities of independent judgment,[50] well know that they can speak out against the government only with caution. As South African playwright, Athol Fugard says, "It's always like that when there is a very powerful, repressive government in place. People are frightened to talk, frightened to see what is happening around them."[51] Under such circumstances, it has been arduous to make known the story of the EPRDF's tyranny.

Cracks in the conspiracy of silence appeared when the tragedy of unintended consequences overtook the EPRDF leaders. President Clinton's visit to East Africa threw a spotlight on the murky underpinnings of the "new generation of African leaders." A few American journalists from the mainstream press joined British colleagues from the BBC and the *Economist* in giving a fair critique of the state of democracy and human rights in the FDRE.[52] The later border squabble between Ethiopia and Eritrea drew further journalistic probes into the records and motivations of the ruling parties of the two nations. Belatedly, the coverage of U.S. media went beyond official pronouncements of the Ethiopian government or the craftily worded apologia of U.S. diplomats.

Exposed was the blatant record of the EPRDF's tyrannical rule by fear. Opened for investigation was what one Ethiopian journalist has called the EPRDF/TPLF's "insidious, all-encompassing, relentless war" on Ethiopia.[53] Ready for further analysis are the weapons—legal, educational, judicial, economic, political, diplomatic, ideological, and military—used by the Front to reduce Ethiopia into "a collection of weak and dependent ethnic homelands."[54] And open to question is the need for United States and Western acquiescence in EPRDF repression—the compost of secret treacheries that are an integral part of diplomatic relations.

With the conspiracy of silence broken, freedom-loving Ethiopians can hope for a more empathetic response to their appeals for support. It should be made clear that there is an alternative to ethnic fundamentalism: that it is democracy with concomitant protection of human and civil rights; political pluralism and dialogue; freedom from harassment, imprisonment, and assassination for one's convictions; free elections; and an independent judiciary.[55] Who, knowing the context of the argument could disagree with the right of the Ethiopian people to decide whether to opt for democracy or to continue with the problematic ethnic federalism?

The lack of freedom of choice has plagued Ethiopians during the twentieth century. The monarchy, the Derg, and the EPRDF have all been self-anointed rulers, who, once in power, have never given the people an opportunity to change the government. It is for such an opportunity to be available to Ethiopians that the opposition political parties make their case. By letting the people decide for themselves what governing arrangements they want, there is hope for a well-ordered Ethiopian society. Then Ethiopia can get on with fulfilling its destiny as the jewel in the crown of Africa. Then there will be a better chance for the government to provide economic security for the people and alleviate the suffering caused by poverty and disease. Then at last the nation can put away its image as a famine-wracked land and become the breadbasket of Africa that it is capable of being.

The people planning this democratic transformation will need wisdom, ability, and vision to create such a society. They also must be carefully prepared and imminently resourceful. Changing the nation's political culture will not be easy. The hard road ahead to democracy will traverse conflict, bargaining and compromise, reverses, new attempts at reform, and possibly violence.[56]

But a critical mass of Ethiopians share a sacred hunger for democracy. They tire of a leavening of malice in their daily bread. With opposition at home and abroad finally organized, pressures for democratic change will mount on the government. An increasingly threatened regime may become overly repressive in an attempt to survive. That will invite a return to civil war. The alternatives make a negotiated attempt at establishing a liberal democracy all the more attractive.

Meanwhile, Ethiopia, having completed its transition from one Marxist-Leninist regime to another, limps on, wearing the thick boot of authoritarianism at the end of one leg, and the iron of ethnic hatred on the other.

NOTES

1. "Highlights of Meles Zenawi' Press Statements," *Ethiopian Register* 5 (February 1998): 11–13.

2. "TPLF/EPRDF Congresses Wound Up Without Addressing Crucial Political Issues," *Ethiopian Register* 5 (February 1998): 13–14; "Government Entertains Opposition Advancing Cause Peacefully: Meles," *Ethiopian Herald*, 27 May 1997, 1, 5.

3. Bureau of Democracy, Human Rights, and Labor, "Ethiopia Country Report on Human Rights Practices for 1997," U.S. Department of State, Washington, DC, 30 January 1998.

4. Lara Santoro, "At the Root of an Odd African War: Money," *Christian Science Monitor*, 22 June 1998; see also, Editorial, "Nakfa and the Transfer of Ethiopia's Wealth to Eritrea," *Ethiopian Register* 4 (December 1997): 2–4.

5. Editorial, "Meles Must Go," *Ethiopian Register* 5 (July 1998): 2–3.

6. "The Economic Causes and Implications of the Ethio-Eritrean War," *Addis Tribune*, Week of 15 June 1998; for the FDRE's explanation of the war, see "The Eritrean Aggression on Ethiopia: A Tragic Turn of Events Leaves the Nation Shocked," *News from Ethiopia*, Embassy of Ethiopia, Washington, DC, June/July 1998.

7. "Ethio-Eritrean Border Dispute on the Brink of an All-out War," *Ethiopian Register* 5 (July 1998): 5–12; United Nations, "IRIN Report on the Eritrea-Ethiopia Conflict," 29 October 1998.

8. EHRCO, "Human Rights Violations Resulting from Eritrean Aggression," Special Report No. 22, 24 August 1998; Ian Fisher, "Behind Eritrea-Ethiopia War, a 'Knack for Stubborness'," *New York Times*, 14 February 1999, 3; Karl Vick, "Old Tactics, New Arms, Lethal Result," *Washington Post*, 31 March 1999, A25.

9. "Highlights of TPLF's Prime Minister Bi-Annual Report to Parliament," *Ethiopian Register* 4 (March 1997): 11–13.

10. James C. McKinley, Jr., "Six Leaders in East Africa Agree to Build Democracies," *New York Times*, 26 March 1998.

11. *The Economist*, 4 April 1998, 53.

12. See David F. Gordon, Overseas Development Council, "Democracy in Africa: The New Leaders," Testimony Before the Senate Committee on Foreign Relations Subcommittee on Africa, 19 March 1998; R. W. Apple, Jr., "Uganda Could be Model for New Africa's Goals," *New York Times*, 26 March 1998.

13. "Clinton Hails the 'New Face of Africa'," *Tulsa World*, 24 March 1998.

14. Felice D. Gaer, "Human Rights: What Role in U.S. Foreign Policy?" *Great Decisions* (New York: Foreign Policy Association, 1998), 31.

15. John M. Broder, "Clinton, in Final China Speech, Calls for Defense of Personal Freedom," *New York Times*, 29 June 1998.

16. Gaer, 32.

17. See Gordon, Testimony.

18. Rich Mkhondo, *The Star*, Johannesburg, 8 January 1998.

19. Gaer, 35.

20. John M. Broder, "Clinton, in Final China Speech, Calls for Defense of Personal Freedom," *New York Times*, 29 June 1998.

21. Ibid.

22. See Anthony Lewis, "Their Suharto and Ours," *New York Times*, 25 May 1998.

23. International Ethiopian Action Committee for Unity and Democracy, "Highlights of Accomplishments," June 1998; "Ethiopians in the Diaspora Protest Against the Repressive Rule of the TPLF," *Ethiopian Register* 4 (July 1997): 8–12; "Ethiopians Protest U.S. Support to the TPLF Dictatorial Regime," *Ethiopia Review* 8 (January-March 1998): 14–15.

24. Keith Grahamm, *The Battle of Democracy* (Brighton, Sussex: Wheatsheaf, 1986), 1.

25. See Theodore M. Vestal, "The Need for United Political Opposition in Ethiopia," *Ethiopia Review* 5 (April1995): 38–39.

26. Habte Giorgis Churnet, "Inauguration of the First Ethiopian National Congress," *Ethiopian Register* 4 (November 1997): 4–7; Yohannes Assefa, "Interview with Dr. Tsehai Berhane-Selassie, Vice Chairwoman, Ethiopian National Congress," *Ethiopia Review* 7 (November-December 1997): 26, 28–29.

27. "The Second Congress of the Ethiopian National Congress (ENC)," *Ethiopian Register* 5 (July 1998): 16–19.

28. "EUCC Created Shengo," *Ethiopia Review* 6 (November 1996): 11.

29. Editorial, "Unity as a Recurrent Theme," *Ethiopian Register* 4 (November 1997): 2.

30. "Opposition Forces to Form Unity?" *Ethiopian Register* 5 (October 1998): 6–7.

31. Habte Giorgis Churnet, "The United Front and its Political Parties," *Ethiopian Register* 5 (September 1998): 35–36.

32. Stephen Holmes, "Gag Rules or the Politics of Omission," in *Constitutionalism and Democracy* eds. Jon Elster and Rune Slagstad, (Cambridge, UK: Cambridge University Press), 70.

33. Ethiopian National Congress, "Joint Declaration of Principles of Ethiopian Opposition Organizations," Bethesda, MD, 6 September 1998 (published in English), "Opposition Forces to Form Unity?" *Ethiopian Register* 5 (October 1998): 6–7; (Amharic) "For Your File," 36.

34. Michael Walzer, *Thick and Thin: Moral Argument at Home and Abroad* (Notre Dame, IN: Notre Dame University Press, 1994), 15.

35. Robert Dahl, *Democracy and Its Critics* (New Haven: Yale University Press, 1989), 242.

36. Holmes, 19–20.

37. John Rawls, *A Theory of Justice* (Cambridge, MA: Belknap Press of Harvard University Press, 1971).

38. Editorial, "A National Dialogue," *Ethiopian Register* 5 (November 1998): 2–3; "From Paris I to Paris II: the Formation of CEOPO," 14, 16–17; CEOPO, "Points of Understanding and Resolutions of the 2nd Paris Conference of Ethiopian Opposition Political Organizations," Paris, 13 September 1998, 29–30; "Opposition Forces Hold Mass Rally in Addis Ababa," *Ethiopian Register* 6 (March

1999): 9–10; Ethiopian National Congress, "Joint Statement of Ethiopian Opposition Political Organizations," *Ethiopian Register* 6 (June 1999): 32–33.

39. See Edmond J. Keller, "The Ethnogenesis of the Oromo Nation and Its Implications for Politics in Ethiopia," *Journal of Modern African Studies* 33 (December 1995): 621– 635; Herbert S. Lewis, "The Development of Oromo Political Consciousness from 1958 to 1994," in *Being and Becoming Oromo: Historical and Anthropological Enquiries* eds. P. T. W. Baxter, Jan Hultin, and Alessandro Triulzi, (Lawrenceville, NJ: Red Sea Press, 1996), 37–47; Mohammed Hassen, "The Development of Oromo Nationalism," Ibid., 67–80; Asafa Jalata, *Oromia and Ethiopia: State Formation and Ethnonational Conflict, 1868–1992* (Boulder, CO: L. Rienner, 1993); Vanni Cappelli, "The Oromo of Ethiopia—Africa's Nation Manquée," *Horn of Africa* 15 (December 1997): 81–91.

40. See, Busha Taa, "A Call for Oromo Deliberation," *Ethiopian Register* 5 (October 1998): 29–30. For historical background, see Donald Levine, *Greater Ethiopia*.

41. See Walzer, 1–7.

42. John Rawls, *Political Liberalism* (New York: Columbia University Press, 1993), xxi.

43. Rawls, *Political Liberalism*, 16.

44. Vaclav Havel, "The Charms of NATO," *The New York Review of Books* LXV (15 January 1998): 24.

45. Holmes, 62–70.

46. Council of Alternative Forces for Peace and Democracy in Ethiopia (CAFPDE), Press Release, "A Diplomatic Coup or a Political Ploy?" Washington, DC, 4 January 1995.

47. Santoro, "At the Root of an Odd African War: Money," *Christian Science Monitor*, 22 June 1998.

48. Editorial, "Meles Must Go," *Ethiopian Register* 5 (July 1998): 2–3.

49. See Adam Przeworski, "Democracy as a Contingent Outcome of Conflicts," in *Constitutionalism and Democracy* eds. Jon Elster and Rune Slagstad, (Cambridge, UK: Cambridge University Press, 1988), 70–78.

50. Individual integrity and independent judgment among those living under oppressive regimes in Ethiopia have long been valued. See Donald Levine, *Wax and Gold* (Chicago: University of Chicago Press, 1965), 286.

51. Athol Fugard, "Notes on 'Valley Song'," *Playbill*, Kennedy Center for the Performing Arts, Washington, DC, May 1997.

52. See, e.g., Stephen Buckley, "Ethiopia: A Rights Violator? Foes Say Foreign Aid Props Up System of Widespread Abuses," *Washington Post*, 13 April 1998, A17; Lara Santoro, "Cracks in Ethiopia's Calm Facade," *Christian Science Monitor*, 23 April 1998; Scott Strauss, "U.S. Aid Flows to Ethiopian Regime that Silences Dissent," *Houston Chronicle*, 4 May 1998.

53. Editorial, "Lessons from the TPLF War on Ethiopia," *Ethiopian Register* 3 (November 1996): 3–4.

54. Ibid.

55. Editorial, "Tyranny and the Friends of Ethiopia," *Ethiopian Register* 4 (July 1997): 4.

56. Marina Ottaway, "From Political Opening to Democratization?" in *Democracy in Africa: the Hard Road Ahead* ed. Marina Ottaway, (Boulder, CO: L. Rienner, 1997), 2.

APPENDIX

Some Business Establishments of the EPRDF/TPLF

1. Guna Trading House SC.
Date Est: Dec. 1991; Address: Addis Ababa.
Activities: Import/export and wholesale trade.

2. Sur Construction SC.
Date Est: Jan. 1992; Cap: 100,000,000 Birr; Address: Addis Ababa.
Activities: Construction of roads, bridges, dams, factory, office and residential buildings, airports, hotels, drainage canals, drilling water, etc.
Manager: Tsegaye Demoz

3. Meskerem Investment SC.
Date Est: Nov. 1992; Address: Addis Ababa.
Board Members: 1. Bereha Haile Mariam 2. Wolday Kidane 3. Worede Gessese
Manager: Solomon Desta
Activities: Construction, mining, import/export, electrical installation, consultancy, agriculture, manufacturing.

4. Tesfa Livestock Development SC.

Date Est: August 1993; Address: Mekele.

Board Members: 1. W/ro Roman G/Sellassie 2. W/ro Shishay Aseffa 3. Mekonnen Tesfahunegn

Activities: Fattening and supplying livestock for local and internal markets, beef and dairy production, fodder production, import of such products, wholesale and retail trade, commission agency, brokerage, transit services, etc.

5. Addis Consultancy House PLC

Date Est: 1995; Address: Addis Ababa.

Activities: Project identification, sector survey, review of technical, mechanical, and electrical designs, project monitoring, preparation and evaluation of bid documents, preparation of contract documents, training project staff, etc.

6. Africa Insurance SC.

Date Est: Jan. 1995; Branches: Addis Ababa, Mekele, Dire Dawa.

Board Members: 1. Yohannes Uqubay Mitiku 2. Tewodros Hagos Tesfay 3. Hibur Gebre Kidan

Activities: Life insurance, annuity, pension, permanent health, sickness, personal accident, general business reinsurance, real estate (mortgage bonds, shares, etc.)

7. Bruh Chemical SC.

Date Est: February 1995; Address: Mekele.

Board Members: 1. Fire T/Michael T/Tsion 2. Isayaas Desta Hailu 3. Berhe Hailu Zerefa

Activities: Manufacture of Caustic Soda, Hydrochloric Acid, Chlorine, industrial salt (coarse or table salt), Hypochlorite and other chemicals marketable locally or abroad.

8. Fana Democracy Publishing PLC

Date Est: May 1995; Address: Addis Ababa.

Manager: Negash Sahle

Activity: Currently produces EPRDF publications such as *Ifoyta*.

9. Radio Fana

The only privately owned radio station in Ethiopia; officially operates as EPRDF's Radio but yet without securing a legal license; started broadcasting from Addis Ababa on November 21, 1995; has broadcasting schedules almost parallel with Ethiopian Radio; programs are both in Amharic and Affan Oromo; freely uses news items which the Ethiopian News Agency acquires either from its salaried agents in the provinces or by buying from news agencies abroad; it has also overtaken Ethiopian Radio in the scale of its advertisement income. Its manager is an Eritrean, Mekonnen Mulugeta.

10. Trans-Ethiopia SC.

Date Est: March 1993; Address: Mekele.

Board Members: 1. Tekle Shiferaw Sahle 2. Tsegay Taimyallew Sebhatleab 3. Gebre Yohannes G/Kidan Engida

Activities: Dry and liquid bulk cargo transportation, public transport, engaging associates in freight or passenger transport, providing engineering and workshop/garage services, importing and selling vehicles, spare parts, tires, workshop/garage equipment and machines, acting as agents for same, providing consultancy and training services related to transport operation. This company now successfully competes with government transport companies such as Woyira and Comet Transport Enterprises. It has also monopolized transportation of bulk freight in the north.

11. Hiwot Agricultural Mechanization SC.

Date Est: March 1993; Address: Mekele.

Board Members: 1. W/ro Kedisan Nega Medhanie 2. W/ro Gebriel Taddese Berhe 3. W/ro Gerima G/Sellassie

Activities: Producing food and cash crops and selling these wholesale or in retail on domestic and external markets, providing rental and repair services of agricultural machinery and equipment, selling agricultural inputs, importing agricultural machinery and acting as agents for or trustees for these, etc.

12. Mesebo Building Materials Manufacturing SC.

Address: Mekele.

Activities: Construction of cement factory in the Mesebo area.

13. Almeda Textiles Manufacturing SC.

Date Est: March 1993; Address: Adwa.

Board Members: 1. W/ro Yomar Asfaw Kidanu 2. Tsegaberhan Hadush W/Mariam 3.Haile Libanos W/Michael

Activities: Manufacturing thread, yarn and any textile using artificial or natural wool, cotton or any other suitable material; manufacturing underwear, shirts, coats, trousers, sports outfits, blankets, bed sheets, towels, fibers, sacks, threads, etc., used for packing; ginning cotton; engaging in agricultural activities that are useful for producing the necessary materials for these; selling products on wholesale or retail basis; importing relevant materials, etc.

14. Sheba Tannery SC.

Date Est: March 1993; Address: Wuqro.

Board Members: 1. W/ro Shishay H/Sellassie W/Sellassie 2. Tekle W/Gebriel Gezzae 3. Shewit G/Kristos Birru

Activities: Processing animal skin to sell on foreign or domestic markets on wholesale or retail basis, producing any goods from hides and skins, importing any material necessary for the production of the same.

15. Mesfin Industrial Engineering SC.

Address: Mekele.

A company named after a deceased veteran TPLF member.

16. Mega-Net Corporation SC.

Date Est: March 1993; Address: Addis Ababa.

Board Members: 1. Berhane Gebre Tsadkan Hagos 2. Berhane Redae Kifle 3. Mebrahtu Kebede Hagos

Activities: Printing any written materials, photographs, and other audio-visual materials; distribution of any publication, photographic works, motion pictures, etc.; translating and dubbing; leasing audio-visual equipment; constructing, expanding, leasing halls for showing films and plays; advertising and promotional work; organizing exhibitions, workshops, symposia, seminars; travel agency, transit work, delivery and dispatch of any goods; training and consultancy in the above fields; exporting and selling on wholesale or retail basis any of its products; engaging in any other profitable business.

Subsidiaries: Mega-Net Corporation was initially established as "Mega-Net Printing and Distribution Share Company" in 1993. A year later, it was restructured as a corporation with subsidiaries operating in different sectors of the economy. Those subsidiaries we have been able to identify so far include Mega Distribution Enterprise, Mega Studio Enterprise, Mega Transit Services (now changed to Express Transit Services), Mega

Creative Arts Center, and Kuraz Publishing Agency (which it bought for birr 13,038,048 when the TPLF government privatized it in 1995). Inside sources claim that Mega Studio Enterprise was set up by confiscating very sophisticated equipment that belonged to Admas Production, an audio-visual unit that was operating under the auspices of the Central Committee of the Derg's WPE. The equipment was bought with public funds for about U.S. $100,000 two years before the fall of the Derg. Mega-Net Corporation is reported to be run by Meles Zenawi's wife, W/ro Azeb, alias *Lemlem*.

17. The Monitor PLC

Date Est: May 1993; Address: Addis Ababa.

Manager: Fitsumzeab Asgedom; some of the other staff include Seye Abraha's family members.

Activities: Publishing, import/export, wholesale and retail trade, commission agency, manufacturing, etc. Currently the company publishes the English newspaper *The Monitor*, which the TPLF senior officials had the audacity to openly recommend to the diplomatic and other expatriate communities at official meetings.

18. Shala Advertizing Enterprise

Address: Addis Ababa, Mesqel Square.

Manager: Assefa Mamo (also Coordinator of EPRDF Information Center).

19. Selam Bus Line SC.

Date Est: May 1994; Address: Mekele.

Activities: Purchasing, taking on lease, selling or exchanging land and premises, buses, machinery, or movables in line with company's objective; providing commercial bus services for a fee; entering into partnership or any other arrangement for sharing profits, union of interest, cooperation, joint venture, reciprocal concessions or otherwise with any company, body or person engaged in any business so as to directly or indirectly benefit from the same.

20. Dessalegn Veterinary Drugs & Inputs Supply PLC

Date Est: January 1996.

Manager: Dr. Maru Aregawi

Activities: Importing and selling veterinary medicine, chemicals, instruments, and livestock production inputs; providing veterinary care and consultancy services; manufacturing veterinary medicine, chemicals, livestock production technical inputs and materials; rental and maintenance of veterinary equipment and instruments; commission agency; engaging in all other profitable activities related to its commercial objective.

21. Dilet Brewery PLC

Date Est: June 1993.

Manager: Kahsay Tewolde Tedla

22. Global Auto And Spare Parts Sales Company

This company has been selling the TPLF's vehicles through auctions in Addis Ababa. Most of the vehicles sold thus are long haul Mercedes and Fiat trucks with trailers. The vehicles are parked in the compound of the former Signal Corps, a military camp about a kilometer to the south of the British Embassy in Addis Ababa, where they are guarded by regular soldiers.

23. Ambassel Trading House PLC

Date Est: Nov. 1995; Address: Addis Ababa.

Manager: Teshome Behailu

Activities: Agro-industrial production, and import/export of such products, wholesale and retail trade, commission agency, brokerage, transit services, etc.

24. Zeleke Agricultural Mechanization SC.

Date Est: May 1996; Address: Delelo, North Gondar.

General Manager: Tewodros Dessuye

Board of directors initial members: 1. Solomon Teqeba, Chairman 2. Kebede Chane 3. Seyoum W/Yohannes (representing Tiret)

(N.B. Solomon Teqeba is a senior member of the ANDM who left Adigrat at the end of March 1983 and became a TPLF fighter until his transfer to EPDM).

Activities: Crop production, agricultural marketing, supply and rent of agricultural tools and machinery, support to agricultural investors, and other activities related to agriculture.

Source: *Ethiopian Register*, July, August 1996.

Selected Bibliography

Adera, Taddesse, and Ali Jimale Ahmed, eds. *Silence Is Not Golden: A Critical Anthology of Ethiopian Literature*. Lawrenceville, NJ: Red Sea Press, 1994.

Aynekulu, Awualom. "The Emerging Monopolies of the TPLF." *Ethiopian Register* 3 (July 1996): 20–32; "The Emerging Monopolies of the TPLF, Part II." *Ethiopian Register* 3 (August 1996): 14–22.

Baxter, P. T .W., Jan Hultin, and Alessandro Triulzi, eds. *Being and Becoming Oromo: Historical and Anthropological Enquiries*. Lawrenceville, NJ: Red Sea Press, 1996.

Bobbio, Noberto. *The Future of Democracy: A Defense of the Rules of the Game*. Minneapolis: University of Minnesota Press, 1987.

Bogdanor, Vernon, ed. *Constitutions in Democratic Politics*. Aldershot, UK: Gower, 1988.

Clapham, Christopher. *Africa and the International System: The Politics of State Survival*. Cambridge: Cambridge University Press, 1996.

Cohen, John M. "Transition Toward Democracy and Governance in Post Mengistu Ethiopia." Harvard Institute for International Development, Cambridge, MA, 1994.

Crummey, Donald. "Ethnic Democracy? The Ethiopian Case." In *Proceedings of the 37th Annual Meeting of the African Studies Association*. Toronto, Ontario, 1–4 November 1994.

Demissie, Ejigou. " 'Privatization' of Public Enterprises in Ethiopia: TPLF Style." *Ethiopian Register* 3 (April 1996): 23–27.

Elshtain, Jean Bethke. *Democracy on Trial*. New York: Basic Books, 1995.

Elster, Jon, and Rune Slagstad, eds. *Constitutionalism and Democracy*. Cambridge: Cambridge University Press, 1988.

Engedayehu, Walle. "Ethiopia: Democracy and the Politics of Ethnicity." *Africa Today* 40 (Spring 1993): 29–53.

EPRDF Central Committee. *Dirijitawi Ma'ekel*. "EPRDF's Organizational Structure and Operation: Lessons for the Opposition." English translation of TPLF/EPRDF Amharic language document, published in six parts. *Ethiopian Register* 4 (September 1997): 16–19; (October 1997): 18– 22; (November 1997): 18–21; (December 1997): 22–27; *Ethiopian Register* 5 (February 1998): 20–24; (March 1998): 18, 20–22, 24.

Finn, John E. *Constitutions in Crisis: Political Violence and the Rule of Law*. New York: Oxford University Press, 1991.

Fukui, Katsuyoshi, Eisei Kurimoto, and Masayoshi Shigeta, eds. *Ethiopia in Broader Perspective*. Kyoto: Shokado, 1997.

Galston, William A. *Liberal Purposes*. New York: Cambridge University Press, 1991.

Gilkes, Patrick. "The Eritrean Referendum." *Ethiopian Review* 3 (April 1993): 59–61.

Gioseff, Daniela, ed. *On Prejudice: A Global Perspective*. New York: Doubleday, 1993.

Gordon, David F. "Democracy in Africa: The New Leaders." Testimony before the Senate Committee on Foreign Relations Subcommittee on Africa, 19 March 1998.

Grahamm, Keith. *The Battle of Democracy*. Brighton, Sussex: Wheatsheaf, 1986.

Haile, Minasse. "Legality of Secessions: The Case of Eritrea." *Emory International Law Review* 8 (Fall 1994): 480–537.

———. "The New Ethiopian Constitution: Its Impact upon Unity, Human Rights and Development." *Suffolk Transnational Law Review* 20 (Winter 1996): 1–84.

Harbeson, John W., and Donald Rothschild, eds. *Africa in World Politics: Post Cold-War Challenges*. Boulder, CO: Westview Press, 1995.

InterAfrica Group. *Proceedings of the Symposium on the Making of the New Ethiopian Constitution, 17–21 May 1993*. Addis Ababa, 1994.

International Centre Against Censorship. *Deadly Marionettes: State-Sponsored Violence in Africa*. London: Article 19, October 1997.

International Human Rights Law Group. *Ethiopia in Transition, A Report on the Judiciary and the Legal Profession*. Washington, DC, January 1994.

Iyob, Ruth. "The Eritrean Experiment: A Cautious Pragmatisim?" *Journal of Modern African Studies* 35 (1997): 647–673.

Jalata, Asafa. *Oromia and Ethiopia: State Formation and Ethnonational Conflict, 1868–1992*. Boulder, CO: L. Rienner, 1993.

Joireman, Sandra Fullerton. "Opposition Politics and Ethnicity in Ethiopia: We Will All Go Down Together." *Journal of Modern African Studies* 35 (1997): 387–407.

Kaplan, Robert D. "Was Democracy Just a Moment?" *Atlantic* 280 (December 1997): 55–80.

Keller, Edmond J. "The Ethnogenesis of the Oromo Nation and Its Implications for Politics in Ethiopia." *Journal of Modern African Studies* 33 (December 1995): 621–635.

Keller, Edmund J., and Donald Rothchild, eds. *Africa in the New International Order: Rethinking State Sovereignty and Regional Security*. Boulder, CO: L. Rienner, 1996.

Levine, Donald. *Greater Ethiopia: The Evolution of a Multiethnic Society*. Chicago: University of Chicago Press, 1974.

———. *Wax and Gold*. Chicago: University of Chicago Press, 1965.

Lyons, Terrence. "The Transition in Ethiopia." *CSIS Africa Notes* (27 August 1991).

Mamdani, Mahmood. *Citizen and Subject: Contemporary Africa and the Legacy of Late Colonialism*. Princeton, NJ: Princeton University Press, 1996.

Marcus, Harold G., ed. *New Trends in Ethiopian Studies*. Lawrenceville, NJ: Red Sea Press, 1994.

Mariam, Alemayehu Gebre. "The Tangled Web of Nationality and Citizenship in Ethiopia." *Ethiopian Review* 3 (April 1993): 75.

Mengisteab, Kidane. "New Approaches to State Building in Africa: The Case of Ethiopia's Ethnic-Based Federalism." *African Studies Review* 40 (December 1997): 111–32.

Muchie, Mammo. "The Surgical Operation of Ethiopia without Anesthetics: Andreas Eshete's Defense of Ethnic Federalism." *Ethiopian Register* 5 (April 1998): 18–22.

Mutua, Makau Wa. "Ethiopia." *Africa Report* (November-December 1993): 51.

Nahum, Fasil. *Constitution for a Nation of Nations: the Ethiopian Prospect*. Lawrenceville, NJ: Red Sea Press, 1997.

National Democratic Institute for International Affairs and the African American Institute. *An Evaluation of the June 21, 1992 Elections in Ethiopia*. Washington, DC, November 1992.

Negash, Assefa. *The Pillage of Ethiopia by Eritreans and their Tigrean Surrogates*. Los Angeles: Adey Publishing, 1996.

Norwegian Institute of Human Rights. *The 1994 Elections and Democracy in Ethiopia: Report of the Norwegian Observer Group*. Human Rights Report. Bergen, Norway, August 1994.

Ofcansky, Thomas P., and LaVerle Berry, eds. *Ethiopia: A Country Study*. Washington, DC: Library of Congress, 1993.

Ottaway, Marina, ed. *Democracy in Africa: the Hard Road Ahead*. Boulder, CO: L. Rienner, 1997.

————. "An Update on the Democratization Process." *Ethiopian Review* 3 (August 1993): 32.

Parker, Ben. *Ethiopia, Breaking New Ground*. Oxford: Oxfam UK, 1995.

Prendergast, John. *Peace, Development, and People of the Horn of Africa*. Washington, DC: Bread for the World, 1992.

Rawls, John. "Justice as Fairness: Political Not Metaphysical." *Philosophy and Public Affairs* XIV (1985): 223–51.

————. *Political Liberalism*. New York: Columbia University Press, 1993.

————. *A Theory of Justice*. Cambridge, MA: Belknap Press, 1971.

Sandel, Michael. *Democracy's Discontent*. Cambridge, MA: Belknap Press, 1996.

Santoro, Lara. "At the Root of an Odd African War: Money." *Christian Science Monitor*, 22 June 1998.

Schlesinger, Arthur M., Jr., *The Disuniting of America*. New York: W. W. Norton, 1992.

Selassie, Alemante G. "Ethnic Identity and Constitutional Design for Africa." *Stanford Journal of International Law* 29 (Fall 1992): 1–56.

Shunkuri, Admasu. "Ethiopians in the U.S." *Ethiopian Review* 5 (March 1995): 22, 24, 26–27.

Spencer, John H. *Ethiopia at Bay: A Personal Account of the Haile Sellassie Years*. Algonac, MI: Reference Publications, 1984.

Tekle, Amare, ed. *Eritrea and Ethiopia: From Conflict to Cooperation*. Lawrenceville, NJ: Red Sea Press, 1994.

TPLF/EPRDF. "TPLF/EPRDF's Strategies for Establishing its Hegemony & Perpetuating its Rule." English translation of TPLF/EPRDF document originally published in June 1993. *Ethiopian Register* 3 (June 1996): 20–29.

"TPLF's Business Influence in the Financial Industry on the Rise." *Ethiopian Register* 4 (June 1997): 10–13.

Unraveling Human Rights Abuses in Ethiopia. Proceedings of a Human Rights Week Observance and Electronic Mail Conference, 3–8 March 1997. Medford, MA: The International Solidarity Committee for Ethiopian Prisoners of Conscience, 1997.

Vestal, Theodore M. "An Analysis of the New Constitution of Ethiopia and the Process of its Adoption." *Northeast African Studies* 3 (1996): 21–38.

————. "Deficits of Democracy in the Transitional Government of Ethiopia Since 1991." *New Trends in Ethiopian Studies*. ed. Harold G. Marcus, 2. (1994): 188–204.

————. "Freedom of Association in the Federal Democratic Republic of Ethiopia," Boston University, African Studies Center, Working Paper No. 210, 1998.

Walzer, Michael. *Thick and Thin: Moral Argument at Home and Abroad*. Notre Dame, IN: Notre Dame University Press, 1994.

Young, John. "Ethnicity and Power in Ethiopia." *Review of African Political Economy* 23 (December 1996): 531–42.

———. "The Tigray and Eritrean Peoples Liberation Fronts: A History of Tensions and Pragmatism." *Journal of Modern African Studies* 34 (March 1996): 105–20.

Zegeye, Abebe, and Siegfried Pausewang, eds. *Ethiopia in Change: Peasantry, Nationalism and Democracy*. London: British Academic Press, 1994.

Zenawi, Meles. Letter to Theodore M. Vestal, 30 November 1995. Published as "Focus." *Ethiopian Register* 3 (August 1996): 26–27.

Zewde, Bahru. *A History of Modern Ethiopia 1855–1974*. Athens: Ohio University Press, 1991.

Index

About the Author

THEODORE M. VESTAL is Professor of Political Science at Oklahoma State University. Professor Vestal went to Ethiopia as a Peace Corps executive in 1964 and has maintained a scholarly interest in the country ever since. Following the fall of the Derg in 1991, he returned to Ethiopia as a consultant to the Council of Representatives of the Transitional Government of Ethiopia and as an international election observer. He is an editorial advisor to the *Ethiopian Register.*

ISBN 0-275-96610-0

EAN

9 780275 966102

90000>

HARDCOVER BAR CODE

12/31/03-1   1999